Torn between a longing for classical forms and the need for new modes of expression, French painting of the revolutionary and Napoleonic eras—still today inadequately investigated—illustrates the style generally described as Neoclassicism, a term basically perhaps inapt, but rich in implications. The neoclassical movement, whose sources and repercussions were international, and whose inconsistencies are becoming better understood thanks to the efforts of present-day art historians to rehabilitate it (as Mannerism has in recent years been rehabilitated), spans the period which witnessed the birth pangs of modern society. It developed steadily from about 1760 to 1830 and passed through several distinct phases variously affecting the different branches of art. Though it modeled itself on sculpture, and though architecture, stimulated by urban development and the discovery of the buried cities of Pompeii and Herculaneum, provided its widest, most distinctive field of application (from Russia to the United States), it was neoclassical painting, in the hands of David, that as early as the 1780s gave the movement its impetus and restored to Paris that primacy in the arts which Rome, historic shrine of the cult of antiquity, was trying to usurp. Brushing aside the dogmas of archaeologists and aestheticians, and relying on his native strength of character, his willpower and impeccable craftsmanship, David created a kind of heroic humanism reflecting the passions, tensions and upheavals of his time. With a strong, unfaltering hand, defying his personal inclinations, he renewed the time-honored tradition of French painting and laid the foundations, both historical and experimental, of a new vision to come, even foreshadowing the fundamental conflicts to which it gave rise.

Last of the great *chefs d'atelier*, he shaped and inspired, among many able pupils, such very different personalities as Gérard, Girodet and Gros, who paved the way from Neoclassicism to Romanticism, while Ingres, his most illustrious and original disciple, whose genius came to fruition under the Empire, continued to uphold his doctrines with a fanatical intransigence that consolidated the strongholds of academicism. Yet Ingres, with his super-sensitive genius for line, achieved bold masterpieces of naturalistic stylization which were destined to cast their spell over Courbet, Degas, Renoir and the painters of the twentieth century; to the utilitarian, expressive, social-minded art of his master, enlisted in the nation's service and dedicated to its best interests, he opposed the pure and abstract beauty of art for art's sake. These two artists, whom it is wrong to dissociate, as is all too often done, pursued by different paths a common ideal, Nature, the Antique, and the Old Masters, which they always held before them; together David and Ingres represent two aspects of the same aesthetic adventure. Neoclassicism, thus traversed by many currents, continually stirred and shaken by obscure forces at work beneath a surface of unruffled calm and reasonableness, oscillated between Roman severity and an Alexandrine grace whose purest representative was Prud'hon.

Jacques-Louis David (1748-1825). Portrait of Madame de Verninac, 1799. (57¼ × 44″)
Louvre, Paris.

criticism. David next made a trip to Flanders to study Rubens and thus round off the experience gained in Italy. With *The Grief of Andromache* (Ecole des Beaux-Arts, Paris), his reception piece at the Academy in 1783, the rift between the sentimentality of the subject matter and the deliberate severity of the design has noticeably widened. True, all the formal elements of David's style are here, but without the powerful simplification that was later to crystallize it. In September 1784 he set out on a second trip to Italy, there to execute the official commission he had received from the king in 1782.

The resulting picture, *The Oath of the Horatii* (Louvre), created a sensation when exhibited in the following year. Everything in it answered to the tastes of a generation brought up on Plutarch and enthralled by Rousseau: the choice of a Roman subject, the sobriety of the

David and his Followers

PROBABLY no other artist has been at once the hero and the victim of his time to such an extent as David. He is the very embodiment of Neoclassicism and all its contradictions, so much so that we run the risk of confusing his program and his temperament —two very different things. The historical limitations of his art, moreover, are liable to blind us not only to its very real originality but also to its intimate connection with the French tradition. The praise and abuse of which he has been the target at different periods have been so extreme, and everything he stood for as an artist, as the leader of a school and as a politician, has been (and still is) so much misunderstood, that it is difficult to evaluate his work on its own merits and to account for its far-reaching repercussions.

Jacques-Louis David was born in Paris on August 30, 1748. Descending from a long line of artisans and shopkeepers, he belonged by birth to that lower middle class from which his loyalty and sympathies never swerved. An orphan at the age of nine, he was brought up by his maternal uncles, Buron, a building contractor, and Desmaisons, an architect, who saw to it that he had a good schooling. But his studies were cut short and his vocation decided by the strong aptitude he showed for drawing. The boy was taken to Boucher, his idol and a distant cousin of his, who gave him an introduction to Joseph Vien (1716-1809), initiator of the Pompeian style, who had opened a school of his own and taught successfully at the Academy. Vien set his pupils to work from the living model (a practice he believed himself to have inaugurated) and inspired them with his own fervent devotion to Nature, the Antique, and the Old Masters—the very ideals that David made his own. During his apprenticeship he lodged in the Louvre with Monsieur Sedaine, a friend of his uncles, poet, librettist, and secretary of the Academy of Architecture. There he met the leading actors and composers of the day, notably Grétry, and developed a keen interest in the theater and music.

Hesitant and mannered, his early works betray a conflict between the new austerity and the blandishments of Rococo, its languor, its fluttering draperies and general dishevelment, its hazy pinks and blues. In 1773, taking over from Fragonard and working in the same spirit, he decorated the magnificent town house in the Chaussée d'Antin designed by Ledoux for the dancer Mademoiselle Guimard, then the star of the Paris Opera. The following year, after three mortifying failures, he competed once again for the Prix de Rome and was at last successful. On October 10, 1775, he left for Italy and, after visiting Parma and Bologna, reached Rome on November 4. At first he was resolved to keep to his French manner and not

Jacques-Louis David (1748-1825). The Oath of the Horatii (detail), 1784. Louvre, Paris.

confronts us with realities of suffering and death, expressed in fresh accents; and the *Equestrian Portrait of Count Potocki* (Warsaw), sketched out at one sitting in Naples and finished in Paris in 1781. Both works go back beyond Rococo to the Baroque tradition, and also contain those Romantic undertones which much later were to find their full expression in Gros, Géricault and Delacroix, each of whom was well aware of their source. But, defying his own temperament and tastes, David chose austerity combined with clear, well-ordered pictorial construction. The nobly draped figures of his *Belisarius* (1781, Lille) are still disposed along the diagonal but, owing to the parallelism of their gestures, tend to form a frieze. Though the composition was unanimously admired at the Salon, the subdued color scheme met with

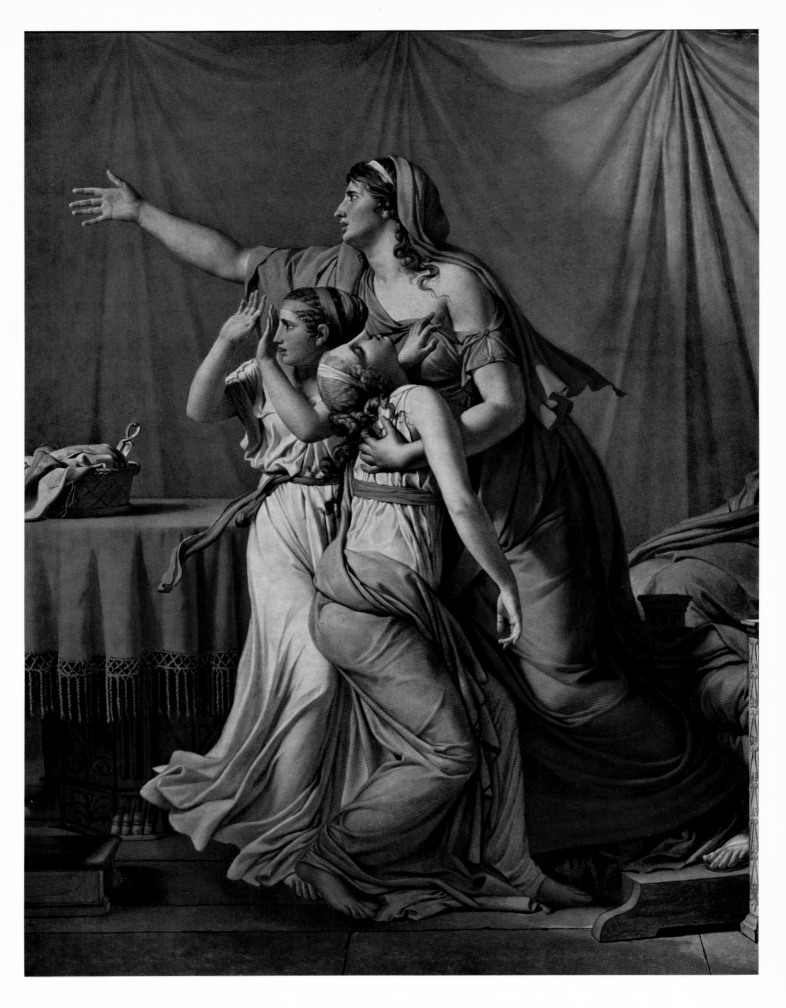

Jacques-Louis David (1748-1825). The Lictors bringing to Brutus the Bodies of his Sons (detail), 1789.

Louvre, Paris.

the break he here is making with the past, a rupture that was to be the crux of nineteenth-century art; the conflict between a desire for stylistic perfection and the urgent need for truth and self-expression. A presage of the Revolution, this work is also one of the finest attempts ever made to come to grips with the fundamentals of pictorial design.

After celebrating the Roman virtue of self-sacrifice in the cause of one's country, David went on to show the serenity of the Greek sage in the face of death. Painted for Trudaine de Montigny, who prided himself on being something of a philosopher, the *Death of Socrates* (Metropolitan Museum of Art, New York) was exhibited at the 1787 Salon where Sir Joshua Reynolds, on his way through Paris, saw and admired it. It remains his supplest, best knit composition; but this very perfection, when all is said and done, is one of virtuoso handling and lacks the spark of life.

David was much more at home in dealing with Roman history and the fierce grandeur of its heroes. The Bastille had already been taken, privileges abolished and the States General convoked, when his *Lictors bringing to Brutus the Bodies of his Sons* (Louvre) was exhibited at the official Salon of 1789—and inevitably hailed as a republican symbol and message of the sublime and intransigent era to come. The theme of the picture is the story of the Roman patriot who, as consul of the Republic, sentenced his own sons to death for conspiring to restore the monarchy. Brutus is seen brooding in the shadows, leaning on the base of a statue. Bringing in the dead bodies on stretchers, the lictors enter from the side in a shaft of light which draws the eye towards the funeral procession. The mother, hugging her two daughters to her breast, as one of them falls into a swoon, looks on in mute horror. At the far right, cut off in part by the picture frame, the weeping grandmother buries her face in her cloak. At the back of the atrium in which the scene is set, rises a Doric colonnade with entablature, from which hangs the grey-blue drapery enclosing the group of grief-stricken women. The foremost column forms the pivot of the three figure groups, each one of which strikes a note of varying intensity. Likewise based on the ancient frieze and bas-relief, the chromatic and spatial arrangement of the picture has become more complex than the severe architectonic patterning of the *Horatii*, but with no loss of clarity in the pictorial design. Angular planes conjoined with compensating curves are multiplied and stabilized by a solid network of verticals and horizontals. The powerful Caravaggesque lighting serves to intensify the color scheme, composed of a wide range of limpid or broken tones, varied in the shadows and lighter blues, the reds, yellows and orange tempered with greys and browns. Again, as in the *Oath of the Horatii*, David concentrates his plastic energy on the male groups exemplifying the stern republican virtues extolled by Corneille, while reserving his tenderest accents for the pathetic figures of the women and children, whose sufferings had been voiced by Racine. The mother who has risen to her feet to form with her daughters a single unit of grief and protest (in contrast to the wilting forms of Camilla and her maids in the *Horatii*), has laid her sewing basket on the table. The blue and grey gleams of the wool shed a faint glow on the blood-red tablecloth. This unexpected still life, worthy of Zurbaran and Chardin, is the only accessory, the only allusion to quiet home life, that breaks in on the bleak and overwrought atmosphere of the tragedy. Neoclassicism, surpassing all its forms and formulas, here attains its full growth and potency, recording for posterity the conflicts and upheavals of an era.

David threw himself body and soul into the events of the French Revolution, which brought him face to face with history in the making. His was the unique experience of a painter who sees his own pictures starting to life before his eyes, his antique heroes stepping from the pages of history into the streets and brushing his shoulders; who sees events conforming to his social and aesthetic ideals. Every actor in those events felt the soul of Brutus stirring within him, kindled by his example and virtues as portrayed by David; the toga of Brutus appeared on the stage, flung over Talma's shoulders, and the furniture represented in David's paintings appeared in every drawing room, while women's fashions took their cue

from the costume and coiffure of Brutus' daughters. The painter's prestige had never stood higher: he was soon to be dictator of the arts, not by royal decree like Lebrun, but by popular consent. Called upon to commemorate the initial act whereby the popular will asserted itself, he sketched out an immense canvas, *The Oath of the Tennis Court*, with all the figures blocked out in the nude. The preliminary design, exhibited at the 1791 Salon, touched off a burst of enthusiasm and inspired an ode by André Chénier. But the painting was never completed; it remains an arresting sketch (Versailles), with only a few of the heads fully individualized and recognizable amid a schematic concourse of athletic bodies.

The theme of a solemn oath, which recurs periodically, almost obsessively, in David's work, symbolizes the immolation of the individual, his absolute subordination to the superior interests of the collectivity. Among the determinant causes of the French Revolution, the aspiration to individual freedom counted far less than the passion for the commonweal— the passion that led David to put his art and his person at the nation's service. As a deputy at the Convention, of which he was twice elected chairman, he voted for the death of Louis XVI. A member of the Committee of General Security, he made speeches and was sent on missions. In 1793 he was instrumental in abolishing the Academy. He reorganized the art schools and teaching methods along more liberal lines, put through legislation concerning museums, monuments, theaters and town-planning, designed uniforms and sabres, engraved medals,

Jacques-Louis David (1748-1825). The Lictors bringing to Brutus the Bodies of his Sons (detail), 1789. Louvre, Paris.

Jacques-Louis David (1748-1825).

Marat Assassinated, 1793. (63¾ × 49¼″) Musées Royaux des Beaux-Arts de Belgique, Brussels.

made a new curtain for the Opera House. Above all, he took charge of organizing the revolutionary celebrations and ceremonies. Here he displayed his incomparable talents as a *metteur en scène*, distributing living masses of figures, arranging processions down to the smallest details, even to the time of day and the line of march, and orchestrating the movements of crowds, such as were to fill his future pictures. Nothing remains of this prodigious, day-to-day activity, apart from the programs and a few drawings. On three occasions, however, for three glorified martyrs whose funerals he organized, he took care to leave a lasting record of the event. Hence the commemorative trilogy of paintings, the *Last Moments of Peletier de Saint-Fargeau* (1793), *Marat Assassinated* (1793) and the *Death of Young Bara* (1794).

The first of these Jacobin ex-votos is lost, probably destroyed; the third, depicting a glowing nude pressing the tricolor cockade to his heart and expiring in the full blush of youth, was presented to the Avignon Museum by Horace Vernet. The famous *Marat Assassinated* (Brussels), which Baudelaire rightly held to be "David's masterpiece and one of the great curiosities of modern art," has become for us the Pietà of the Revolution—a secular, not to say a political painting lifted to the religious plane in the very year when Goya, by very different means, was leaving decorative art behind him and giving full scope to his genius. Two extremes here strangely meet—uncompromising realism and the most skillfully contrived pictorial construction—and combine to transmute the horrible into the sublime without sparing us any of its crudity. The acid colors in contrasting zones of light, yellows, greens and red-tinged greys, serve to emphasize the taut precision of the design and the geometric network of horizontals and verticals running parallel to the picture frame. The almost hypnotic "close-up" of the dead man is accentuated by the unrelieved emptiness of the background. Shrouded in livid shadow, the chest emerges from the bathtub as if from a coffin and slumps back on the towels like some element of a still life. In contrast to the hard flat tones of the picture as a whole, and the angular arms and trunk bathed in a pallid light, the face and Madras headdress are modeled with a full brush and an almost poignant mildness. Baudelaire noticed this when he wrote, "There is something both tender and poignant about this work; in the chilly air of this room, between these cold walls, around this cold and funereal bathtub, hovers a soul." And it is the soul of David as well as that of his friend Marat, "a soul as bitter and despotic as the Revolution which gave birth to it." This is a painting that stands alone in its century, that prefigures Courbet and Manet, and harks back by way of Caravaggio to the Primitives. We should probably have to go back to Mantegna's *Dead Christ* in the Brera to find a work of like intensity and concision.

After the 9th Thermidor (July 27, 1794), when Robespierre finally fell and the Reign of Terror came to an end, David was arrested. Confined on August 2, 1794, in the Hôtel des Fermes, he was transferred on September 15 to the Luxembourg prison. Devoid of imagination, he had never painted without a model before him. His compositions, nearly all suggested by some visual experience, a scene of real life or a stage or ballet performance, had always been carefully worked out on the basis of elaborate studies and designs. Now, during his detention, thrown back on his own resources in a small room in the Hôtel des Fermes, he recorded with scrupulous fidelity his own image, as seen in a mirror; then, when moved to the Luxembourg, with the same fidelity he recorded the view from his window over the gardens. These astonishing creations are both in the Louvre. The self-portrait, in which no hint of the regicide or the art dictator transpires, reveals on the contrary the full-blooded warmth and humanity of a painter who dominated his emotions by the conscious perfection of his workmanship. The landscape, the only one to come from his hand (if we except those in his Italian sketchbooks), is a marvel of easy naturalness and timeless freshness; it forms a link between the landscapes of the late medieval illuminators and those of Corot.

Released on December 28, 1794, he was imprisoned again on May 25, 1795, then banished from Paris on August 4 and placed on probation in the home of his brother-in-law Sériziat at

Tournan, near Melun. Finally, on October 26, 1795, he was amnestied and reinstated in his official post, with his prestige intact. But the dissolute society of the Directory was not for him, and now that the storm was over he withdrew to his studio, returning to his pupils and the projects he had abandoned for politics. The decade 1784-1794 is that of his greatest works, inspired by the ideals and the passions of the times. The years 1795-1800 mark a temporary pause, an interlude of quiet thought, and also of stylistic purification. Whenever the turn of events restored him to the leisure of private life, his mind reverted to antique subjects; no others seemed to him so worthy of cultivation.

In 1799 he finished the *Rape of the Sabine Women* (Louvre). This extraordinary composition, a trifle cold in its very perfection, which exerted a fascination on the Cubist painters, represented for David the supreme expression of his ideal, the synthesis between style rigorously applied and nature truthfully recorded, for these antique statues had been posed for by living models. The rhythmic crystallization of volumes and gestures is slightly impaired by the confused mass of the fortress, the rather pedantic concern for archaeological exactitude, and the frenzied, overcrowding intrusion of the male nudes among the superb figures of women and children, perhaps the finest figure paintings in the whole of David's work.

In the long sequence of portraits that mark every phase of his evolution, David threw off the bonds of his aesthetic and made no attempt to imitate the antique. He looked with his own eyes, steadily and directly, and drew on the best of his natural gifts (largely excluded from his big figure compositions in which he aimed at careful finish): his power of imparting a rich and full-flavored texture to the painted canvas. Of all his portraits of relatives, friends and public figures whom he knew and admired, scarcely one was done to order and several have almost miraculously come down to us in the form of unfinished sketches, thus revealing his incomparable craftsmanship and command of the painter's means. From the very outset, in his portraits of the Buron and Sedaine families of 1769, David displayed his probity and penetration, and his infallible technique. The well-known figures of *La Marquise d'Orvilliers* (1790), *Madame Trudaine* (1791), *Monsieur Sériziat* and *Madame Sériziat and her Son* (1795), and *Mademoiselle Tallard* (1795), a particularly delightful work, all in the Louvre, stand out against a neutral ground, intimate and withal monumental, complete and satisfying in their utter simplicity. The *Portrait of Madame de Verninac* (Louvre) offers, without any loss of breadth, the same plastic density and plenitude as the *Rape of the Sabine Women* painted in the same year (1799). This opulent brunette in a low-necked white dress set off against a uniform grey background by the yellow spiral of a scarf patterned with palmettes, sits with quiet self-assurance on a chair in the antique style ornamented with gilt-bronze fittings. Delacroix (who owned this portrait of his elder sister, wife of the Prefect of Lyons) found fault with its placid, unassuming perfection: "There is no center of interest, the eye is drawn to the head no more than it is to the draperies or the chair." This was a failing that Ingres and Matisse were later to recognize as a quality, as a token of the supreme inner harmony of the picture. The following year, with ineffable grace and felicity, David recorded the winsome gaze and attitude of *Madame Récamier* (Louvre), bare-headed, bare-footed, resting on her couch. The tall slender lamp-stand (drawn perhaps by Ingres, then his pupil) emphasizes by contrast the lithe body forming a supple diagonal across the blue and yellow cushions.

"A man of instinct, but always carried away by the ideas that successively dominated his mind" (Delécluze), and even more by the leaders whose personality fascinated him, David came under the spell first of Robespierre, then of Napoleon. As early as 1797, fresh from the battle of Rivoli which brought the Italian campaign to a close, General Bonaparte paid a visit to David's studio, captivated the painter and granted him a brief sitting, at which David succeeded in committing to canvas that tawny, feverish face, glowing with the inner fire of the man, now in the Louvre. The final equestrian version of 1801, *Napoleon crossing the St Bernard Pass* (Versailles), created the prototype of all the Napoleonic portraits to come.

After the proclamation of the Empire (May 1804), Napoleon tore David away from his visions of the antique, appointed him official painter of the régime and again plunged him into the current of contemporary history by commissioning him to commemorate the events of the day on a grandiose scale. Of all the scenes he was to glorify, only two were actually painted, the *Coronation of Napoleon in Notre-Dame* (Louvre) and its military pendant, the *Distribution of the Eagles on the Champ-de-Mars* (Versailles). David had attended the coronation ceremony on December 2, 1804, watching it from a place of honor in the tribune, and carefully noted, on a plan of the cathedral prepared in advance, the respective positions of all who took part. Then, following his usual practice, he made individual portraits of every figure, studied the costumes and accessories in minute detail, and reconstituted, with the help of a pasteboard model, the choir of Notre-Dame, down to its very lighting effects.

Brought to completion in November 1807, after three years of uninterrupted work, this canvas, as vast and sumptuous as Veronese's *Wedding at Cana*, is not—as might have been feared—a mere assemblage of glittering portraits, an ostentatious record of court pageantry. Thanks to a scrupulously truthful reconstitution, it achieves an ordered presentation of a great event. The distribution of figure groups and skillfully contrived back-lighting serve to focus attention on the central scene and the Emperor's gesture as, standing on the steps of the altar and already wearing the imperial diadem, he holds forth the crown he is about to

Jacques-Louis David (1748-1825). Portrait of Madame Récamier, 1800. (68⅛ × 95¾")

Louvre, Paris.

Jacques-Louis David (1748-1825).

The Coronation of the Emperor Napoleon and the Empress Josephine (detail), 1806-1807. Louvre, Paris.

place on the head of the kneeling Josephine; over her robe of white silk braided with gold, the Empress wears a crimson mantle spangled with golden stars and lined with ermine, upheld by two maids of honor. The simplicity of the composition throws into relief the blond and blue-green radiance of a dazzling palette inspired by Rubens and the Venetians. The pomp and splendor of the setting, enhanced on all sides by the glitter of gold on velvet, in no way detracts from the truthfulness of the rendering, which brings before us, as they really were, all these men and women with fear, envy or complacency written on their faces. To justify his quite unnecessary presence in the picture, Pope Pius VII—of whom David had already painted an admirable half-length portrait in 1805 (Louvre) during the Pope's confinement at the Tuileries—makes a half-hearted gesture of benediction. The Versailles Museum possesses a replica of the *Coronation* (begun in 1808, finished in 1822), of the same size, with many variants in the costumes and above all in the colors, but the quality of the painting, despite the beauty of the colors, cannot quite compare with that of the original. It hangs on the opposite wall from its military pendant, the *Distribution of the Eagles* (1810) or, more exactly (for this picture too represents a collective oath solemnly administered), the *Oath sworn by the Army before its Chief*, a ceremony held on the Champ-de-Mars on December 5, 1801, after the distribution of the eagles, which flap in the wind and are lowered before the Emperor, while the marshals raise their batons. David attempted here to recapture something of the fervor that had swept through the revolutionary assembly of the Jeu de Paume, but his efforts fail to carry conviction and the picture remains lifeless and theatrical.

The composition of his own choice, begun in the early days of the Empire as a symbol of Greece and male nudity, *Leonidas at Thermopylae* (Louvre), was continually interrupted by the official commissions showered upon him. Finished at last in 1814, when enemy armies were converging on Paris, it is even more coldly contrived, and fatally cramped by archaeological preoccupations, than the *Rape of the Sabine Women*. The youths bearing garlands and the warrior engraving the epitaph on a rock stand out nobly, majestically from the grey, wooden figure group, but without ever rising above the level of what Delacroix, discussing this very work, aptly called "vigorous manly prose"—and indeed that fitly describes David's style as a whole. Such grace and poetry as were in him are reserved for his intimate portraits which, beneath the outward trappings of fine clothes, preserve the fresh and natural charm of a sketch. Besides the little known portrait of his wife (1813, Private Collection, Paris) in a low-cut satin gown, with plumes and blond-lace in her hair, there are those, much more famous, of his daughters, of whose social position he was so proud: *Baroness Meunier*, in a red velvet robe, and *Baroness Jeanin*, smiling, in pink court dress, with white flowers in her dark hair (both painted about 1812, both in the Cailleux Collection, Paris).

Exiled from France upon the restoration of the Bourbons, the former regicide was forbidden to reside in Rome and found asylum in Brussels, where he was received with honor. But this final period of exile (1816-1825) brought with it a steady decline in his art. He reverted to the graceful amatory themes of his early work and, under Flemish influence, stepped up his colors, which grew shrill and showed up the increasing slackness of his drawing. From *Cupid and Psyche* (1817, Collection of Princess Murat, Paris) to *Mars disarmed by Venus and the Graces* (1824, Brussels), whose very title is tantamount to a confession, the quality of his work fell off rapidly, tainting even his last portraits in which the keen penetration of old gives way to a desire to please.

David was a great teacher. His studio was painted in 1814 by the young Cochereau (1793-1817), in a canvas of inestimable documentary value (Louvre), and described at length by the elderly Delécluze in a valuable volume of recollections (1855). David trained and sent forth through the years about four hundred aspiring artists, some of whom were the as yet unidentified authors of portraits attributed to the master himself. Notable among his most devoted followers and assistants were J. G. Drouais (1763-1788), David's favorite pupil;

1748-1825).

athedral of Notre-Dame, 1806-1807. (20 ft × 30 ft 7 in.) Louvre, Paris.

François Gérard (1770-1837).
Portrait of the Miniature Painter Jean-Baptiste Isabey and his Daughter, 1795. (76⅛ × 51⅛″) Louvre, Paris.

J. B. Wicar (1762-1834) and F. X. Fabre (1766-1837), now chiefly remembered for their generous bequests to the museums of Lille and Montpellier; P. A. Hennequin (1762-1833); A. L. C. Pagnest (1790-1819); and Georges Rouget (1784-1869), who was responsible for much of the *Coronation of Napoleon* and even more of the replica of it. But apart from Ingres and Gros (who will be studied separately), the two outstanding personalities schooled in his studio and stimulated by his example—though both drew away from him under the pressure of new art currents—were Girodet and Gérard. Neoclassical precepts are combined in their work with realist and pre-romantic elements.

Anne-Louis Girodet de Roucy-Trioson (1767-1824) won the Prix de Rome in 1789 and, mourned for by his friend Gros, died in 1824, the year of Delacroix's *Massacres at Chios*, which he accepted with mixed feelings. Highly cultivated, himself a poet after the manner of Abbé Delille, he practised an art which reveals the underlying dissension, typical of the age, between his literary aspirations and his means of expression. He renewed the thematic repertory, but without any readjustment of his technique, merely enveloping his strictly Davidian contours in airy vapors and nocturnal lighting effects. His *Sleep of Endymion* (Louvre) attracted attention at the 1792 Salon, and Prud'hon was haunted by its melancholy grace. After painting a portrait of Chateaubriand (1807, Saint-Malo Museum), he found inspiration in Chateaubriand's writings for one of his most popular compositions, the *Funeral of Atala* (1808, Louvre), which, despite its medieval atmosphere and noble fervor, reduces the impassioned cadences of the writer's glowing style to the level of a sentimental vignette. He scored his greatest success with his *Flood Scene* (1806, Louvre); here he tried his hand at awesome and terrible effects which may have chilled the spines of his contemporaries, but smack today of an ostentatious academicism bordering on the ridiculous. His best work is unquestionably to be found in his stylized drawings of nudes, in his all but forgotten landscapes of the Cadore Alps (Musée Magnin, Dijon) and in the Ossianic episodes (anticipating the Pre-Raphaelites) executed in 1801 for the ceiling of the Château de la Malmaison (preliminary sketch in the Louvre) which displeased David and delighted Bonaparte.

Born in Rome, where his father was a steward in the household of Cardinal de Bernis, François Gérard (1770-1837) was a friend and follower of Girodet, with whom he collaborated on the Malmaison decorations. He proved, however, more faithful to the spirit of David, to which he added an intellectual refinement peculiarly his own. As a thanks-offering to J. B. Isabey (1767-1855), a highly successful miniature painter who had generously helped him at the start of his career, he painted in 1795 the penetrating portrait of the artist and his daughter (Louvre) in a warm brown color scale, with light effects reminiscent of the Dutch masters, but handled with an unconstrained authority and vividness that revealed his mastery and the gift for portraiture that was to make his fortune. Discouraged by the failure of his mythological scenes (*Cupid and Psyche*, 1798, Louvre) and his vast, mediocre historical compositions (*Austerlitz*, 1810, and *Henri IV*, 1817, both in the Versailles Museum), he cultivated the art of the portrait and there found fulfillment, taking the place vacated by the émigrés, in particular by Madame Vigée-Lebrun (1755-1842), who, exploiting by rote a clever and pleasing technique much indebted to David, developed a lucrative practice in all the courts of Europe. Gérard particularly excelled in feminine silhouettes shown with grace and purity against hazy landscape backgrounds, for example the *Comtesse Regnaud de Saint-Jean d'Angely* (1798, Louvre), *Madame Récamier* (1802, Musée Carnavalet, Paris) and the *Marquise Visconti* (1810, Louvre). All these portraits were based on vivid, delicately tinted preparatory sketches, handled with unfailing skill, and the small galleries at the Versailles Museum in which they have been brought together reveal the most exquisite and delightful aspect of his art. After painting all the leading figures of the Empire, Gérard received in his famous Parisian salon the social and artistic élite of the Restoration. He gave a friendly welcome to the young Delacroix, to whom he lent his support, and indeed opened his own work to the new influences of the day.

Pierre-Paul Prud'hon (1758-1823). Portrait of the Empress Josephine, 1805. (96⅛ × 70½″)
Louvre, Paris.

Charm of Prud'hon

THE last artist of the eighteenth century (as the Goncourts called him), Pierre-Paul Prud'hon (1758-1823) was also, by virtue of his extreme sensitivity and unhappy fate, a precursor of the Romantics. In spite of his isolated position, he reflects the many-sidedness of neoclassical painting in the late eighteenth century. Like the poet André Chénier, he represents its strain of Hellenic distinction and Alexandrine grace as against its cult of Roman austerity and theatrical grandeur.

Born at Cluny on April 4, 1758, Prud'hon was the thirteenth child of a poor stone-mason and soon an orphan. He was trained at first as an artisan until, in 1774, he was awarded a grant enabling him to study at the art academy in Dijon, where he was fortunate in receiving the guidance of a remarkable teacher, François Devosge, founder of the Dijon museum and the master of Rude. Here, in a region famous for its medieval sculpture, Prud'hon may have gleaned "the secret of full-bodied and supple forms at the very time when line was on the point of drying up, drained of all content" (Henri Focillon). After an initial stay in Paris (1780-1783), where letters of introduction to the painter Pierre and the engraver Wille from his patron, Baron de Joursanvault, stood him in good stead, the States of Burgundy awarded him a further grant and sent him to Italy (1785-1788), commissioning him to make a copy of Pietro da Cortona's ceiling in the Palazzo Barberini. He arrived in Rome in the year (1785) of David's triumph with the *Oath of the Horatii*; but he was little affected by it, realizing as he did that his own path was to be a very different one. He became friendly with the sculptor Canova (1757-1822), who had not yet lost the Venetian charm of his early work; he discovered Antiquity with his own eyes and heart, not from the reconstructions of learned archaeologists; and among the masters of the Renaissance he fixed his choice on Raphael and, even more, on Leonardo and Correggio, whose mysterious and tender *sfumato* he soon assimilated, finding it particularly congenial to his own tastes.

Returning to France, he stopped for a time at Cluny, where he contracted a disastrous marriage which embittered his whole life. In November 1789 he settled in Paris, became a militant member of the Jacobin clubs, earned a meager living with his drawings and minia-tures, and revealed a gift for portraiture in his likenesses of *Cadet de Gassicourt* (1791, Musée Jacquemart-André, Paris) and his friend *Saint-Just* (1793, Lyons). The texture of these works, still thin but richly worked up, departed radically from the smooth modeling of David and even at this early stage had acquired a silky, velvety sheen.

In the autumn of 1794, driven from Paris by the food shortage and the triumph of the moderate party (Thermidoreans) after the fall of Robespierre, he took refuge in the region of Gray, in Franche-Comté, where he painted a fine series of portraits, among them *Georges Anthony* (Dijon) and *Madame Anthony and her Children* (Lyons), works contemporary with David's famous portraits of *Monsieur Sériziat* and *Madame Sériziat and her Son*, and by no means inferior to them in freshness and sureness of touch. Late in 1796 he returned to Paris, produced some delightful illustrations for the printer Didot (for editions of Racine, Tasso, Rousseau, *Daphnis and Chloe* and other works), and at last made his name with the general public at the 1799 Salon with his first large-scale composition: *Truth and Wisdom descend to Earth and the Darkness enveloping it is dispelled at their Approach*. This was originally intended for Versailles, then adapted as a ceiling panel at the palace of Saint-Cloud, and finally installed in the Louvre. The wealthy army contractor Lanois now commissioned a large decorative painting (unfortunately dismembered) for the Hôtel Saint-Julien, for which he designed the noble and gracious figures symbolizing Wealth, the Arts, Pleasure and Philosophy, together with the Dance of the Hours and Seasons (sketches at Montpellier, drawings at Chantilly and Gray). For the new society of the Directory, enriched by speculation and eager to enjoy itself after the convulsions and hardships of the Revolution, he revived the graceful tradition of eighteenth-century painting, adapting it to the taste of the day and the vogue for the antique, and gave new life and vigor to the emasculate art of allegorical painting.

In 1800, reverting for the nonce to the manner of Mantegna, he sketched out his *Triumph of Bonaparte* (Lyons), which remained unfinished—a frieze of glowing colors and sweeping breadth, unique in his output for its technique and presentation. Standing in a red uniform between Victory and Peace clad in white, Bonaparte is preceded by a troop of Cupids gamboling and dancing along, one of them bearing an olive branch. A group of women in shimmering drapery closes the triumphal procession, outlined in harmonious rhythms against a background of blue-tinged mountains and a slate-grey sky. The lovely ceiling painting for the gallery of archaic Greek sculpture in the Louvre, *Diana imploring Jupiter not to subject her to the Laws of Marriage*, showed the mastery he had attained by 1803 of flying figures and vaporous skies. Favorite painter of the Empress Josephine, he represented his brilliant patroness in 1805 amid the autumnal leafage of the garden at Malmaison. Despite the diadem and the spangled white gown, this work captures better than any other the dreamy charm of manner of the beautiful Creole, uneasily lifted to the summit of glory, yet overshadowed by a presentiment of evil days to come. The expressive curve of the arms called for many preliminary studies. A disciple of Jean-Jacques Rousseau, a close friend of Bernardin de Saint-Pierre, and hailing from the same part of France as Lamartine, Prud'hon had an innate psychological grasp of landscape and its human correspondences.

At the 1808 Salon he exhibited the two works that established his reputation: *Justice and Divine Vengeance pursuing Crime* (Louvre), ordered by the Prefect of the Seine for the Assize Court in the Palais de Justice, a novel synthesis of grace and power, Antique in inspiration, Romantic in mood, a work later to be copied by Géricault; and *Psyche carried off by the Zephyrs* (Louvre), with its vibrant undertones of Correggio. While most of his paintings have seriously deteriorated owing to his liberal use of bitumen, his admirable pencil drawings on ash-grey or blue-tinted paper, with their delicately blurred tracery of lines, as if glowing from within, transmit intact the essence of his art, the wealth and variety of his imagination, the melody of a form suavely yet briskly handled, and the silvery tenderness of a light which Corot was often to remember. Fine sets of these drawings can be seen in the Louvre, the Musée Condé at Chantilly and the local museum at Gray (Haute-Saône).

Even after Josephine fell into disgrace, Prud'hon continued to enjoy the patronage of Napoleon and gained the confidence of the new Empress Marie-Louise, who employed him as drawing master, art counsellor and decorator. He designed the furniture and decorations of

her bridal suite, the cradle of the King of Rome and the seal of the Empire; he decorated the Hôtel de Ville for a commemorative fête and gave what life and warmth he could to the chilly ceremonial of the Imperial court. At the 1812 Salon he exhibited *Venus and Adonis* (Wallace Collection, London), ordered by Marie-Louise for the Tuileries; at the 1814 Salon appeared his *Young Zephyr hovering over the Water* (Louvre), his last venture into the realm of Greek fable. His *Venus at her Bath* or *Innocence* (Louvre) he left unfinished, as the Restoration led him to concentrate on portraiture, which he had never ceased to practise, and religious painting. The tragic suicide in May 1821 of Constance Mayer, who since 1802 had been his pupil and devoted friend, consoling him for the misery of his married life, broke his spirit and darkened the last months of his life. In 1822 he painted the portrait of *Madame Jarre* (Louvre), her brow encircled with vine leaves and a Leonardesque smile playing about the corners of her mouth; this was followed by his last nightpiece, a poignant *Crucifixion* (Louvre), symbol of his own distress. "Happiness," he wrote to his daughter Emilie shortly before his death on February 11, 1823, "has never formed any part of my existence." But his entire œuvre, so delicately sensual, so steeped in melancholy, nostalgically reflects the dream of happiness that haunted his mind. Stendhal invites us to share the peculiar flavor and resonance to be got from that nostalgia: "Enjoy the emotion that comes of a picture by Prud'hon, a strain of Mozart, or a certain singular glance of a woman who is often in your thoughts."

Pierre-Paul Prud'hon (1758-1823). The Triumph of Bonaparte, 1800. Sketch. (35½ × 69″)
Musée des Beaux-Arts, Lyons.

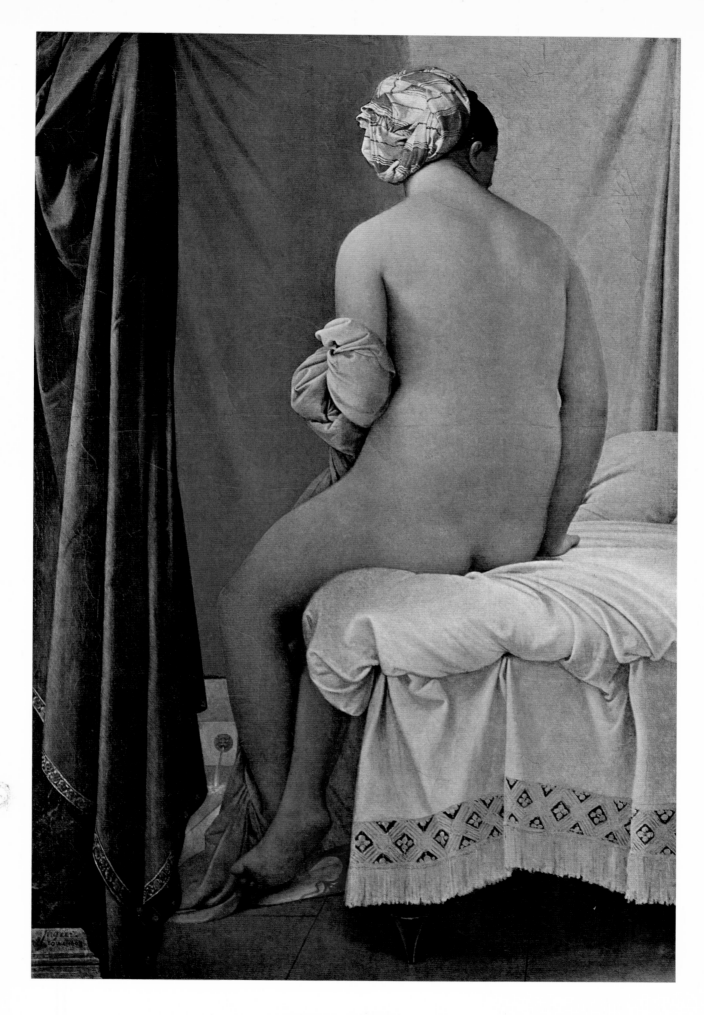

Jean-Dominique Ingres (1780-1867).
La Baigneuse de Valpinçon, 1808. (56¾ × 38¼″) Louvre, Paris.

Ingres and Stylization

INGRES was just twenty when the nineteenth century opened and his technical mastery was even then astonishingly evident. When he died in 1867, a few months before Baudelaire, Impressionism was already on the rise and Manet had already painted the *Déjeuner sur l'Herbe* and *Olympia*. Throughout this long period of time, an age in France of so many social and artistic upheavals, Ingres remained obstinately faithful to "the one true way," the Neoclassicism of his youth, which he prolonged far beyond its historical limits—with results which, despite the powerful unifying effect of his style, could not but be unequal, now anachronistic, now boldly inventive. The large-scale compositions, on which he thought to base his future glory, have become lifeless period-pieces, while the drawings, portraits and nudes, regarded in their day as secondary, incidental works, have fascinated modern painters from Seurat onward, Matisse and the cubist generation in particular. This contradiction is usually explained by describing Ingres as a Romantic in spite of himself; a would-be Classicist who, while abiding by classical principles and disciplines, was actually at the mercy of an unruly temperament and passionate instincts. Much has been made of this alluring paradox, but it may well be that it betrays a misconception of both types of art, without shedding any light either on the real underlying conflict in Ingres between doctrine and vision (which is not a case of Classical versus Romantic) or on the singular quality of a style directly stemming from that of David. Ingres must be seen clearly in relation to David, his master, before his position with respect to his future adversary Delacroix can be understood.

Born at Montauban, in southwestern France, on August 29, 1780, Jean-Dominique Ingres inherited both his artistic vocation and his love of music from his father, a decorator of great skill and versatility. At the age of eleven he began his apprenticeship at nearby Toulouse, a city proud of its Roman origins, its medieval churches, its Renaissance buildings, its tradition of learning. There he received a thorough grounding in the arts from three professors: the painter Joseph Roques, the sculptor Vigan and the landscape painter Briant. In August 1797, a few months after his arrival in Paris, he entered David's studio and, though only seventeen at the time, at once attracted attention by his earnestness, maturity and strength of character. "His character was cast in a single block, like a bronze statue," wrote half a century later his fellow pupil, Delécluze, who found him in 1854 exactly as he had known him in 1797, and noted in his first figure study the distinctive qualities of his life's work: finesse of outline, firm modeling, a true sense of form, and—revealing detail— a tendency to exaggerate.

Jean-Dominique Ingres (1780-1867). The Painter Granet (detail), 1807. Musée Granet, Aix-en-Provence.

Jean-Dominique Ingres (1780-1867). Portrait of Madame Devauçay (detail), 1807. Musée Condé, Chantilly.

the beginning of the misconception that was henceforth to weigh on his official career, and the beginning of his unfortunate orientation towards large-scale figure compositions. Elected a member of the Institute (1825) and appointed to a professorship at the Ecole des Beaux-Arts (1829), he also opened a school of his own which attracted large numbers of pupils and where, in reaction against current trends, his methods and ideas hardened into set doctrines. He undertook and rapidly completed the *Apotheosis of Homer* (1827), conceived as a ceiling panel for the Egyptian rooms in the Louvre; and worked hard and long over the *Martyrdom of St Symphorian* (Autun Cathedral), which he himself regarded as his *magnum opus*, but which met with a cool reception at the 1834 Salon. Out of spite he returned to Italy as director of the Villa Medici (1835-1841), which he administered with exemplary efficiency.

At last, on his return to Paris in 1841, he enjoyed the triumph he had so long hungered for. The despotic old man was loaded with honors, and the "legend" (and also the "caricature") took form that still clings to his name. Honors and social privileges he accepted naïvely, without discrimination, as an artist's due, indeed as the legitimate recognition of his genius and of the outdated tradition which, all his life, in the face of every innovation, he not only clung to but stubbornly, even haughtily, championed. "I may to some appear hard and harsh," he wrote as late as 1864 (at the age of eighty-four), "but desperate ills call for desperate remedies. I am bound to say how much I feel the rightness of my steadfast convictions and of that sincere love of art which, I venture to think, no one will gainsay me. Queer, crotchety, intolerant I may well seem. But as my exalted tastes are to me a religion, and as I can justify the loftiness of what I love and worship, it will be easy—leaving aside the whole question of my sensitive nerves—to account for my intolerance and my alleged peculiarities."

How, then, in this orthodox fanatic, are we to explain his fecund moments of unwitting deviation from the principles he held sacred; the puzzling oddities, both in his character and in his art, of which his contemporaries were so acutely aware? Wherein, for example, is he to be distinguished from David? By what evolutionary process do we move on from David's *Portrait of Madame Sériziat* to Ingres' *Portrait of Madame Rivière* (1805, Louvre), or from David's *Madame de Verninac* to Ingres' *Madame Devauçay* (1807, Chantilly), apparently so closely akin yet so different in spirit?

Ingres accepted all the principles that guided David—"the truest, the strictest and the purest," he called them—but he shifted their accent and modified their relationships. Again and again he reasserted the fundamental identity between nature, the antique and the Old Masters. "Always copy nature and learn to see things as they are. Hence the necessity of studying the antique and the Old Masters, not to imitate them but here again to learn to see." Yet each of these three bases of style, though still taken as a whole by David, were inflected by Ingres in parallel directions: the antique towards archaism, the Old Masters (i.e. the Renaissance masters) towards primitivism, and nature towards visual appearances and a "naïve" acceptance of sensations. The scale of references on which he based his work, in accordance with the tastes of the First Empire and his own partialities, was widened and better differentiated in proportion as he deepened his contacts with nature. His notion of nature, in the end primordial for an understanding of his art, remains complex and difficult to grasp, for it includes both the material reality of objects and the psychological truth of portraits. Baudelaire, with more insight than anyone else has shown, singled out what he called the "naturalism" of Ingres and its affinities with the early Courbet. In 1827, at the Ecole des Beaux-Arts, Ingres reacted against the *beau idéal* of Quatremère de Quincy and laid down this astonishing precept: "Style is nature."

The idealistic force that overcomes the constraints imposed by "nature," and the force that gives vitality to his style, is line. Ingres stands apart from David in assigning an even more tangible and active role to line. Line, for David, meant outline, strictly cleaving to

volumes, respecting human anatomy and recording visual reality. For Ingres, line generates form and movement (even smoke he conveys in terms of line); determined not so much by the model as by his own sensory responses to the model, his line tends to flow freely, obeying creative laws of its own. Ingres, as his pupil Amaury-Duval put it, "made a line of his own... which renders his impression and compels us to share it." Thanks to this expressive, musically contained stylization, which is a creation of his own and the secret of his novelty, he transposed the subject into a rhythmic motif, far overshot the simple goals of nineteenth-century realism, and showed himself a modern of the moderns in achieving the abstract equivalence of signs. In this sense, while keeping well within his own system, he departed from the classical canon and became the ancestor of those whom Maurice Denis was ineptly to call the "distorters," and who in point of fact were the imperious inventors of new forms, complete in themselves, self-sufficient and self-justifying.

Ingres' really creative work was done in his early period when, in isolation and obscurity, he courageously pursued a vision of his own in the teeth of academic hostility whose sarcasms and blindness he was the first painter of the century to suffer from. A particular accent or bias can be detected in the successive phases of his youth, varying with the mood and influence of the moment: "Etruscan" and Gothic before his departure for Italy, Quattrocentesque during the years in Rome, frankly Raphaelesque during his stay in Florence. After 1824, sudden recognition and fame forced an official role upon him which, however, affected not so much his style as his program. Apart from these fluctuations, there can scarcely be said to

Jean-Dominique Ingres (1780-1867).
Antiochus and Stratonice, 1866. (24 × 36¼") Musée Fabre, Montpellier.

be any evolution in his style or in his manner of conceiving and rendering form. To historical relativism he opposed the absolute cult of beauty; he represents an art of perfection, in contradistinction to an art of invention. This being so, the quality of his work varies little chronologically; such differences as there are stem rather from his interests of the moment, from the subjects he chooses.

Faithful (like David) to the hierarchy of genres, the very foundation of classicism, Ingres regarded himself as "a painter of history and not an illustrator of the middle classes." But devoid of imagination (like David), he proved the more incapable of giving life to large figure groups as he was wholly unsustained by any collective élan, any vivid ideal. He artificially worked out for himself a kind of autocratic humanism, based on the glorification of gods and heroes, masters of themselves and the world: Oedipus, Jupiter, Homer, Napoleon. His literary sources are made perfectly clear in his notebooks, and in his interpretations of them, based on ancient prototypes, critics have found it easy to detect his borrowings; indeed he never made any secret of these, admitting that his aim was "to be original by imitating." The resulting works as a rule are stiff and formal, lacking conviction and unity, flagrantly so in the *Vow of Louis XIII*, in which celestial vision and regal majesty fail to unite. The

Jean-Dominique Ingres (1780-1867). The Turkish Bath (detail), 1862.
Louvre, Paris.

P. Fr. 22

—   —

Jean-Dominique Ingres (1780-1867). The Turkish Bath (detail), 1862.
Louvre, Paris.

transcendence of a theme pre-eminently Baroque dissolves into a genre scene undistinguished except as a display of expert workmanship. As early as 1813 he was brooding over the difficulties of such a composition for a meticulous executant like himself, nourished on intellectual disciplines, habitually proceeding by juxtaposition and apt to linger over details. "For a good painter who is a master of his craft and has learnt to imitate nature, the longest part of his task is to think his picture out in full, to have it all in his head as it were, in order thereafter to throw himself wholeheartedly into the actual work and set it down at one go. Then, I think, the thing will be felt to be a whole." Even the *Apotheosis of Homer*, his manifesto, so much celebrated and one of his few large-scale works actually executed in the glow of its initial conception—even this has receded today into a make-believe empyrean in which only the admirable figures of the Iliad and the Odyssey retain a semblance of life. Worse was to come when Raphael again served him as a model for some sadly tedious political and religious allegories, which lapse into academicism and even truckle to officialdom. In these Ingres betrayed the supreme warrant for all he did: his own superlative gifts and that pure ideal of art for art's sake which Théophile Gautier praised him so feelingly for embodying, as the ultimate expression of Romanticism. The *Martyrdom of St Symphorian*, which engrossed him for ten years, brings to mind, on a less exalted plane, the *Rape of the Sabine Women*, on which in fact it is patterned; a few moving fragments, for example the woman embracing a child,

Jean-Dominique Ingres (1780-1867). The Turkish Bath, 1862. (Diameter 42½″) Louvre, Paris.

help to redeem the nerveless astringency of the picture as a whole. But these ambitious compositions are so carefully contrived, so highly finished, that the intended effect of monumentality utterly miscarries. Delacroix complained of the great ceiling panel of 1853 in the Hôtel de Ville, the *Apotheosis of Napoleon* (destroyed during the Commune in 1871), that it was but an enlarged cameo. The small easel pictures on "modern" (i.e. medieval and Renaissance) subjects, of which he made so many slightly differing versions, were much better suited to his gifts: the historical sequences on *Raphael, Aretino, Henri IV,* and the delightful legend of *Paolo and Francesca,* motifs very much in the "troubadour" taste of the time, treated all in subtle arabesques and that glowing preciosity of tone that one associates with miniature painting. He even went so far as to paint a contemporary scene, to which he was understandably attracted by the pomp of the ceremony and the magnificence of a setting he was familiar

with: *Pope Pius VII officiating in the Sistine Chapel*, a kind of *Coronation of Napoleon* in miniature, with the same gorgeous costumes and the same fidelity of portraiture. An initial version (1814), treated lengthwise, is in the National Gallery, Washington, and a later variant (1820), in a vertical format, is in the Louvre. Both have an exceptional brilliance of coloring, steeped in a luminous atmosphere of purple and gold.

Apart from the drawings, the most vital portion of Ingres' output consists of two series of works: the portraits, painted from sheer necessity as a means of livelihood; and the odalisques and bathers, which sprang from his deepest instincts. In both cases, avoiding set formulas and abstract schemes of composition, he created his style direct from life, a style answering to the innermost promptings of his nature, voiced and crystallized with magisterial power. Here, too, he drew more fully on a palette deliberately restricted in his larger, artificial compositions, and invented a personal color scheme admirably suited to his way of seeing —local tones of the same pitch and clarity as the flawless linework enveloping them. For, as he said, "there has never been a great draughtsman who failed to find the coloring exactly suited to the character of his line." From Delacroix to Cézanne, as we shall see in the following pages, the two terms of the equation were reversed, and it was a case of the great colorist finding exactly the right line. The perfection achieved by Ingres rests on a supreme harmony between form, expression and color, purity of design fusing with intensity of expression in the strictest economy of the painter's means. The very words in which he defined his method might have been uttered by Matisse (who in fact, as Jean Puy writes in describing the confrontation of the two pictures at the Louvre in 1907, was more attracted by Ingres' *Odalisque* than by Manet's *Olympia*). "Expression, which is the essential part of art," Ingres wrote, "is intimately bound up with form. The expression will be good only if it has been formulated with absolute accuracy. The simpler the lines and forms, the greater the force and beauty of the work."

His only source of livelihood as a young man, and his redeeming claim to fame in old age, the portraits are nearly all of them felicitous and successful paintings, though on different levels of achievement. Ingres was the last great portraitist to leave us, like Holbein, a complete gallery, intimate, official and cosmopolitan, of the men and women of his time. The *Portrait of Monsieur Bertin* (1832, Louvre), perhaps the most famous of them all, virtually the pictorial equivalent of some character in Balzac, so tellingly records the type figure of a social class then in the ascendant that its symbolic value almost exceeds its artistic value. The society portraits, in which he had to observe the proprieties of an exacting aristocracy and keep his powers of invention well under control, are nevertheless prodigies of technique and expression, those in particular in which the device of a mirror is used to broaden and mysteriously perfect the composition: *Madame de Senonnes* (1816, Nantes), the *Comtesse d'Haussonville* (1845, Frick Collection, New York), or *Madame Moitessier* (1856, National Gallery, London). Other portraits are presented against landscape backgrounds lyrically and architectonically attuned to the model's personality: *Mademoiselle Rivière* (1805, Louvre), *Monsieur Cordier* (1811, Louvre), or *Count Gouriev* (1821, Hermitage, Leningrad). The *Portrait of Madame de Senonnes*, a languorous, full-blown beauty in a robe of garnet-red velvet with lace ruching, is often held to be his masterpiece, but some may understandably prefer the three marvels of his youth, *Madame Rivière* (1805, Louvre), all undulating grace bound in a perfect oval, and above all, unsurpassable in their vitality and concentration, their plenitude and rigor, the *Portrait of Granet* (1807, Musée Granet, Aix-en-Provence) and the *Portrait of Madame Devauçay* (1807, Musée Condé, Chantilly). Abandoning the scumbles of David and the play of transparent shadows over light glazes, he employed here, though applied in thin, smooth coats, dense and contrasting pigments which, after a century and a half, have acquired a mellow golden patina. The sober distinction of the tones, yellows and blacks, olive greens and red browns, exalts the ivory and bistre flesh-tints and accords perfectly with an energetic poetry of form and expression.

In his first study of Ingres, written in 1846, Baudelaire noted the distinctive strain of feeling that runs through all his work, "love of woman," which his linear stylization transforms into outright eroticism. "His libertinage is earnest and carries conviction. Monsieur Ingres is never so happy, never so powerful, as when his genius can come to grips with the physical charms of some young beauty... If the island of Cythera were to inspire a picture from Monsieur Ingres, we may be sure that it would not be blithe and smiling like that of Watteau, but robust and substantial like antique love." After painting his *Apotheosis of Homer*, the epitome of all his doctrines, Ingres toyed for years with the idea of a complementary apotheosis of sensual pleasure. The opportunity of realizing it finally came when he was commissioned to decorate the great hall in the Château de Dampierre. He chose the theme of the Golden Age, picturing the innocence and nakedness of the Garden of Eden, the nostalgic myth of humanity before the Fall. The many preliminary designs number among the most beautiful things of their kind in all art, but after a decade of planning and preparation (1840-1850) the work came to a standstill, never to be resumed. No doubt the real reason for the failure of the project lay in the artist's congenital inability to organize a large surface, in the conflict between ideal transposition and naturalistic experience that dogged all his efforts, and in his stubborn concentration on details. The erotic obsessions of a lifetime found expression in the sensuous and exhilarating masterpiece which he finished and signed at the age of eighty-two, *The Turkish Bath* (1862, Louvre), a compact and circular concourse of female nudes.

Ingres renounced the "correct" anatomic proportions and design on which the heroic character of the male nude had long been based, even in the hands of David. The female form alone lent itself to swaying arabesques, to the sinuosities of line at its freest; the female form alone enabled him to reconcile his pagan sensuality and his plastic obsessions. "Beautiful forms," he said, "consist of straight planes rounded off." Many a composition of his would have lapsed into academicism but for the saving grace of some female figure—for example *Jupiter and Thetis* (1811, Aix-en-Provence) and *Roger and Angelica* (1819, Louvre). Jupiter, for all his gigantic proportions, is ridiculously insignificant, a mere support for the ingratiating caresses of Thetis, herself a plastic creation of unparalleled boldness and mastery. Roger is a stiff mechanical figure encased in over-elaborate armor, but Seurat was to copy the breathless nude of Angelica. Ingres himself set great store by his *Antiochus and Stratonice*, a subject very much in vogue in the late eighteenth century (it was treated by David), which he interpreted first in 1840 (Chantilly) and again in 1866 (Montpellier), with the layout reversed, a version perhaps superior to the first in its lesser insistence on details. The composition is rather spoilt by too searching an effort at archaeological reconstruction and by the melodramatic lifelikeness of the scene. But the figure of Stratonice herself, a Racinian heroine gripped by the hand of fate, the very soul of feminine charm and modesty, is a sublime creation, the happiest Ingres ever conceived. Thirty-five preparatory studies were required to work out the arresting pose of the arm, folded against the breast, which closes the pensive silhouette in all its statuesque perfection.

Romantic Exaltation

Eugène Delacroix (1798-1863). Scenes of the Massacres at Chios (detail), 1824. Louvre, Paris.

NEOCLASSICISM coexisted from the very beginning with certain antagonistic forces and cross-currents usually designated by the term Pre-Romanticism—a term hardly appropriate and indeed misleading, for what we have in each case are independent trends, not merely resurgences or anticipations. Pre-Romanticism is above all a literary phenomenon which colored, without changing them, the forms of neoclassical painting, whose break-up in any case was inevitable. Associated by Baudelaire with the very notion of modern art, Romanticism was the first really revolutionary development of nineteenth-century art, and it still conditions our emotional responses to a large extent. Historically speaking, Romantic painting in France represents the prevailing style of the period 1820-1850, sponsored by a generation still smarting under the fall of the Napoleonic Empire and bent on converting into spiritual energy the physical energy to which it aspired. The scope and significance of the movement are as vast as they are vague, and "one would have to violate every rule of clear thinking in order even to attempt to define it" (Paul Valéry). But its character can be brought out pretty clearly by contrasting it with Neoclassicism, to which it stands irreconcilably opposed by the new emphasis it lays on emotion, individual freedom, and ceaseless change. Neoclassicism had professed to observe absolute laws which, in reality, were no longer justified by any transcendental principle, and to serve a collectivity whose cohesion had actually been broken. Romanticism was the art of the individual giving uninhibited expression to his sense of solitude and freedom, his restlessness and private yearnings, his estrangement from society and his longing for mystical communion with nature. Poetry, painting, and music above all (to the subjective condition of which, as Walter Pater said, all art aspires) constitute its privileged means of expression. Throwing off the influence of sculpture and rigid contours, painters began to glory in the suggestive power of color. The soul had burst the limits of the body and gone forth to confront the unknown.

Despite the restraints imposed upon him by David, Gros, wrote Delacroix, "owed to himself alone the strong, original qualities which place him in the forefront of our school of painting." Endowed with visionary powers and a fine sense of color, he glorified the romantic hero *par excellence*, Napoleon, whose "life is the epic of our century for all the arts" (Delacroix).

Géricault's brief and brilliant career answered perfectly to Victor Hugo's description of the man of genius as "a mettlesome courser." Fired (to use his own words) with "a wild enthusiasm that overcomes and masters every obstacle," he embodied in his life and art the Byronic myth of Mazeppa. Near akin to Goya in many ways, he is at times a high Romantic, at times an uncompromising Realist.

Highly educated, gifted with superior powers of mind, a poet among painters, and the exalted interpreter of Dante and Shakespeare, Delacroix renewed the pictorial idiom of his time by assimilating the non-classical cultures. He transformed Romanticism from a fashion to a universal state of mind and founded the modern psychology of color. He was also the century's greatest decorator and its greatest exponent of Oriental themes.

Antoine-Jean Gros (1771-1835).
Bonaparte at the Battle of Arcola, 1796. (28¾ × 23¼″) Louvre, Paris.

Gros and the Napoleonic Saga

F AVORITE disciple of David and an ardent supporter of the young Delacroix, Gros was not a man of sufficient character to overcome the contradiction implied by these attachments. Hence the glaring inequalities of his work and a checkered career that ended in suicide. But during the glorious period in which he was at one with the spirit of the age and his gifts found their natural outlet, in the period, that is, between his unsure beginnings and a tragic end, he speeded up the transition from Neoclassicism (in which he had been schooled) to Romanticism, of which his temperament and instincts made him a pioneer.

Antoine-Jean Gros was born in Paris on March 16, 1771. At fourteen he was admitted to David's studio; the master had just returned from his second stay in Rome and was scoring a triumph with his *Oath of the Horatii*. Gros quickly distinguished himself among David's pupils, and won his esteem and affection. In January 1793, through the good offices of David, he obtained a passport for Italy. After visiting Florence, Milan and Venice, he settled at Genoa where, in the rich local collections, he saw and admired works by Puget, Van Dyck and Rubens. He supported himself by his brush, and his warm sensibility and handsome, melancholy features, as we see them in the early self-portraits of 1791 (Toulouse) and 1795 (Versailles), made him a favorite in local society, particularly with the ladies. In December 1796 he met Josephine Bonaparte, who took him with her in her carriage to Milan and presented him to Napoleon, fresh from the battle of Arcola. He at once made a portrait of the victorious general, showing him in the thick of the fight, his characteristic silhouette forming a sweeping curve as he looks back at the troops he is leading to victory; the initial study is in the Louvre, the finished painting in the Versailles Museum. In this inaugural work Gros seized on and vividly rendered those epic qualities of Napoleon's first Italian campaign which Stendhal so well conveys in the opening pages of the *Chartreuse de Parme*, in which the painter rightly plays his part. His glory was henceforth to be bound up with that of the hero "whose first steps had just shaken the world" and who now, before turning to fresh campaigns, appointed Gros a member of the commission set up to select (i.e. confiscate) works of art from Italian collections for shipment to France, where they went to enrich the Louvre.

It was a great disappointment to him that he missed the opportunity of following the "new Alexander" to Egypt. Out of deference for David he executed some cold and painstaking works on antique subjects, *Alexander and Bucephalus* and *Timoleon and Timophanes*. Returning to Paris after eight years' absence, he exhibited at the 1801 Salon his *Bonaparte at Arcola,*

which shows his spirited brushwork at its best, and *Sappho leaping into the Sea from the Leucadian Promontory*, Davidian in conception but with moonlight effects in the manner of Girodet. Gros, oddly enough, though after the Italian campaign he stayed at home and saw none of the distant battles and foreign lands which he was asked to paint, excelled all the military chroniclers of his time and produced a series of battle pictures no less admirable for their historical exactitude—vouched for by eye-witnesses—than for their purely pictorial qualities. For each picture Gros documented himself with the utmost care and transposed in imagination the experience he had gained during the Italian campaign. It is, first and foremost, by virtue of this visionary power, which no other of David's followers possessed, that he belongs to the romantic movement. Before Goya, Géricault and Delacroix, he renewed the artistic and moral interpretation of a particularly difficult type of painting, showing modern warfare as it really was. Delestre, his friend and biographer (1845), and a frequent visitor to his studio, made a careful record of his doctrines and working methods, very different from those of David. He laid stress on the dynamics of design, the virtue of color, and concern for the general unity. As against the fragmentary studies and individuation of the neoclassical painters, he recommended "developing each part simultaneously" so as constantly to maintain the homogeneity of the execution. Lastly, it was Gros who reintroduced color as an expressive force and a connecting principle. He spoke out against excessive austerity and strictness in painting. To the forthright tones of light and contrasting tones of shadow, he added, freshly and firmly brushed in, the intermediate half-tones, here and there bringing out local texture with transparent scumbles. Following his example, Géricault, Delacroix and Daumier built up their works around internal masses and not in terms of contours, while his conception of color was taken over by the Impressionists and Cézanne.

The initial picture of this sequence, which also marks the beginnings of Orientalism in nineteenth-century painting, is the *Battle of Nazareth*. The order for the work was rescinded, and only the preliminary sketch was actually carried out (1801, Nantes Museum). Géricault paid a thousand francs for the privilege of making a copy of it (presented by Horace Vernet to the Avignon Museum). Gros stressed the tension between the hero he set out to glorify and the multitude engaged in battle. Highly colored cavalry units are seen grouped around General Junot, wearing a tricolored uniform and slashing with his sword at the Turkish cavalry squadrons in their white burnouses, as they turn and fly under the bright Palestinian sky. "To those who are unacquainted with this admirable sketch," wrote Delacroix, "it is impossible to give an idea of the vigor, the brilliance, the sweep, and at the same time the compositional skill that it reveals. The painter here proves himself a consummate master." Gros developed his style and enjoyed a complete success at the 1804 Salon with a second Oriental episode, of a very different character: *Bonaparte visiting the Plague-House of Jaffa* (Louvre). Beneath the arches of a mosque converted into a lazaretto, threading his way among the dead and dying, the young Napoleon renews the healing gesture of the miracle-workers of all ages and touches with his outstretched hand the sores of one of the plague-stricken. Using the firsthand information supplied him by Denon, he recreates the exotic setting with almost uncanny accuracy. Discarding both the pyramidal design and the bas-relief conception of David, he composed the picture in terms of dark masses and contrasted lighting. The *Battle of Aboukir* (Versailles), commissioned by Murat and exhibited at the 1806 Salon, reverts to and develops on a vast scale the theme sketched out in the *Battle of Nazareth*, but with an even greater turbulence in the mêlée of men and horses.

By 1808 Gros had attained the summit of his powers, and at the Salon of that year, alongside David's *Coronation of Napoleon*, he exhibited his *Napoleon on the Battlefield of Eylau* (Louvre), a funeral symphony illustrating not so much the victory bought at too high a price as the pity and compassion inspired by the horrors of war. The immensity of the plain and the wan and eerie daylight of a Polish winter, conveyed no less truthfully than the scorching sunlight of the East, emphasize the bleakness of the scene. Delacroix admired everything

about it, even its disproportions, and particularly what he called "the poetry of the details" in this tragic work, of which he himself gave a perfect description. "Entire ranks of the regiments fallen in battle are lying on the snow like sheaves evenly spaced out in this cruel harvest of young manhood. The village of Eylau is still burning on the right... Here and there dying horses, shaking off the night frost, struggle to their feet in a final effort and fall back over the bodies of their dead masters... This sinister picture, made up of a hundred pictures, seems to appeal to the eye and the mind from all sides at once; yet all this is but the setting for the sublime figure of Napoleon."

The compositions that followed, the *Taking of Madrid* (1809), the *Battle of the Pyramids* (1810) and the *Battle of Austerlitz* (1812), all in the Versailles Museum, abound in admirable details, with costumes and ethnic types scrupulously differentiated and local atmosphere tellingly conveyed; but they lack the epic sweep and dramatic character of the *Battle of Eylau*. In addition to these large-scale compositions, Gros painted many separate portraits of the French war leaders, proudly silhouetted against the scene of their exploits: *General Lasalle* (1808, Collection of the Marquise de Champeaux, Toury Lurcy) and *Count General Fournier-Sarlovèze* (1812, Louvre), brilliant equestrian portraits of Napoleon's dashing cavalry officers. Outstanding among the full-length portraits is his posthumous likeness of *Christine Boyer* (c. 1800, Louvre), a wraithlike figure in a romantic woodland setting. He excelled, too, in such intimate half-length portraits, even more hauntingly expressive, as *The Young Amalric* (1804, Private Collection, Paris) and *Madame Récamier* (c. 1825, Zagreb Museum) in her riper years. As for *Charles V received by Francis I at the Abbey of Saint-Denis* (1812, Louvre), in

Antoine-Jean Gros (1771-1835).
Napoleon on the Battlefield of Eylau, 1808. (210 × 315″) Louvre, Paris.

which he deployed the full resources of his palette, its style and dimensions make it the first notable success in a field, that of French history and archaeological evocation, that was to be much cultivated by the little masters of the romantic movement. The Restoration inspired his last two works on contemporary themes: the *Departure of Louis XVIII from the Tuileries* (1817, Versailles) and the *Embarkation of the Duchesse d'Angoulême* (1819, Bordeaux).

David, driven into exile upon the return of the Bourbons in 1815, made over his studio to Gros, exhorting him to maintain his doctrines in their pristine purity and to return to the antique and mythological subjects. As early as 1822, Gros recognized and paid generous tribute to the genius of Delacroix and the painting of the future, but he himself, alas, took David's counsels to heart, succumbing to the baneful influence of a tyrannical master and an outmoded art. He accepted commissions for large mural paintings, but his cold and spiritless decorations for the Panthéon (1811-1824) and his ceiling panels for the Egyptian rooms in the Louvre (1827) show a decline and a marked unfitness for this type of work. He found himself despised by the triumphant Romantics, for whom he had prepared the way, and by the classical-minded followers of Ingres, who robbed him of most of his pupils. In 1834 he declined a commission to paint the Battle of Jena for Versailles, which would have afforded him an opportunity of returning to his earlier and happier vein. Stubbornly persisting in the path marked out for him by David, he staked everything on a final effort: his *Hercules and*

Joseph-Ferdinand Boissard de Boisdenier (1813-1866).

Episode in the Retreat from Russia, 1835. (63 × 88⅝″) Musée des Beaux-Arts, Rouen.

Nicolas-Toussaint Charlet (1792-1845).
The Retreat from Russia. Undated. (43⅛ × 82½") Musée des Beaux-Arts, Lyons.

Diomedes (Toulouse), exhibited at the 1835 Salon. But it was sharply criticized and he gave way to despair. On July 26 he was found drowned in the Seine near Meudon. "The suicide of Gros," wrote Delacroix, "is one of the saddest events in the annals of human passion."

Gros disappeared from the scene just as the romantic generation was awakening, with keen nostalgia, to a sense of the glory and grandeur of the Napoleonic era. The 1835 Salon, so tragic for Gros himself, gave an enthusiastic reception to one of the most brilliant battle pieces produced in imitation of his own—by one of his pupils, as it so happened—and esteemed by all to be superior to Gros's in "dramatic intensity": the *Episode in the Retreat from Russia* (Rouen) by Boissard de Boisdenier (1813-1866). This artist, a sophisticated dilettante, painter, poet, musician and linguist, presided over the famous gatherings at the Hôtel Pimodan, attended by Gautier, Balzac and Baudelaire among others. He produced little else besides this exceptionally fine canvas, a tragic scene apparently based on a detail in the foreground of Gros's *Battle of Eylau*, enlarged and treated on a monumental scale. The following year, at the 1836 Salon, the most successful exhibitor was again a pupil of Gros's, Nicolas-Toussaint Charlet (1792-1845), known chiefly for his lithographs; and again the successful work was *The Retreat from Russia* (Lyons), in which the Grande Armée was virtually destroyed. Ney, Murat, Eugène de Beauharnais, all the great leaders and even Napoleon himself, have made their escape, leaving the wretched troops to their fate in the numbing cold and blinding snows of the Russian winter. Both Alfred de Musset and Delacroix commended the fine intensity of this poignant canvas, unsustained by any particular structural power, but vigorously executed in slanting or whirling strokes of the brush, with sweeping tracts of cold colors.

Théodore Géricault (1791-1824).
Cavalry Officer of the Imperial Guard, 1812. Sketch. (20⅝ × 15¾″) Louvre, Paris.

Brilliance of Géricault

LIKE Giorgione and Seurat, Géricault died at the age of thirty-two. A mysterious and fascinating figure, he represents far more than a connecting link between Gros and Delacroix, the role to which his brief career has often been reduced by undiscerning critics—though even so this would suffice to justify his fame. True, his work promised more than it achieved. Experimental, many-sided, disconnected, it consists largely of sketches, projects and designs; immense in its projected scope, it failed to reach fruition and remains but a mighty fragment. Nevertheless, he prefigured most of the subsequent developments of the century and his art contained synthetic elements which, as we now can see, link Poussin with Cézanne, Michelangelo with Daumier, Caravaggio with Courbet, and Impressionism with its English sources.

Born at Rouen on September 26, 1791, Théodore Géricault moved with his parents to Paris shortly before 1800. An only child, hypersensitive and unruly, gentle and excitable by turns, he lost his mother when he was only ten years old, and this bereavement clouded his childhood, already deeply marked by the turbulent aftermath of the French Revolution. During his schooldays at the Lycée Impérial, he neglected his studies in his enthusiasm for painting and horses. The two heroes he then worshipped were Rubens and the circus rider Franconi, manager of the Cirque Olympique. Possessed of private means enabling him to live as the fancy took him, he disregarded the opposition of his father, a lawyer who had gone into business, and flung himself into his vocation with juvenile enthusiasm. "Whatever stands in the way of the triumphant march of genius," he wrote in a manuscript that outspokenly summed up the ideas behind the new aesthetic, "acts as an irritant and fills the artist with a feverish enthusiasm that overcomes and masters every obstacle... Genius is the fire of a volcano which must and will burst forth, because the truly creative artist is constrained by a law of his being to shine, illuminate and amaze the world."

In his lifetime Géricault exhibited but three pictures, the only ones he considered finished works: the *Cavalry Officer of the Imperial Guard Charging* (1812), the *Wounded Cuirassier* (1814) and the *Raft of the Medusa* (1819), which latter created a sensation at the 1819 Salon. These famous paintings, dated and fully documented, are however only the salient landmarks of a much larger body of virtually unknown works, of whose rich diversity they give as a matter of fact but little indication. Charles Clément, in the valuable monograph (1867) in which, indignant with the way Géricault's work had been neglected over a long period, he

sought to "pay homage and do justice to the greatest artist of our time" and "focus the eyes of an indifferent public on his noble figure," divided the artist's brief and fruitful career into six phases corresponding to his successive activities and interests: the formative years (1808-1812), the period of military themes (1812-1816), the Italian interlude (1816-1817), the *Medusa* period (1817-1819), the visit to England (1820-1821) and the final years (1822-1824). This is a clear and helpful classification, but it does not exactly tally with the complex evolution of the artist's style, further complicated by the many problems of attribution and chronology which remain unsolved. It is unfortunate that no official retrospective exhibition has ever been organized. This alone would afford the opportunity for a systematic regrouping of his work and demonstrate the importance of a painter whom Michelet regarded as the most expressive of his period, but whose real admirers today are limited to a small and discriminating élite.

From 1808 to 1810 Géricault worked under Carle Vernet (1758-1825), a witty and fashionable painter of horses and racing scenes, an admirer of the English school and an observer too of contemporary life. From him Géricault learned more about living and using his eyes than he did about painting. He became friendly with his teacher's son, Horace Vernet, who successfully carried on the family traditions of this dynasty of painters; and in this milieu, superficial no doubt but genial and stimulating, he received an impress by no means so negligible as is commonly supposed. "An amazing man, this Carle Vernet," wrote Baudelaire. "His work is a world in itself, a *Comédie humaine* in miniature." In 1810, acting as always on impulse, Géricault changed teachers and entered the studio of David's former pupil Guérin, who—in spite of himself—trained the Romantic generation, just as Gustave Moreau was to train that of Matisse and the Fauves. Among his pupils were Champmartin, Léon Cogniet, Henriquel-Dupont, Paul Huet, the Scheffer brothers, Riesener, Delacroix and many more. We know nothing of Guérin's student-in-charge, the enigmatic Champion, who according to Delacroix exerted a considerable influence on the group and, in particular, on Géricault himself and his bosom friend Dedreux-Dorcy. The first requisite for a fuller understanding of Géricault's background and beginnings as an artist would be a thorough study—unfortunately beyond the scope of this volume—of Guérin's studio, whose atmosphere is so tantalizingly evoked in Balzac's *La Rabouilleuse* and *Un Ménage de Garçon*.

Géricault embarked on a series of powerful figure studies of the male and female nude, painted from life, planned a number of vast mythological compositions (never carried out), and spent long hours observing the horses in the Versailles stables and the Old Masters at the Louvre, then temporarily enriched with many of the greatest masterpieces in Europe brought to Paris by Napoleon. He was the first modern painter to realize the encyclopedic value of the museum as a direct means of private tuition and self-development, and his example was followed by Delacroix, Courbet, Manet, Degas, Cézanne and Seurat. Clément lists thirty-two copies, but the catalogue of the Géricault sale (at the Hôtel Bullion, November 2 and 3, 1824) recently exhumed by L. Eitner (*Gazette des Beaux-Arts*, February 1959), lists more than sixty; most of these works, all of the utmost interest and of high quality, were purchased by fellow artists, notably Delacroix, and a few enlightened collectors. Including copies both of contemporaries (David, Gros, Prud'hon, Guérin, Carle Vernet) and Renaissance and Baroque masters, they reveal a very wide field of interest and range of taste, centering chiefly however on the Flemish and Venetian colorists, the Mannerists and the Caravaggeschi. The most arresting (now in the Bühler Collection, Winterthur), both in its theme and its breadth of treatment, is his copy of Caravaggio's great *Deposition*, which had been removed from the Vatican and placed in the Louvre in 1797 (it was restored to the Vatican after 1815). It is a curious fact that, while for the most part Géricault chose to copy highly emotional religious subjects, usually episodes of the Passion, his own work was secular throughout, in open reaction against the clerical bias of the Restoration. His sketchbooks (all of them torn apart except those in the Louvre and Chicago) contain parallel and complementary studies after Michelangelo's sculptures and the bas-reliefs on Hellenistic sarcophagi; in many

ways they recall Poussin and anticipate Cézanne. Géricault aspired to combine plastic energy with pictorial verve, densely compounded masses with moving lights. His historical role was not so much to create a new style as to deepen and enrich the pictorial design he inherited and believed in, revitalizing it and rendering it amenable to the new modes of expression. "Let him go his own way," Guérin shrewdly commented, disarmed by his gifts and versatility, "he has the makings of three or four painters."

At the age of twenty-one he tried his luck at the 1812 Salon, not with an antique theme but with a contemporary subject. At the last moment he submitted his *Cavalry Officer of the Imperial Guard Charging* (Louvre), which the jury accepted and proceeded to hang alongside Gros's much-admired equestrian portrait of Murat. The two works have certain affinities, but Géricault's canvas after all was not so much a portrait as a symbolic glorification of war painted with an ardor and sweep that took David by surprise when he caught sight of it: "Where can this come from? I fail to recognize this brushwork." Clément, touching on the creative processes of the artist, whose work was always based on visual experience, tells how this picture took shape in his mind while he was on his way to the Fête de Saint-Cloud on September 13, 1812. "He saw on the road one of those large covered wagons which Parisian artisans share the expenses of renting and convert into an omnibus on these occasions. It was drawn by a grey horse, by no means a handsome one, but high-mettled and beautifully colored. Unaccustomed to the harness, with bloodshot eyes, foaming mouth and wind-blown mane, the spirited animal was plunging and rearing in the dust under a bright sun. That sun was

Théodore Géricault (1791-1824). The Death of Hippolytus. Undated. (10¼ × 15″) Musée Fabre, Montpellier.

the sun of Austerlitz. That dust was the smoke of battle. That horse was the mettlesome charger, maddened by the smell of powder, the flash of gunfire, the roar of the cannon. He saw it mounted by one of those bold and brilliant young officers, one of those sons of Mars, the heroes and demi-gods of the age. It was like a vision. He went home and at once set to work." That was on the 13th of September. The official Salon was to open on November 1 and all entries had to be submitted before October 12. Géricault therefore had less than a month in which to paint his picture—a vast composition requiring a large number of sketches, many of which have been lost, but the finest, most brilliant of which is preserved in the Louvre.

In spite of its size (nearly ten feet high), unusual for a single figure, the final painting preserves all the warmth and freshness of the initial inspiration—a real bravura piece in its vigorous design, bold movement, light effects and coloristic brio. The horse's head, wild-eyed and defiant, together with the bristling mane, is particularly fine. Géricault was awarded a medal and warmly praised (the only public recognition he received in his lifetime) but no one bought the picture. He exhibited it again at the next Salon, held in November 1814, after the fall of the Empire, with Napoleon in exile and Paris occupied by the Allied armies; and this time it was accompanied by a contrasting pendant, the *Wounded Cuirassier* (Louvre), a work unevenly handled and more striking than really successful. The theme here had not been thrust upon him in a flash of inspiration, but had had to be worked out by trial and

Théodore Géricault (1791-1824). Horse-Race on the Corso in Rome, 1817. Sketch. (17¾ × 23⅝″) Louvre, Paris.

Théodore Géricault (1791-1824). The Bull Market, 1817. (23⅛ × 19¾″)
Courtesy of the Fogg Art Museum, Harvard University. Bequest of Granville L. Winthrop.

error; its genesis and maturation have been analysed, each time in the light of newly discovered documents, by René Huyghe (*L'Amour de l'Art*, February 1931), L. Eitner (*Burlington Magazine*, August 1954) and L. Johnson (*Burlington Magazine*, March 1955). Its emotive impact springs from the contrast between the glum resignation of the defeated warrior, who has set foot on the ground and is about to come down the slope, and the agitation of the horse, still excited by the action of the battle. Thus, without either allegorizing or idealizing, simply by his epic magnification of reality and his intuitive grasp of the vital moments of history in the making (and these were his two finest gifts), Géricault symbolized the rise and fall of the French Empire in two telling images of horsemen, one charging, the other unhorsed. The two works differ not only in conception but in technique, the first fluid and colorful under the influence of Rubens and Gros, the second massive and somber, built up with dense, fully modeled pigments which are handled with even surer strokes in the two versions of a half-length *Cavalryman* (Louvre and Rouen). In the interval between these works, which mark two changes of style, Géricault painted, first, a great many studies of horses, the most extra-ordinary of them representing twenty-five *Hindquarters* on a single canvas (Vicomtesse de Noailles Collection, Paris), arranged in three rows, in all the variety of their different coats,

Théodore Géricault (1791-1824).

The Raft of the Medusa, 1818. Unfinished Sketch. (25½ × 32⅝″) Louvre, Paris.

a masterpiece of documentary accuracy and pictorial vividness; and secondly a series of small military portraits, as refined and daintily handled as miniatures, among them the *Trumpeter of the Polish Lancers* (Glasgow), the *Seated Trumpeter* (Vienna) and the *Red Lancer* (Collection of Baron Elie de Rothschild, Paris).

After the Salon of 1814, acting on a sudden impulse wholly at variance with the liberal ideas he was later to profess, he enlisted in a regiment of Grey Musketeers raised by Louis XVIII and followed the king to Béthune during the Hundred Days. (This curious episode, which has given rise to various interpretations, was ingeniously novelized by Aragon in *La Semaine Sainte*.) Between March 1815, when his regiment was disbanded, and September 1816, when he left for Italy, he was entangled in a mysterious and hopeless love affair whose exact circumstances can only be guessed at. Presumably he fell in love with a married woman, older than himself; but the only evidence we have (pointed out by K. Berger) is his obsession with the idea of a mother who has compromised herself, and the unconscious motivation that can be read into the small dramatic canvas in the Musée Fabre, Montpellier, the *Death of Hippolytus*, a theme that had not been treated since Rubens and Poussin. It was during this period of emotional involvement and slackened output, as he turned for mental relief towards antique themes (sketching out a *Battle of Giants* and a *Mars and Venus*), that he probably painted the three recently discovered *Landscapes* (Walter P. Chrysler and H. Hartford Collections, New York), larger in size than the Louvre *Flood*, built up on traditional foundations and yet, thanks to their spirited brushwork and flickering lights, full of a lyrical power that strikes a wholly modern note. Géricault took over classical forms and, recasting them in the heat of his imagination, compelled them to express romantic feelings. "Whatever he touches," wrote Delacroix, "he lifts up and charges with new life."

While the state of his feelings may have driven him to seek a change of scene, the fact remains that his trip to Italy came at that time as a natural sequel to the evolution of his style since 1814, increasingly affected by French influences (Poussin, Coustou, Clodion, Prud'hon and even Girodet). Géricault reached Florence on October 10, 1816, where he studied Michelangelo and discovered the Tuscan Mannerists. In November he went on to Rome, where the Sistine Chapel held him fascinated—at the very time when it was fascinating Stendhal, whom he may well have met there (and whom he resembles in many ways). He made friends with Auguste and Victor Schnetz. He paid a visit to Ingres and admired his drawings, but outstayed his welcome and had to be shown to the door. He drew and sketched in the streets (one of these sketches represents an execution) and the Campagna.

In the spring of 1817, during the Carnival, he was particularly struck by one of the popular amusements described by Goethe and evoked by Berlioz, the famous race of riderless horses held on the Corso amid the wild cries of the crowd. He chose to represent the moment before the departure, as the young grooms strain every muscle to hold back the restive, high-stepping animals at the starting gate. He began an immense canvas some thirty feet high, working up each part, as usual, on the basis of numerous drawings and some twenty sketches. The sketch now in the Louvre (the latest in date according to Clément) enables us to gauge the progressive crystallization of the theme from the first impulsive jottings (Walters Art Gallery, Baltimore), through the transition from a direct Baroque vision, tautly extended along the diagonal, to a classical design in terms of echeloned bas-reliefs. The famous version in the Rouen Museum, distinct from the others, shows but a single prancing courser held in check by four nude athletes. In a sober, timeless setting of blue hills and clouds, it matches the rhythmic grandeur and purity of Poussin and the friezes of the Parthenon. Géricault here combines to perfection the two themes—symbols of vital energy and plastic beauty—that were to haunt Degas: the horse and the nude. Yet he remained faithful (he was the last to do so) to David's conception of the male nude. The *Bull Market* (Fogg Art Museum, Cambridge, Mass.), preceded by some admirable drawings, is closely related in spirit and

Théodore Géricault (1791-1824).
The Insane Kleptomaniac, about 1822. (24 × 20″) Musée des Beaux-Arts, Ghent.

method to the *Horse-Race on the Corso,* except that the urban setting of the latter has been changed into a landscape. He contrived to combine the vividness of a direct impression with reminiscences of the bulls on Mithraic sarcophagi. Bright touches of green, red and blue traverse the rich modulation of greys and browns that bring out volumes.

In a year's time Géricault saw all he wished to see in Italy. By the autumn of 1817 he was back in his studio in the Rue des Martyrs. Located in this same picturesque quarter of Paris was the Café de la Nouvelle Athènes, where the leaders of the Opposition party gathered in the evenings to air their views. Géricault sympathized with them wholeheartedly. He inveighed against the hypocrisy of the Restoration, loathed (as he put it) "cool heat and the sensibility which responds only to winds, storms and moonlight," and turned with generous sympathies to the realities of contemporary life. He tried his hand at lithography almost as soon as he heard of the process (invented in 1798) and quickly made himself a master of it. Always a keen, scientific observer of animal life, he studied the wild beasts at the Jardin des Plantes long before Delacroix and Barye. Though without the Spaniard's visionary faculties and powers of insight, Géricault had much in common with Goya: the same insatiable curiosity, the same consuming interest in scenes of violence and horror. He executed, for example, an enthralling series of drawings (Rouen Museum and Private Collection, U.S.A.) illustrating the successive episodes of the Fualdes Affair, a famous political crime of the day.

Another contemporary event, of wider implications and highly damaging to the régime, had already attracted his attention. On July 2, 1816, the French frigate *Medusa* bound for Senegal was wrecked off the west coast of Africa owing to the incompetency of the captain, a reinstated émigré. The ship's officers and passengers took to the few available lifeboats, while the one hundred and fifty crewmen were taken in tow aboard a makeshift raft. The tow-lines snapped and the raft remained adrift on the ocean for twelve days with neither water nor provisions of any kind. By the time it was sighted and picked up by a passing ship, the *Argus,* there were only fifteen survivors, more dead than alive. Two of them, Corréard, who had built the ship, and Savigny, a doctor, published a detailed account of the catastrophe, but its sale was forbidden by the government. Géricault sought out the two men and interviewed other survivors, whom he invited to pose for him. In his studio he installed an exact model of the raft on a reduced scale and at the neighboring Hôpital Beaujon he painted a series of "still lifes" of human heads and severed limbs, astounding in their almost clinical accuracy and poignant intensity (Louvre, Stockholm, Montpellier, etc.). By these means he thoroughly familiarized himself with his subject, for which he made over fifty sketches and preparatory designs; these, could they ever be brought together, would in themselves form an exhibition of the highest interest. For a time he hesitated between several episodes—the mutiny of the sailors, the rescue of the castaways—and finally fixed on the climax of the odyssey, the moment when the survivors on the drifting raft sight a sail on the horizon. In November 1818 he shut himself up in his studio and for the next eight months worked on the picture uninterruptedly, except for a brief trip to Le Havre for another look at the sea. Exhibited at the 1819 Salon, it is by far his most ambitious and monumental work, and is still the painting by which he is best known. Despite the painstaking thoroughness of his documentation, he was unable to dominate so vast a surface without resorting to an occasional artifice, and what we find on this raft are the tormented souls of the Sistine Chapel, the dead of Eylau, and even a few of Rosso's macabre figures. Years before Michelet drew attention to it, Batissier, the artist's first biographer (1842), pointed out the historical implications of the painting: "the struggle of our powerless country, the drama of a leaderless generation." All influences have been absorbed and unified by an imperious grip galvanizing form, making the most of texture, and imparting to the whole a modern pathos. With its Caravaggesque lighting divided into two zones, the composition combines the Baroque diagonal and the classical pyramid, sweeping the eye upward towards the look-out and the promise of salvation, and compelling it by the same movement to cross the area of despair in the foreground.

Eugène Delacroix (1798-1863).

The Execution of the Doge Marino Faliero, 1826. (56⅞ × 44⅜″)

Reproduced by Permission of the Trustees of the Wallace Collection, London.

Delacroix and the Poetry of Color

Delacroix, anyhow in his early work, followed the path traced out by Gros and Géricault but deviated from that of David—to whom Gros and Géricault were still to some extent indebted—and found in Ingres a necessary rival. David was a consummate technician, Ingres a great master, Géricault a magnificent temperament. Eugène Delacroix, himself one of the favored few of that Almighty God whom he invokes so movingly in the last pages of his *Journal*, reigned supreme over the art world of his day, thanks to the rare advantage of possessing both high intelligence and a gift for painting unique of its kind. There is no separating the influence exerted by his work, due both to its brilliant technique and its spiritual impact, from the distinguished personality of the man himself, who won the allegiance and affection of his contemporaries, even of those who thought little of his painting, and who showed himself in his writings the peer of Stendhal in searching self-analysis and of Leonardo in aesthetic speculation. To this may be added, as a crowning factor predisposing us in Delacroix's favor, the eloquent appreciations of Baudelaire. Cézanne, who so profoundly mistrusted art criticism, dreamed all his life of composing an *Apotheosis of Delacroix*, and a few weeks before his death (as we learn from a letter to his son dated September 28, 1906) was reading Baudelaire's studies of his hero.

Born at Saint-Maurice, near Paris, on April 26, 1798, Eugène Delacroix is believed, on strong evidence, to have been a natural son of Talleyrand's. His mother came of families closely related to the famous eighteenth-century French cabinet-makers Oeben and Riesener. His childhood was spent at Marseilles and Bordeaux, where his legal father, who died in 1805, held the post of Prefect. He showed a precocious taste for drawing and took music lessons from an old friend of Mozart. From 1806 to 1815 he received a sound classical education at the Lycée Impérial in Paris and paid those frequent visits to the Louvre which decided his vocation. In 1813 he spent his summer holidays near the ruined abbey of Valmont, near Fécamp, on the English Channel, and this romantic spot, which he often revisited after 1829, made a strong impression on his mind, inspiring him, as he wrote to his friend Louvet, "with a host of wholly romantic ideas." The death of his mother in September 1814 was a cruel blow; thereafter he lived with his sister Henriette de Verninac, of whom David had painted the magnificent portrait reproduced on page 12. In the spring of 1816 he entered the famous studio of Baron Guérin, where Géricault (whose fervent admirer he soon became) occasionally put in an appearance. "It was here," he later wrote, "that the seeds were sown of that so-called Romantic art of which, if public opinion is to be trusted, I am now the moving spirit.

If by Romanticism is meant the free expression of my personal feelings, my aloofness from the standardized types of painting prescribed in the Schools, and my dislike of academic formulas, I must confess that not only am I a Romantic but that I already was one at the age of fifteen! Even then I much preferred Prud'hon and Gros to Guérin and Girodet."

By 1820 he felt the first onset of that slow fever which in the end consumed him, and which almost from the start constrained him to husband his resources and direct all his energies into his painting. In 1821 he finished the *Virgin of the Sacred Heart* (Ajaccio Cathedral), a religious commission passed on to him by Géricault; painted an allegorical series of the seasons to decorate the dining room of the new town house built by the actor Talma in the Rue de la Tour-des-Dames; and portrayed himself, a dark, mysterious figure, a brooding but imperious presence, in the so-called *Portrait of Delacroix as Hamlet* in the Louvre.

On April 15, 1822, Delacroix confided to his friend Soulier (from whom he learned English and watercolor technique): "I have just finished a back-breaking piece of work which has taken up every minute of my time for the past two and a half months. In this space of time I have made a picture of considerable size which will be shown at the Salon. I was very keen on figuring in it this year, and so I've decided to try my luck." The result was a storm of controversy around his name, which in fact did not subside until his death. A visionary transposition of the *Raft of the Medusa*, the *Dante and Virgil in the Inferno* (Louvre)—later to be copied by Corot, Courbet, Manet and Cézanne—is the first landmark on that lifelong journey of self-exploration which was to lead Delacroix out of the Styx, towards the light, by way of the sufferings and agony of the Damned. Guérin flew into a rage when he saw the picture and disowned his pupil; Delécluze dismissed it contemptuously as a "daub." But Gros was won over at once and had it framed at his own expense, while Thiers acclaimed his genius in *Le Constitutionnel*. "No work," he wrote prophetically, "could better reveal the makings of a great painter than this picture. Its author flings his figures on it, groups them and bends them to his will with the boldness of Michelangelo and the fecundity of Rubens."

On September 3, 1822, anniversary of his mother's death, Delacroix began the admirable *Journal* which he kept assiduously until October 5, 1824, then systematically resumed after a long interruption on January 19, 1847. The entry for February 27, 1824, contains this significant confession: "What for me is most real of all are the illusions I create with my painting. The rest is shifting sand." He was then engrossed in the execution of the master-piece of his youth, the work which for the first time gave full scope to his style and his temper-ament, and which, like Picasso's *Guernica*, was painted under the immediate impact of an event that outraged the conscience of the entire civilized world. This was his *Scenes of the Massacres at Chios* (Louvre), depicting the atrocities committed by the Turks on the Greek island of Chios in 1822. Delacroix planned the picture in May 1823, and from January to July of 1824 he worked on it in successive bursts of enthusiasm, momentarily interrupted but in the long run stimulated by news of the deaths of Géricault (January) and Byron (April). In June, under the influence of Constable's *Hay Wain*, which he saw in the window of a Parisian picture dealer, he freshened up his colors, making them vibrant, and entirely repainted the background, deepening its translucency and intensifying its modulations. The finished work appeared at last on August 26, at the opening of the 1824 Salon, in the same room with Ingres' *Vow of Louis XIII*, and it consummated the breach between the two opposing camps. "Those harrowing scenes," Théophile Gautier later recalled, "that violent color, the fury of that brushwork, all excited the indignation of the classicists... and fired the enthusiasm of the younger painters." Both Stendhal and Thiers, again, took up the cudgels in defense of Delacroix against the biting sarcasms of the established critics. But for Gros it was too much; he recanted and this time condemned what he saw, perhaps out of spite at finding his own ideas developed so boldly and sweepingly. The composition, in the form of an inverted triangle, rests on the tension and emotional impact of *color*, further amplified

Eugène Delacroix (1798-1863).

The Emperor Justinian composing his Institutes, 1826. Sketch. (21⅝ × 17⅞″) Musée des Arts Décoratifs, Paris.

Eugène Delacroix (1798-1863).
Scenes of the Massacres at Chios, 1824. (164½ × 139½") Louvre, Paris.

by the vast landscape burnished with copper-tinted gleams. What in fact the painter was aiming at, and achieved, was not so much a dramatic action as a contrasting presentation of fierce pride and shattering disaster and, above all, the multiple echoes thus aroused in the spectator's mind.

The 1824 Salon included a large section of English paintings, among them a portrait by Sir Thomas Lawrence, watercolors by Copley Fielding, studies by Bonington, and three large landscapes by Constable whose luminous freshness created a sensation. Already influenced to some extent by English art, English literature, and even English fashions (for he was at that time something of a dandy), Delacroix paid a visit to England from May to August 1825, at a time of active and fruitful cultural intercourse between England and France. In London he fell in with his friends Fielding and Bonington and found a whole colony of young French artists at work there, among them Poterlet, Isabey, Lami, Colin and Champmartin. Turner and Constable were out of town, but he was received by Lawrence, Etty and Wilkie, made the round of the museums and collections, gazed admiringly at the English countryside and

Eugène Delacroix (1798-1863).
The Taking of Constantinople by the Crusaders, 1840. (161½ × 196¼″) Louvre, Paris.

Eugène Delacroix (1798-1863). Liberty

ople, 1830. (102½×128″) Louvre, Paris.

acquainted himself with English ways, tried out some of the horses in the Elmore stables, sketched the armor in the collection of the well-known antiquary Dr Meyrick, and attended performances of Shakespeare and of Goethe's *Faust*. From this memorable trip to England, which he mused over in retrospect in a moving letter to his friend Silvestre of December 31, 1858, he brought back a freer and easier technique and a deeper appreciation of the literary and poetic sources on which he was to draw so heavily for his inspiration.

Returning to Paris he was soon hard at work again. But at the same time he frequented both the drawing rooms of Restoration society and the avant-garde circles of the Paris art world, making many new friends. For a few months he shared lodgings with Bonington, whose radiant watercolors ("diamonds of their kind," he called them) he so greatly admired. In May 1826, the proceeds going for Greek relief, he exhibited at the Galerie Lebrun two resplendent paintings, in which his new English palette stood triumphantly revealed: *Giaour and Pasha Fighting* (Art Institute of Chicago) and *Marino Faliero* (Wallace Collection, London). Their themes reveal the influence of Byron, which was then almost universal. The first theme, taken from the *Oriental Tales*, was treated repeatedly in several versions and variants. The second was inspired by Byron's tragedy, published in 1820. Beheaded for having conspired against the Republic, the Doge Marino Faliero lies on the steps at the foot of the staircase in the Ducal Palace, the focal center of the scene, observed with impassive haughtiness by the justiciary dignitaries in their glowing robes. Delacroix often confessed his personal predilection for this sumptuous composition on a tragic theme, which Sir Thomas Lawrence offered to buy, and "which stands out," wrote Baudelaire, "among our fondest memories." Warm half-tones and purple shadows (observed, as Charles Blanc reports, in the play of sunlight on a canary-yellow gig) sustain the red and gold harmony, suggestive of Venice, of the lakes and chrome yellows. In June 1826, working with the same chromatic verve on the country estate of some friends near Bourges, he painted the dazzling *Still Life with a Lobster* (Louvre), a work that stands apart in his œuvre, governed by a deep-toned color scheme of scarlet and blue tempered with transparent greys and browns. Hunting trophies and a haul of fish, grouped in the decorative manner of Jan Fyt and Frans Snyders, are displayed against a vast landscape of plains, on a cloudless day, with the tang of the sea in the wind. Later in the same year he received two very different commissions: one from the City of Paris for a *Christ in the Garden of Olives* for the church of Saint-Paul, "one of the finest works of the master and of our century" (Léon Rosenthal); and for the State, intended to decorate the chamber of the Conseil d'Etat in the Hôtel de Ville (where it was destroyed by the Commune in 1871), a vast canvas representing *The Emperor Justinian composing his Institutes*, of which all that remains is a magnificent sketch (once owned by Corot, now in the Musée des Arts Décoratifs, Paris), a gem of red and emerald on a deep brown background, resuscitating the ostentation and splendor of Byzantium.

In Paris, on September 11, 1827, the English troupe of Henrietta Smithson and Charles Kemble gave a performance of *Hamlet* at the Théâtre de l'Odéon. In the audience that night were Delacroix, Berlioz and Victor Hugo, the three young "ringleaders" of French Romanticism, brought together for a brief moment—before drawing apart and holding aloof from each other—by their common cult of Shakespeare. On November 4 was inaugurated the Egyptian Museum of Charles X. On the same day opened the Salon impatiently awaited since 1824, and there, three years in advance of the writers, the combined forces of the new school of painting fought their own "battle of Hernani." Except for the dainty *Portrait of Baron Schwiter* (later owned by Degas, now in the National Gallery, London), which was rejected by the jury, Delacroix exhibited most of his recent works, headed by a symbolic allegory, transcending historical painting: *Greece expiring on the Ruins of Missolonghi* (Bordeaux), his homage to the heroic homeland of the arts and freedom, and a tribute to the memory of the great English poet who gave his life in her cause. When this canvas and *Marino Faliero* were taken to London in February 1828, Delacroix replaced them with the *Death of Sardanapalus* (Louvre),

Eugène Delacroix (1798-1863). Hamlet and Horatio in the Graveyard, 1839. (32 × 25¾″) Louvre, Paris.

a vast "machine" again of Byronic inspiration, but owing to its boldness it was an almost complete failure. Admittedly its pathos and lush sensuality, the over-abundant accessories and the mannerism of the tones somewhat unhinge the composition, which holds together much better in the sketch (Louvre). But surely, in this extraordinary operatic finale, we have the most arresting illustration of the Romantic complex of violence and lust, inextricably bound up together, which obsessed the nineteenth century, from the orgies of the Marquis de Sade to the Wagnerian drama of *Axël*. "There was an old rankling, a dark underside, that had to be satisfied," wrote Delacroix in May 1824 with reference to the *Massacres at Chios*. And the *Sardanapalus*, which he liked to call his Massacre No. 2, points even more insistently to the dark substrata, the demoniacal erotic urge, that made him associate, unforgettably, the imploring slave-girl and the rearing horse, in themselves marvels of the painter's art; and made him, furthermore, impart to the unfeeling detachment of the Oriental despot ordering the holocaust—a dream projection of his innermost self—the deep-seated pessimism which Kierkegaard detected in his study of Nero. A work, in short, of dubious artistic value, but a revelation of the artist's personality. It is contemporary with a delightful series of Odalisques, the pearly gleams of their flesh-tints set off by glistening silks, as in the gorgeous *Woman with a Parrot* (Lyons), a motif taken up again by Courbet and Manet. And then—henceforth more obsessive than the nudes sacrificed in the funeral holocaust of Sardanapalus—came the first studies of wild animals at the Jardin des Plantes, made in the company of Barye. These studies appeared, significantly enough, at the same time as the historical cycle of battle pictures, inaugurated by the tumultuous sketch of the *Battle of Nancy* (1828, Ny Carlsberg Glyptotek, Copenhagen).

"The tiger, stalking his prey, has less light in his eyes and a less impatient tremor of the muscles than had our great painter himself when his whole soul had darted after an idea or gone in pursuit of a dream." Baudelaire and all who approached Delacroix have remarked on this striking resemblance to the felines in whom he delighted, and in whom, under the veneer of his high breeding, he recognized his own savage instincts. In a penetrating essay (*Lettres*, October 1943), the French poet Jean Jouve, following Baudelaire, surveys Delacroix's art and points to the deadly eruption everywhere of the beast—the wild animal or the human animal. But in order to restrain "culpable eroticism" and its sanguinary lust, the carnage, for all its vividness, is imbued with an indivisible melancholy; the world of violence is contained in a greater world of calm and beauty. "In many canvases we find a dead man under a blue sky. The conflict is brought out with the utmost breadth and solemnity, as if death were always attended by the splendor of light." Thus it is in the masterpiece of 1830, *Liberty leading the People* (Louvre), which sums up and concludes his romantic youth, and vibrates with a passionate realism unique in his art. Endowed with the epic powers of Gros and Géricault, master besides of a far wider range of effects, Delacroix transfigures the grim days of July 1830, raises into the grey and yellow sky of Paris the invincible Goddess brandishing the Republican tricolor over the paving stones and the overshadowed dead. The excited street urchin and the resolute student in an opera-hat—none other than the painter himself, who in fact was actually on the barricades, though less through political conviction than revolutionary idealism—stand at her side, spurring on the mob at their heels, while a wounded worker in front drops to his knees and expires among the scattered corpses, gazing up ecstatically at the supreme vision of Liberty.

Liberty leading the People has become the symbol of the Eternal Romantic and his own generous aspirations. The ephemeral Romanticism of 1830, which triumphed at the Salons while the whole artillery of contemporary criticism was leveled at Delacroix, drew on French history and the so-called Troubadour style, while in its ventures into literature "it dealt more with Hamlet's cloak than with his terrible dilemma" (Léon Rosenthal). The subject, in other words, was limited to the anecdotal, and style to the picturesque. The leading lights of the 1827 Salon were Eugène Devéria (1805-1865), whose *Birth of Henri IV* (Louvre, sketch

at Montpellier), a glittering, overcrowded canvas, raised high hopes which were never fulfilled; Ary Scheffer (1795-1858), with his *Suliote Women* (Louvre), a pale reflection of the *Massacres at Chios*; Louis Boulanger (1806-1867), Victor Hugo's favorite painter, who made his debut with a theme pre-eminently romantic and Byronic, *Mazeppa* (Rouen), already treated by Géricault (1822), Delacroix (1824) and Horace Vernet (1826), and taken up again by Chassériau in 1851. After 1830 all the major successes were reserved for the academic Romanticism of Horace Vernet (1789-1863). Equal success attended the efforts of Vernet's no less celebrated son-in-law, Paul Delaroche (1797-1856), who turned out a steady flow of melodramatic history paintings. On the other hand, even apart from some excellent landscapists, Orientalists and illustrators, there were a number of little masters whose works, though now forgotten, are by no means without interest: Champmartin (1797-1883), Poterlet (1803-1835) and Riesener (1808-1878), all influenced by Delacroix; in the lineage of Gros, the vigorous Franche-Comté painter Jean Gigoux (1806-1894); and the enigmatic Leroy (1820-1846), who made a portrait of the young Baudelaire (1844, Versailles Museum).

In 1831 Delacroix took part in the competitions, sponsored by the government, for the decoration of the Chamber of Deputies, treating two of the three subjects proposed to the competitors: *Boissy d'Anglas at the Convention* (Bordeaux Museum; sketch at Smith College, Northampton, Mass.) and *Mirabeau before Dreux-Brézé* (Ny Carlsberg Glyptotek, Copenhagen; sketch in the Louvre). In both cases he sketched out the tumultuous scene with inspired ardor and synthetic accents that powerfully convey the rising fury of the mob and the resolute

Eugène Delacroix (1798-1863). The Drawing of Lots in the Boat at Sea (from Byron's "Don Juan"), 1840.

(53⅛ × 77¼") Louvre, Paris.

mood of the Assembly massed behind its orator. But to satisfy the jury he was obliged in the end to produce highly finished paintings, treated in minute and painstaking touches. Such is particularly the case with the second. Yet these concessions, so degrading in his own eyes, were insufficient in those of the jury and he received no award. In a letter of March 1, 1831, to *L'Artiste*, a lavishly illustrated review recently launched by his friend Ricourt as the mouthpiece of French Romanticism, he lucidly exposed the baneful effects on all participants of the methods imposed by such competitions. In the autumn he consoled and recruited himself in the solitude of Valmont where an unexpected proposal reached him.

The French Ambassador to Morocco, the Comte de Mornay, about to return to his post, invited the artist to come with him. Delacroix accordingly spent six delighted months in Morocco, from January to June 1832, with an excursion in May to southern Spain, Cadiz and Seville. The sights he saw there came like a revelation. We can follow his movements and share his impressions almost day by day thanks to his correspondence and above all his notebooks (preserved in the Louvre and at Chantilly), covered with notes and sketches jotted down on the spur of the moment, often on the pommel of his saddle while riding ("I could do with twenty arms and forty-eight hours a day!" he exclaimed), and touched up with watercolors in the evening, in his tent. He drew a picture of himself in his traveling outfit, "with his large dark eyes screwed up and blinking from the intensity of his gaze, and seeming to drink in the light" (Baudelaire) under his visored cap. The studio dreamer, hitherto nourished on literature, suddenly discovered, without even leaving Tangier, "the sublime come to life, walking the streets and overpowering you with its reality." After the ride to Meknes, penetrating to the heart of the Moslem world of North Africa, which opened his eyes simultaneously to Antiquity, the Bible and the real Orient, intact in its timeless grandeur and shining bright under the Mediterranean sun, he summed up his impressions as follows, writing on the eve of his departure to the critic Augustin Jal: "You have seen Algiers and you have some idea what these countries are like. There is something here even simpler and more primitive; there is less of the Turkish intermixture. The Greeks and Romans are here on my doorstep; I laugh heartily at the thought of David's Greeks... I know the Greeks at present; the statues are the truth and nothing but the truth—only you must know how to read them, but not like our poor moderns who see in them only hieroglyphs."

Thus Delacroix, who all his life dreamt of visiting Italy and never went, found Greece and Rome in Morocco. By an inspired insight that enriched his style and reversed the teachings of David, he experienced the ideal of the antique in the realities of daily life; he saw the statues of antiquity brought to life in the majestic Berbers clad in white "like the maidens on the Panathenaic frieze of the Parthenon," more nobly draped in their tattered garments than "Roman consuls." This decisive experience transformed his art and, evolving on much the same lines as Poussin and Cézanne, between whom he forms a mighty link, he moved on now from an initial Romanticism to a broad Classicism, towards a lofty unity in which all distinctions of school fade away—a unity based on the radiance and power of color, on its poetry, its musicality. To the revival of antique form successfully achieved in their happiest moments and in different ways by Ingres, Prud'hon and Géricault, there corresponds in Delacroix an intuitive understanding of, and sympathy with, the great masters of color and Baroque luminism, Rubens, Veronese, Titian, Rembrandt.

To Delacroix's constant study of the Old Masters and the best painters of the generation or two before his own, notably Goya, Gros and Constable, was added an acute analysis of the phenomena of color, of the effects of sunlight and shadow on the objects around him. "On the way home in the omnibus I observed the effect of the half-tone on horses, like bays and blacks, with shining skin" (February 4, 1847). His *Journal* abounds in similar remarks revealing a ceaseless observation of reality, and fruitful comparisons constantly being made between nature and painting. "Coming back I carefully studied the leafage of the trees... This study

of the trees on my way has helped me to tone up my picture of the *Lion Killers* which, being out of sorts yesterday, I rather made a mess of, although all was going well the day before" (April 27, 1854). Delacroix took a keen interest, moreover, in Chevreul's optical theories, set forth orally from 1828 on, published in 1839, and much discussed in *L'Artiste*; these confirmed his own experiments and the intuitions of the great colorists of the past. The subtle laws of contrasts and complementaries, the division of the brushstroke by hatchings, and the interweaving of brushstrokes by *flochetage*, all went to enrich the essential principle of his technique: the shading of reflected light—a principle which was already dividing painters into opposite camps in the time of Leonardo. For Ingres "reflected light is unworthy of historical painting"; for Delacroix "everything in nature is reflected light."

Delacroix gathered in the heritage of the great colorists with but one end in view: to deepen and differentiate his own color. In handling color he brought out unsuspected possibilities which all modern painters have since turned to account. He inaugurated a whole new era of color. Seurat's disciple Paul Signac (in *D'Eugène Delacroix au Néo-impressionnisme*, 1899) and Matisse's friend René Piot (in *Les Palettes de Delacroix*, 1931) traced and pointed out the technical scope of his revolutionary methods and their immense consequences, exemplified simultaneously in Gauguin, Van Gogh and Cézanne. Silvestre and above all Baudelaire have paid tribute to the spiritual value of Delacroix's use of color, summed up as follows by Odilon Redon: "Venice, Parma and Verona saw only the material side of color. Delacroix alone has grasped the moral and human aspect of color; therein lie his achievement and his claims on posterity." His inexhaustible imagination, in its choice of themes, embraces dream and reality to the widest possible extent and variety, and transposes them chromatically into a mysterious world governed by laws of its own for which there is scarcely any equivalent in art but the world of El Greco, who at that time had still to be rediscovered. But for Delacroix, would Baudelaire, almost alone of his generation, have had eyes to see the eight El Grecos in the collection of Louis-Philippe?

"The great quality in the drawing of supreme artists is truthfulness of movement." With this profound observation Baudelaire cleared up the misunderstanding that militated so much and so long against Delacroix, whose gifts as a colorist came in time to be recognized, his powers as a draughtsman however being all the more stubbornly denied. The fact is that his passionate colors call for a darting, swift-flowing line bursting with energy and built up, like Gros's and Géricault's, around internal nuclei, not in terms of outlines. No modern artist before Cézanne (and Degas) pondered so deeply on the eternal conflict between color and line which set Delacroix up against Ingres, and on the necessity of achieving a synthesis based on the dominant pole. If, as Ingres would have it, "there has never been a great draughtsman who failed to find the coloring exactly suited to the character of his line," the very opposite is no less true. "When the tones are accurate," wrote Delacroix himself, "the lines all but draw themselves" (March 4, 1847). In addition to the thousands of drawings and sketches full of Baroque dynamism and dramatic chiaroscuro, made in connection with his paintings, Delacroix composed, with a line as hard as iron or a touch as soft as velvet, several independent sets of lithographs, illustrating *Faust* (1827), *Hamlet* (1834-1843) and *Götz von Berlichingen* (1836-1843). All testify to the living force of his literary inspiration and to his genius as a graphic artist.

On his return from Morocco in 1833, he was occupied with a continuous program of mural decorations which included several cycles and was not to be brought to a conclusion until 1861, a few years before his death. This gigantic program—which will be dealt with presently in a separate chapter—by no means interrupted his regular studio work, in which large-scale Salon pieces alternate with small easel paintings. One's preferences may well go spontaneously to the latter, gems of concentrated power and homely intimacy, sometimes in their quiet tenderness bringing to mind Chardin (*The Stove*, c. 1830, Louvre), or again, as in a simple *Study of*

Turkish Slippers (1832, Louvre), suggesting all the glamour of the Orient. But this is to do an injustice to the large compositions, for we must not let ourselves be daunted by a certain grandiloquence and indeed a certain amount of stagecraft, rendered necessary by their size and subject matter.

At the 1834 Salon appeared the *Algerian Women in their Quarters*, shown in all their gorgeous finery and dreamy languor. Today little remains to be said about this masterpiece. Its genesis, the secret world it reveals, its documentary value, the almost scientific knowledge of color that went to its making—all this has been studied in full. As for its powers of attraction and stimulation, these are attested, after Renoir, by the entire œuvre of Matisse and the fifteen variations on the *Algerian Women* made a few years ago by Picasso (1954-1955). "Here orange, blue, red, and green sing their most mysterious song. The women's clothes combine the subtlest and richest of color harmonies, the red turban and dark skin of the maid-servant ring out deep chords, the blood courses through the veins under the golden complexion of these Arab brides, as languorous, as marvelous, as silent as the painting itself, figures symbolic of Colors, incarnation of Princess Color" (Jean Cassou). One of them, the woman in the center with her head tilted into shadow, has dropped her hand on to her bare leg and conveys to the spectator's eye, already replete with color harmonies, a strange and disturbing sense of touch. In 1956 the canvas was taken to Venice for an exhibition, where in the light of the lagoon it glowed like a Giorgione or a Carpaccio. Yet here the step was taken that led to Manet's *Olympia*.

Turning from the Oriental seclusion and heavily scented atmosphere of the harem, Delacroix revealed something of the extraordinary range of his art when, in the following year, 1835, he painted his first *Calvary* (Vannes), to be followed in time by several more. In 1836, with a delicate brush, he made a fresh interpretation of that fine Caravaggesque theme *St Sebastian succored by the Holy Women* (Church of Nantua). To the 1837 Salon he submitted his most ambitious battlepiece, the *Bridge of Taillebourg* (Versailles, sketch in the Louvre), a wild mêlée of strident colors dominated by the regal figure of St Louis. Contemporary with this vivid evocation of medieval warfare is a scene of pastoral life in Bible times, *A Woman of the Tribe offering Milk to the Kaid* (Nantes). In 1838, shortly before a trip to Belgium and Holland, he exhibited his *Medea* (Lille) at the Salon, a leonine personification of fury, and painted, in an arresting monochrome faintly tinged with blue, the inspired face of his friend Chopin (Louvre) improvising at the keyboard. The famous *Self-Portrait with a Green Waistcoat* (Louvre) may well date from the same year, a mighty head bespeaking rugged energy, stamped with the two hallmarks of genius: "immense passion, plus formidable will-power" (Baudelaire). His most moving version of a theme that particularly appealed to him, *Hamlet and Horatio in the Graveyard* (Louvre), is that of 1839. "No one has framed this hero of suffering, indignation, doubt and irony in a more poetic light and posed him in an attitude more real" (George Sand). The *Jewish Wedding in Morocco* (Louvre), an evocation of a scene he actually witnessed, dispenses with accessories and literary overtones and is presented solely in terms of the rhythm of attitudes and the purity of its color harmonies, "the first work in which that anxious imagination of his comes to rest at last, feels for its way, meditates and ponders on the powers of his palette and the resources of his tones" (Odilon Redon).

Delacroix's art achieved full expression in the three outstanding works of 1840: the *Justice of Trajan* (Rouen), the *Drawing of Lots in the Boat at Sea* (Louvre) from Byron's *Don Juan*, and the *Taking of Constantinople by the Crusaders* (Louvre). All the picture elements concerted together answer to the necessities of pictorial expression which he himself defined as follows: "If, to a composition on a subject interesting in itself, you add an arrangement of lines which sharpens the impression it makes, a chiaroscuro which strikes the imagination, and a color scheme suited to its character, you have solved a most difficult problem and you rank high. The result is a harmony whose combinations are adapted to a single melody, a picture

Eugène Delacroix (1798-1863).

Apollo subduing the Python, 1849. Sketch. (51¼ × 38⅜″) Musées Royaux des Beaux-Arts de Belgique, Brussels.

that tends to be musical." The color orchestration and its dominant tonality, themselves full of suggestive power, further magnify the scope of the subject, whether historical or visionary. The *Drawing of Lots in the Boat at Sea* situates the human drama in the livid immensity of a storm-tossed sea, such as Delacroix had just seen off Dieppe. Take away the drifting boat carrying Byron's hero, and what remains is the finest seascape of the nineteenth century prior to Courbet. As for the *Justice of Trajan*, handled with a dramatic suspense that is Delacroix's alone, it is a masterly synthesis of rhythm and light, of Rubens and Veronese. Baudelaire hesitated between the *Trajan*, whose commanding figure on a rearing horse amid the tumult he has provoked sums up the grandeur of the Roman Empire, and the even grander, more mysterious sweep of the *Crusaders*, a solemn dramatization justified by "the emphatic truthfulness of the gesture in the great circumstances of life." On their snorting war-horses, the baffled, disillusioned conquerors ride roughshod over victims and booty alike and drink to the full the bitter cup of violence. The upright spears, the fluttering banners, and the helmets adorned with lions and eagles, silhouetted against the outspread panorama of the greatest city of the East, set the rhythm of a strange and haunting ballet enacted on the ruins of an expiring civilization. The dead woman on the left, with the funereal, decomposed tones of the face, and the strikingly foreshortened body clad in blue, orange and green, together with the magnificent blonde on the right, a sister of the captives of Chios, kneeling half-naked

Eugène Delacroix (1798-1863).
Lion Hunt, 1861. (29¼ × 38″) The Potter Palmer Collection, The Art Institute of Chicago.

before the stern warriors, her bare back an expanse of light emerging from the purple, gold-fringed robe, her long hair streaming over the head of her prostrate companion—these incomparable details have often been reproduced. Night falling in the distance and smoke from the burning city darken the sky over the Bosporus, and the far-flung scene resolves itself into a deep-toned harmony of purple and somber azure-blue.

Delacroix spent the summer of 1842 with George Sand, in her country house at Nohant, in Berry. There he painted his first studies of flowers while listening to the improvisations of Chopin, which he likened to "dew-sprinkled flowers." In 1844 he bought a country place of his own at Champrosay, on the edge of the forest of Senart, just outside Paris. Pausing in the midst of a steady output of flower pieces, landscapes and vivid scenes of animals fighting, he painted another picture on a Roman theme, forming a pendant to the *Justice of Trajan*: the *Death of Marcus Aurelius* (Lyons), exhibited in 1845 with a large Moroccan composition, the *Sultan surrounded by his Guard* (Toulouse), a scene of Oriental pomp which he himself had witnessed before the gate and walls of Meknes, a dazzling harmony of sunny greys beneath the relentless clarity of the African sky. At the 1846 Salon he exhibited three medium-sized paintings, literary in inspiration: the *Abduction of Rebecca* (Metropolitan Museum, New York), from Sir Walter Scott's *Ivanhoe*; *Gretchen in the Church* (Wallace Collection, London), from Goethe's *Faust*; and *Romeo and Juliet* (Collection of Baron von Hirsch, Basel).

The year 1847 marks a turning point. Delacroix resumed his *Journal* and finished his monumental decorations for the Luxembourg and the Palais Bourbon (Chambre des Députés); in the latter, represented on opposite walls, are *Orpheus bringing Civilization to Greece and the World* and *Attila trampling underfoot Italy and the Arts*. The theme of the struggle of life against the shackles that trammel it is one that haunted him all his life—but the hope of deliverance now grows stronger. His *St George and the Dragon* (1847, Louvre), with its glowing, phosphorescent hues traversed by the sharp thrust of the lance, implied and included for him —as it had for Raphael—the related themes of Perseus delivering Andromeda and Roger delivering Angelica. His great ceiling panel for the Galerie d'Apollon (1849-1851), of which we reproduce the fantastic sketch, *Apollo subduing the Python* (Brussels), imparts a cosmic breadth to the vault of the Louvre and celebrates the triumph of light over darkness. Taking over a subject that was not of his own choosing, and keeping to a tradition of decorative painting which he enriched and extended, Delacroix at the same time sublimated his deepest instincts in glorifying the universal myth that epitomized the underlying significance of his own life and work ever since the "descent into Hell" in the Barque of Dante. While the best of the painting, on his own showing, is admittedly the nocturnal zone teeming with monsters and strewn with corpses, the catharsis is nevertheless achieved. "Delacroix's," as Jouve has said, "is a transforming imagination. What is imagination? It is a relationship between liberty and the unconscious, and a spell cast over the monster: it is a conquest by the image, and that means a *demon subdued*." The wall paintings in the Chapelle des Saints-Anges of the church of Saint-Sulpice, in Paris, bring to a close his almost lifelong series of monumental decorations and constitutes his spiritual testament. The theme is Jacob wrestling with the Angel. Here Delacroix, like Jacob, meets the angel and fights within himself the supreme battle, to accede to what Maurice Barrès called *le mystère en pleine lumière*. Delivered from the beast that lurks within us all, Delacroix was free to treat his favorite subjects: hunting scenes and animals fighting. Apart from sketches and replicas, there exist three masterly versions of the *Lion Hunt* (1855, Bordeaux; 1858, Boston; 1861, Chicago) in which the influence of Rubens, revived by another trip to Belgium in 1850, is combined with the impressions produced by enthusiastic visits to the Jardin des Plantes (recorded in his *Journal*) and obsessive memories of Morocco. The final version above all, reproduced here, is so powerful an explosion of rhythms and colors against the majestic expanse of a far-flung landscape that it absorbs us irresistibly in its intense and fatal magic. "A good picture," said Baudelaire, "to be faithful to the dream that engendered it, must be produced like a world."

Théodore Chassériau (1819-1856). The Toilet of Esther, 1841. (17⅞ × 14″) Louvre, Paris.

Orientalism and Decoration

ELACROIX towers above all his rivals both in the field of Orientalism, chiefly cultivated by the little masters of Romanticism, and in that of large-scale mural painting, the special preserve of Ingres' pupils. Chassériau, who attempted the difficult synthesis of Ingres and Delacroix, and in doing so successfully avoided the pitfalls of eclecticism, also made his mark in these two branches of art, each of which had its special danger: the first, with its exotic subject matter, tended to lapse into the picturesque; the second, owing to the technique and working methods employed, tended to be cold and lifeless.

Three important political events were instrumental in making Orientalism fashionable in the arts (though the way had been prepared by the *turqueries* and *chinoiseries* in vogue in France since the time of Louis XIV): Napoleon's campaigns in Egypt and Palestine, of which Gros was the finest interpreter; the Greek war of independence against the Turks, which had literary repercussions all over Europe but inspired painters only in France; and, lastly, the French conquest of Algeria, which from 1830 on focused attention on North Africa. So in addition to Constantinople, Asia Minor and the Levant, places long associated with the Bible and the Crusaders, there emerged a second source—soon to be preponderant—of "Orientalism," a term in this case geographically inexact, but ethnographically justifiable.

Ingres himself sometimes showed a touch of Romanticism in his choice of subjects, and particularly in that singular streak of Orientalism which once led him to be described as "a Chinese painter astray in Athens." As early as 1814 he began transforming his Bathers into Odalisques (one of the first, if not *the* first, to treat this theme) by placing them in an exotic setting and above all by emphasizing the "arabesques" of their sensuous curves. The *Odalisque with a Slave* of 1839, which reflects the influence of Persian miniatures and suggests "the mystery, silence and seclusion of the seraglio" (Théophile Gautier), corresponds in Ingres' œuvre to the *Algerian Women* in Delacroix's. It is a more intimate, Orientalized version of the large *Odalisque* of 1814 which, despite the accessories, still conformed to the Italian canon. "The earlier one was an Italian girl in disguise," noted a critic writing in *L'Artiste* in 1855, when the two pictures were being exhibited together at the Paris World's Fair, "while the later one is a real sultana." For the final composition of his *Turkish Bath* Ingres based himself on the firsthand descriptions given in the letters of Lady Mary Wortley Montagu, wife of the British Ambassador at Constantinople, and on French and English prints of Turkish scenes going back to the eighteenth and even to the sixteenth century.

Jules-Robert Auguste (1789-1850).
Nude Woman mounting a Horse. Undated. (8⅝ × 5½") Louvre, Paris.

Like the epic East of Gros, the sensual East of Ingres is a product of the artist's imagination. The true creator of an authentic Orientalism in the Romantic vein, and one of the most curious figures among the little masters of Romanticism, was Jules-Robert Auguste (1789-1850), respectfully known to his friends and fellow artists as Monsieur Auguste. Son and grandson of famous jewelers, he was led by his private fortune, gifts and personal inclinations to adopt an independent mode of life, traveling when and where he liked, painting and sketching as the fancy took him, unhampered by the need to sell his works. Awarded the Prix de Rome for sculpture in 1810, he went to Italy, met Ingres and lingered on there for several years. In 1816 he became friendly with Géricault, who advised him to concentrate on painting. He set off on a long, leisurely journey to the Levant, visiting Albania, Syria, Greece, Egypt, possibly the Barbary Coast as well, and returned to France about 1820 with a large collection of Eastern weapons, costumes and curios, which he let his artist friends use for local color in their pictures, notably Delacroix in the *Massacres at Chios*. Delacroix much admired Auguste's watercolors and pastels, his studies of horses and scenes of Oriental life (of which the Orléans Museum owns a fine series, presented by Baron Schwiter). The dusky *Nude* in the Louvre, about to mount a spirited white horse against which her dark sensual form strikes a piquant contrast, was long attributed to Delacroix himself. In his studio in the Rue des Martyrs, near those of Géricault and Horace Vernet, Monsieur Auguste gathered round him a circle of artists and writers that included such men as Delacroix and Mérimée.

The leading exponent of Orientalism after 1831 was Alexandre-Gabriel Decamps (1803-1860) who, in the course of a stay in Constantinople and Asia Minor (chiefly at Smyrna) in 1827, had completely yielded to the glamour of the East. His extraordinary success with both public and critics (from Delécluze to Baudelaire) he owed in part no doubt to the prevailing vogue for Oriental subjects, but also and above all to the virtuosity of his execution, with its skillfully worked up impasto and its vigorous contrasts of light and shade. He was sensitive to textural effects, to light and its reflections, but his form remained traditional under a technique that tends to be labored. Decamps also ventured into the field of history painting and his *Defeat of the Cimbri* (1833, Louvre) is a worthy period piece ably combining the tumult of battle with a dramatically but rather ponderously handled landscape. To his famous Oriental pieces (e.g. *The Punishment of the Hooks*, 1837, Wallace Collection, London) present-day taste prefers his humble rustic scenes (like the *Farmyard*, 1856, Louvre) which, painted toward the end of his life, show him drawing closer to the Realists and the Barbizon group. Another Orientalist, attracted by Syria, Palestine, and particularly Egypt, was Prosper Marilhat (1811-1847), whose first canvas came to Théophile Gautier like a bolt from the blue and filled him with a desire to see the East; but Marilhat's style is very different from that of Decamps. Adrien Dauzats (1804-1868), an archaeological painter, traveled in both Egypt and Algeria depicting the monuments and their natural setting with grandeur and precision.

Eugène Delacroix (1798-1863).
Algerian Women in their Quarters, 1849. (33 × 43¾″) Musée Fabre, Montpellier.

Delacroix, too, at once realized the implications, both for himself and for painters to come, of all he saw in Morocco, and the change of approach and methods thus brought about. In the letter to Augustin Jal of June 4, 1832, from which we have already quoted, he wrote prophetically: "If our pundits persist in imposing on our young nurselings of the Muses such subjects as the household of Priam or Atreus, I am convinced (and you'll certainly agree with me) that we'd do far, far better to send them out as cabin-boys on the first ship to Barbary than to go on exploiting the worn-out classical soil of Rome. Rome is no longer to be found in Rome." Henceforth, instead of the traditional trip to Italy, painters got into the habit of making a trip to the East—and the consequences were immediately visible in their style and, above all, their palette. For the resurrection of color dates from this time. Besides the major transformation which we have described, Delacroix brought back from Morocco not only the documentary material of his future work, but the very color and atmosphere in which that work took its rise. "Notice," says Baudelaire, "how much the general color scheme of Delacroix's pictures partakes of the colors peculiar to Oriental landscapes and interiors." He reverted years afterwards to his favorite Oriental themes which, as if purified in retrospect, gain in depth and spareness what they lose in anecdotal picturesqueness. "It was not until I had forgotten the details and could only record in my pictures the striking and poetic side of things," wrote Delacroix himself in 1853, "that I began to make something tolerable out of my trip to Africa." Thus the smaller variant of the *Algerian Women* painted in after-years (1849, Montpellier)—which made so deep an impression on Van Gogh when he saw it in the autumn of 1888—is even superior to the brilliant initial version (1834, Louvre) in the unity of its lighting effects, its appealing intimacy and more sparing use of accessories. The essential difference between them is the light, in the earlier version arbitrary and glancing so as to bring out the gorgeous range of colors in the costumes, in the later natural and subdued so as to leave the suppler forms afloat in semi-darkness, their subtly graded tones softened and slightly blurred in the recessive perspective of time and memory. "The glow of desire," writes Louis Gillet, "gives place to its after-glow of regret and nostalgia."

Delacroix was delighted not only with the costumes, the way of life and the living quarters of the natives, but also by the grandeur and magnificence of a primitive land wholly unspoilt. And the rugged and noble landscapes which he saw on the way from Tangier to Meknes, in the shadow of the Atlas mountains, which he sketched in watercolors in his notebooks and stored up in his memory, also became the setting for the antique and Biblical scenes he painted on the walls of the Palais Bourbon, the Palais du Luxembourg and the church of Saint-Sulpice, which they imbued with a luminous majesty. Among the Orientalists later drawn to North Africa in the wake of Delacroix, the two most notable are Fromentin and Dehodencq. Eugène Fromentin (1820-1876), a sensitive and cultivated man, much more important as a writer than a painter, traveled in Egypt and paid three long visits to Algeria (1846, 1848, 1852). He was particularly successful in conveying the atmosphere of the desert in subtle shadings of grey. Alfred Dehodencq (1819-1882), a powerful colorist who owed much to Delacroix (though he was also an admirer of Géricault), made an enthusiastic painting trip to Andalusia (1848) before discovering Morocco (1854). He took a keen interest in the life of the country, its customs, ceremonials, and ethnic types. Among his best works are the *Farewell of Boabdil* (1869, Roubaix) and the *Jewish Wedding at Tangier* (1870, Poitiers).

Frowned upon by David in the revolutionary period (his own large canvases were intended to hang in museums), large-scale mural painting was restored to favor under Napoleon. It was lavishly patronized after the Restoration, for political and religious reasons, but Géricault and Prud'hon, who had a real aptitude for this type of painting, were ignored and the official commissions were bestowed on mediocre artists. Gros, to be sure, is an exception, but the complete failure of his work in the Panthéon and the Louvre only showed up the decadence into which mural painting had fallen. A turn for the better—due to several causes— occurred during the reign of Louis-Philippe (1830-1848). Ingres and Delacroix set the example,

re-embodying two opposing traditions of decorative art: Florentine and classical, Venetian and Baroque. Artists and critics alike proclaimed the superiority of mural painting, as an expression of the social mythos, over easel painting, dismissed as a narrow reflection of modern individualism, and lively discussions took place as to the specific exigencies of its style, technique and subject matter. Several fruitless attempts were made to rediscover the technical secrets of true fresco painting (which in any case was ill-suited to the transalpine climate). The use of wax, on the other hand, by attenuating the over-glossy effects and opaque shadows of oil paints, produced excellent results and preserved the freshness and low pitch of tones. Whatever the technique, it became customary to execute murals on the spot, in so far as possible, even when lighting conditions and available installations left much to be desired.

"My heart beats faster," confessed Delacroix, "when I stand before large wall surfaces ready to be painted." If such was his heart's desire, then his wishes were amply fulfilled, for from 1833 to 1861 he received a long series of orders for mural decorations, one or more of which he always had in hand: the Salon du Roi (1833-1837) and the library (1838-1847) in the Palais Bourbon; the library (1840-1847) in the Palais du Luxembourg; the *Pietà* (1843) in the church of Saint-Denis du Saint-Sacrement; the ceiling of the Galerie d'Apollon (1849-1851) in the Louvre; the Salon de la Paix (1849-1854) in the Hôtel de Ville (which was burned down in 1871 during the Commune); the Chapelle des Saints-Anges (1849-1861) in the church of Saint-Sulpice. This vast and varied production, one of the most grandiose of its kind, including both secular and religious subjects, on which for thirty years he lavished the treasures of his palette and imagination, has yet to receive the recognition and attention it deserves. All his decorations in the Hôtel de Ville (including the *Justinian* of 1827 in the chamber of the Conseil d'Etat) were of course destroyed, while the great complementary ensembles in the Palais Bourbon (Chamber of Deputies) and Palais du Luxembourg (Senate) are all but inaccessible to the public and extremely difficult to photograph. The admirable *Pietà* of Saint-Denis du Saint-Sacrement, with its poignant harmonies of red and blue, executed to the sound of music during the Divine Service, remains invisible (like the *St Sebastian* in the church at Nantua), lost in the obscurity of a humble church in the Marais district of Paris. Few are the visitors to the Louvre who look up at the ceiling panel in the Galerie d'Apollon (a marvel of the painter's art, unforgettable to those fortunate enough to see and study it when it was taken down for restoration), which fits without any incongruity into the sumptuous setting designed by Lebrun. And if the two wall paintings in Saint-Sulpice—in the first chapel to the right of the entrance—constitute, as they surely do, the crowning achievement of the artist's career and the only work in France comparable to the great Italian frescoes, how many art lovers are even aware of their existence? It is much to be hoped that the centenary celebrations of 1963 will facilitate access to, and encourage the study of, these decorative paintings which perhaps illustrate better than any others the evolution of Delacroix's style and mind in his ripest, most productive years. He himself—who judged his own work by the strictest standards—set great store by them, as we know from his correspondence, and was chagrined to see them pass unnoticed. While he by no means invariably overcame all the difficulties inherent in such large-scale works, their success or failure did not depend solely on technique or size or the laws of the genre, but (as in all the rest of his work) on the inscrutable underlying relationships between the imagination and the unconscious, between what comes of traditional culture and what goes back to the deepest instincts. What he always dreamed of, in his concern for pictorial unity, was the opportunity of decorating an entire edifice on his own, from beginning to end. In each case nevertheless, despite the claims of different commissions on his attention and the mediocrity of contemporary architecture, he perfectly mastered the decorative and mural requirements of his task, within the illusionist system of Baroque decoration to which he adhered, with a polyphonic range of colors of his own invention. He took his lead from the supreme examples of Veronese and Rubens, as well as from the best French tradition of Poussin, Lesueur (whose work in the Cabinet des Muses in the Hôtel Lambert he restored in 1844), Lebrun and Prud'hon.

Appointed a minister in 1833, Thiers commissioned him to decorate the Salle du Trône, or Salon du Roi, in the Palais Bourbon, a square vestibule difficult to deal with. He did away with the heavy frieze and made the best of the available space, painting allegories of "the vital forces of the nation" (Justice, Agriculture, Industry, War) on the coffered ceiling and personifications in grisaille of the Rivers of France on the elongated piers between the doors. In a statement written in 1848 he set forth the aims and conception that guided him in this initial work, expressing regret that it should be inaccessible to the public and disfigured by tawdry furnishings which falsified the color relationships.

In the library of the Palais Bourbon, where he was inspired by Veronese and used oils and wax, and the library of the Palais du Luxembourg, painted with the so-called Van Dyck palette of nine tones, Delacroix found for the first time a wall space adequate to his encyclopedic program, his "mnemotechny of the grandeur and natural passion of the universal man" (Baudelaire) at grips with the dark forces which he must and will overcome. On the two opposite niche-shaped hemicycles of the Palais Bourbon, Orpheus, bringer of civilization to the world, and Attila, war and barbarism personified, face each other in dramatic suspense. Twenty pendentives supporting the five bays of the ceiling, decorated in accordance with a methodically established plan, illustrate signal episodes from the history of the Sciences, Philosophy, Legislature, Theology and Poetry. "This is Delacroix's masterpiece, perhaps the masterpiece of French painting," wrote Joubin at the sight of this great poem epitomizing the trials and sufferings of humanity in its progress from darkness to light. The powerful, turbulent hymn resounding beneath the vaults of the Palais Bourbon reaches its climax in the central cupola of the Luxembourg. Dante, guided through the lower worlds by Virgil, accedes to the Elysian Fields of the poets presided over by Homer, attended by a company of illustrious Greeks and Romans. Delacroix, disregarding conventional schemas, laid in a luminous landscape (such as he had seen with his own eyes in Morocco) that brings the antique world vividly to life in all its pristine freshness. He achieved a harmonious synthesis between his romantic temperament and his will to classicism, while at the same time the thinker is as much in evidence as the painter, and a yearning for the past prevails over the conquest of the present. Rhetoric has not been ruled out, but Delacroix is at home with the sublime and handles it with a freedom of the brush which the happiest creations of his easel were to profit by. With the ceiling panel in the Galerie d'Apollon at the Louvre, painted in oils (with no admixture of wax) in a dazzling scale of rich, full-bodied colors, he faced again the evil spirits of the inner man and exorcised them, exploiting the possibilities of Baroque turbulence to the utmost limit. The constituent duality of his decorative work is again manifested in his "last testament" in the Chapelle des Saints-Anges at Saint-Sulpice. On the righthand wall is *Heliodorus driven from the Temple* which, for all the energy of the execution and the splendor of the coloring, remains an image of the past, a brilliant reinterpretation of Raphael. On the lefthand wall is *Jacob wrestling with the Angel*, a solemn yet exotic and mystical vision which, both technically and poetically, opens a window on the future, transcending the eloquence and theatricality of Baroque in the silent majesty of the forms and the spiritualization of pure tones governed by the intimate rhythm of shadows and lights, of half-tones and reflections.

Ingres' contempt for the easel picture ("an invention of periods of decadence") has been recorded by Amaury-Duval and Delaborde quotes him as saying in 1840, "Art should be devoted to the decoration of churches, public buildings, and temples of Justice; that is its only true function." Yet he repeatedly declined the commissions offered to him for decorations in the Panthéon, the Luxembourg and many churches. The compositions ordered for the cathedrals of Montauban and Autun were executed in his studio, with little consideration for the actual conditions of the building. The *Apotheosis of Homer* (1827), intended as a ceiling panel for the Louvre, is presented frontally, while its political counterpart, the *Apotheosis of Napoleon* (1853), a ceiling panel for the Hôtel de Ville (destroyed in 1871), was more in the

Eugène Delacroix (1798-1863). Jacob wrestling with the Angel (detail), 1858-1861.
Chapelle des Saints-Anges, Church of Saint-Sulpice, Paris.

nature of an enlarged cameo. In Rome in 1812 he had painted in tempera his *Romulus and Acron* (Ecole des Beaux-Arts, Paris) for the Quirinal palace, and resolved then and there (a resolution he failed to keep) to use this technique in the future for his large-scale works, describing it as "the equal of fresco painting, or anyhow the worthiest substitute for it." In September 1839, perhaps in emulation of Delacroix who was then at work in the Palais Bourbon, he accepted a proposal from the Duc de Luynes to decorate the great hall in the Château de Dampierre. He set to work with an ardor that gradually slackened until in March 1850 he had the contract canceled and abandoned the project. For a time, from 1843 to 1847, he went to live at Dampierre and tackled the wall directly, after the manner of the Tuscan frescoists. On one side of the hall he more or less completed *The Golden Age*, his myth of the youth of the world in its naked innocence, but barely sketched out its contrasting pendant, *The Iron Age*, on the opposite wall. We have referred to the stylistic reasons that led him to abandon the work, which, though a noble effort, must also be written off as a technical failure. The Dampierre fresco is today no more than a ruin, but with it begins that renewal of mural painting in the strict sense, as distinct from ceiling panels and the Baroque division into compartments, which was carried through by Chassériau and Puvis de Chavannes.

Religious decoration became the almost exclusive prerogative of Ingres' pupils, many of whom belonged to that curious Lyonese school of mystical painters, akin in many ways to the German Nazarenes and the English Pre-Raphaelites, but of more interest for the history of taste and sensibility than for that of painting. One of the local precursors was Victor Orsel (1795-1850), a pupil of Guérin and a friend of Overbeck and the Nazarene group in Rome. His ideal, realized with dreary suavity on the walls of Notre-Dame-de-Lorette in Paris, consisted in "watering down Greek art." A more expressive and spirited artist, who studied first under Ingres, then under Delacroix, was Louis Janmot (1814-1892), in whom Delacroix even found "a remarkable Dantesque fragrance." He made portraits of the great apostles of Catholic regeneration (Lacordaire, Ozanam, Montalembert), decorated the churches of Saint-Etienne-du-Mont (Paris) and Saint-François-de-Sales (Lyons), and also painted the *Poem of the Soul* (in the Château de Bertaud), one of the longest, most singular and ethereal cycles in the strange annals of Romantic painting. The cold, austere imagery of Hippolyte Flandrin (1809-1864), academically inspired by Assisi, Pisa and Ravenna, with hieratic processions and gold backgrounds, proliferated over the walls of the Parisian churches of Saint-Séverin (1840-1841), Saint-Germain-des-Prés (1842-1846, 1856-1861), Saint-Vincent-de-Paul (1849-1853)—which a misguided enthusiast went so far as to call the "Christian Parthenon"—and those of Saint-Paul at Nîmes (1847-1849) and Saint-Martin d'Ainay at Lyons (1855). Flandrin however, like all Ingres' disciples, was a good portrait painter, excelling in women's faces. Less prolific but more gifted, Victor-Louis Mottez (1809-1897) took advantage of the years he spent in Italy (1835-1842) to make a systematic study of the fresco technique, and in doing so was led to translate Cennino Cennini's treatise on painting. In 1840, on the wall of his studio in Rome, he frescoed the pensive silhouette of his wife—a work which Ingres so much admired that he had it detached and transferred to canvas (it is now in the Louvre). And a fine piece of painting it is, firmly and freely handled, at once intimate and monumental. The Parisian climate and some rather too thorough cleanings have impaired his religious frescoes in Saint-Germain-l'Auxerrois (1846), Saint-Séverin (1846) and Saint-Sulpice (1862). Besides inspiring a school of Christian mystics, the mists of Lyons lent their peculiar flavor to the humanitarian mysticism of Paul Chenavard (1807-1893), more of a philosopher than a painter, though in spite of its Ingresque tendencies his work was admired by Delacroix. Chenavard's project for a "Universal Palingenesis" on the walls of the Panthéon, in Paris, was accepted in 1848, but the commission was canceled in 1852 before it could be carried out.

Born at Santo Domingo in the West Indies, son of the French consul and a Creole mother, Théodore Chassériau (1819-1856) came to Paris with his parents in 1822. His career was a short one, but he was so precocious that at the age of eleven he was admitted to the studio

of Ingres, who marveled at his gifts, and he remained there until the master's departure for Italy in 1834. He made a successful debut at the Salon of 1836 and at that of 1839 exhibited two canvases already perfect of their kind, revealing a mature personal style and a new type of womanhood, one mythological, the *Venus Anadyomene* (Louvre), the other Biblical, *Susanna and the Elders* (Louvre). These works convey, with engaging reticence, the charm at once elegiac and sensual of a Prud'hon of the islands, that refined, slightly perplexing combination of Hellenism and exoticism which characterizes all his art. He paid a visit to Italy lasting from July 1840 to February 1841. He admired the monuments of Rome, found them sublime, but the place seemed to him like a tomb. He saw Ingres there, and though he went his own way he never repudiated the lessons of his great elder. His intense and sober portrait of *Lacordaire* (1840, Louvre) in the white Dominican habit, and that of *Two Sisters*

Théodore Chassériau (1819-1856). Peace, 1848. (134 × 142⅝″) Louvre, Paris.

(1843, Louvre), so severely refined in the pose and tones (greens, bistre, reds)—which Degas thought the best portrait of the century—make clear both what he owed to Ingres, particularly to the portraits of *Granet* and *Madame Devauçay*, and what was peculiarly his own, the muffled fire of his colors, the subtly slanting axes of volumes, the nostalgic ardor concealed under the fine economy of his means. The *Toilet of Esther* (1841, Louvre), shown in the mysterious ritual of adorning her amber-colored, honey-hued body between two dark-skinned slave-girls, strangely combines the savor of a Persian miniature, which the picture resembles even in its small format, with the compact design of a Greek metope and the curvilinear rhythms of the Fontainebleau Mannerists. It marks a point of equilibrium and full bloom in the initial phase of the artist, who leaned thereafter more and more towards Delacroix, interpreting Shakespeare in his turn, both in paintings and engravings (series of etchings for *Othello* in 1844). At the 1845 Salon his equestrian portrait of the *Caliph of Constantine* (Versailles) was hung beside Delacroix's *Sultan of Morocco surrounded by his Guard* (Toulouse). In 1846 he set out on a long journey to Algeria. But in the Oriental scenes which from now on formed the bulk of his output, horsemen fighting and interiors of harems, he succumbed to the lure of the picturesque, and his intenser, heavier colors grow vulgar and meretricious. In 1846 he painted a radiant portrait of *Mademoiselle Cabarrus* (Quimper), clad in white, garlanded and dreamy, and in 1848 he met the actress Alice Ozy, the model of his dreams, with "the body of a Greek goddess and the head of a sultana" (Théophile Gautier), who inspired some of his finest drawings and one of the most beautiful Giorgionesque nudes in French painting, the *Bather sleeping beside a Spring* (1850, Avignon).

Pierre Puvis de Chavannes (1824-1898).

Marseilles, Port of the Orient, 1868. Sketch. (38¾ × 57½″) The Phillips Collection, Washington, D.C.

From 1843 to 1854 Chassériau devoted most of his time to mural painting, the field that gave best scope to his originality and fine technique. Choosing Christian subjects with an Oriental setting, he decorated the Chapelle de Sainte-Marie l'Egyptienne in the church of Saint-Merri (1844) and the Chapelle des Fonts Baptismaux in Saint-Roch (1854), in Paris, and painted a moving *Descent from the Cross*—in which the Holy Women look like Arab girls—in the vault over the altar of Saint-Philippe-du-Roule (1856). Undoubtedly his greatest work was the fresco decoration for the Cour des Comptes (1844-1848), ravaged by fire during the Commune in 1871 and abandoned in the ruins of the building, until finally the remnants were salvaged by experts from the Louvre and remounted on canvas. Figures in grisaille, personifying Silence, Meditation and Study, led up the staircase towards the majestic symphony formed on the first floor, between the friezes and pendentives, by the scenes of Peace, War and Commerce. Chassériau here followed Ingres—the Ingres of the *St Symphorian* and above all of Dampierre—but developed his work in terms of suppler cadences, free of rigid symmetry and orthogonal projection, in which at times he rises to the forcefulness of Géricault, at times subsides into the milder key of Prud'hon. The best preserved group, reproduced here, comes from the left side of the scene depicting Peace. Under the olive branch, in a serene golden light, a group of young women are suckling or dandling their children, while harvesters lie resting on sheaves and in the background herdsmen urge on their brawny animals. These are not the allegories of fable, but—according to the humanistic program Chassériau drew up for himself on the eve of the 1848 revolution—"quite simple subjects drawn from the history of mankind and human life... enabling one to be emotional, true and free." The result is a monumental transposition of familiar realities, attuned to the solemn rhythm of Works and Days.

The outstanding decorator of the second half of the century was Pierre Puvis de Chavannes (1824-1898). Although the art of his later years, when he subscribed to the symbolist aesthetic, lies outside the scope of this study, his early work calls for mention in view of his direct connection with Chassériau, who helped him to find himself and pointed out the path he was to follow. He came of an old family of Burgundy, but was born at Lyons and his style bears the Lyonese imprint. He prolonged and crystallized the Ingresque idealism peculiar to the school of that city, and his evolution ran parallel—on a higher plane—to that of Flandrin. He was already in his twenties, preparing to be an engineer, when after a serious illness he went to Italy to recuperate and there realized where his true vocation lay. After studying erratically under several antagonistic teachers, he met Chassériau. This was decisive. From him he learned to discipline his style and was oriented towards large-scale mural painting. His earliest attempts in this field date from 1854 (Château de Brouchy) and his first successful decorations, inspired, even in their themes, by those of Chassériau in the Cour des Comptes, were the *War* and *Peace* of 1861 (Amiens). These inaugurated the vast series of decorative paintings which, alternating with many easel pictures, of which the most famous is the *Poor Fisherman* (1881, Louvre), occupied him for the rest of his life: Marseilles (1867-1869), Poitiers (1871-1875), Lyons (1883-1886), Rouen (1890-1891) and, in Paris, the Panthéon (1874-1878, 1898), the Sorbonne (1887) and the Hôtel de Ville (1891-1894). In these murals he created "the moral landscape which suited the ideas, admirations, finely clouded spirits and fond optimism of the last two generations" (Focillon). Departing from the practice of his predecessors, he executed his decorations in the studio, on canvas, and they were then mounted in place on the wall surface; but he always prepared them with sketches made in harmony with the local tones of the building to be decorated, and painted them in flat colors with simplified drawing to give something of the effect of fresco. His first monumental paintings in a fully personal style are the two panels he made for the staircase of the Musée des Beaux-Arts of Marseilles, in the Palais Longchamp: *Massilia, the Greek Colony* and *Marseilles, Port of the Orient*. The latter, of which we illustrate the vivid sketch (1868, Phillips Collection, Washington), significantly combines the two tendencies examined in this chapter. Representing the ultimate development, purified but all too often insipid in its transparent serenity,

of the styles of Ingres and Chassériau, the Mediterranean Arcadia of Puvis de Chavannes also forms the tenuous link connecting Poussin with Gauguin and the Nabis, and earned for its creator a much inflated reputation towards the end of his life. Although his qualities are those of an assimilator, occasionally a precursor, rather than a true creator, the discredit into which he has fallen today seems no less excessive. While his nobly concerted allegorical compositions are lacking in visionary energy and suggestive power, they include some landscape backgrounds—no doubt the most vital part of his work—imbued with real feeling and reflecting the noble example of Corot and other masters in the all-important domain to which we now must turn.

The Rise of Landscape Painting

Camille Corot (1796-1875).

The Cathedral of Mantes, 1865-1869. (20 × 12½″) Musée des Beaux-Arts, Rheims.

LIKE the taste for portraiture, a feeling for landscape is one of the purest, most abiding qualities of the French genius. Rococo culminated in a profusion of leafage which already contained intimations of the future. After a partial eclipse during the Revolution and under the Empire, and an incubational phase (inadequately studied), landscape gradually, from 1830 on, achieved its emancipation and celebrated its final, all but exclusive triumph with the advent of Impressionism. This trend was not peculiar to France, but gained ground everywhere in Europe. England played a pioneering role, and Germany, though standing outside the main stream, made a characteristic contribution to the movement. In this Europe-wide flowering of landscape art (our present-day familiarity with which tends to make us forget how singular it then was) Ruskin rightly saw the major, most distinctive art form of his age.

Here, as with most of the changes that have come over art in modern times, we must look back to the previous century when we seek to trace the origins of this phenomenon. The scientific and philosophical investigations of the Age of Enlightenment led to a new conception of nature, which took effect on both literature and painting. In Diderot's *Salons*, nature is envisaged as a "model," capable like the human body of being imitated, but (he insisted) the artist's approach to nature should be unsophisticated and naïve, no longer intellectual. Newton had published his treatise on *Optics* and Berkeley followed up with his *New Theory of Vision*, basing perception on passive receptivity to light and colors. Kant, by separating the *phenomenon* from the *noumenon*, incited the painter to direct his gaze solely to visible appearances. Jean-Jacques Rousseau vaunted the delights of country walks (which were to inspire several generations of French painters, from Corot to Bonnard), and of lonely meditation in the heart of nature, which his successors were to treat as a two-faced goddess, now wild and ruthless, now serene and benevolent. In 1794 an English aesthetician, Sir Uvedale Price, added to the categories of the Beautiful and the Sublime that of the Picturesque, domain *par excellence* of the landscape painter. And it was from England that in the following year Chateaubriand wrote his seminal letter on landscape art, publication of which was, however, deferred until 1828, when the climate of taste, now that David had had his day, favored its reception.

In the nineteenth-century landscape we find an intermingling and an interaction of all the art currents of the age. The neoclassical tradition, the only trend officially endorsed —its evolution stage by stage from the days of Joseph Vernet (1714-1789) onwards still awaits a chronicler—led up to the glorious revelation of the art of Corot. It included a series of Italianizing specialists, as delightfully simple and forthright in their sketches made from nature as tedious and inert in the laborious compositions they concocted in their studios.

The Romantic trend in France, after being held in check over a long period, benefited from English influences, but still tended to take inspiration from Flemish and above all Dutch precedents. None the less it had autochthonous sources and a lineage of French precursors. Those intrepid pathfinders, the Barbizon group, worked in the heart of nature and landscape now became the vehicle by which Romanticism was transformed into Realism.

From Neoclassicism to Corot

Focusing its attention on man, Neoclassicism took little notice of landscape and assigned it the lowest place in the artistic hierarchy. "It is a type of art that has no right to exist," said the author of the *Lettres critiques et philosophiques* (with reference to the 1796 Salon) and accordingly refused to discuss it. Yet, in spite of these theoretical objections and official disdain, the Free Salons of the Revolutionary period were suddenly invaded by landscapes without figures which, to the horror of the critics, won favor with the public. It was the success of these pictures that galvanized the opposition against them and led to a restatement of the classical doctrines of the Italianizing, neo-Poussinesque landscape, whose leading exponents were two southerners: Pierre-Henri de Valenciennes (1750-1819) from Toulouse and Jean-Joseph-Xavier Bidauld (1758-1846) from Carpentras. In the seclusion of the studio they methodically pieced together composite landscapes which have long since ceased to figure on the walls of art galleries, whereas the preliminary studies from nature that they kept hidden in their portfolios are now being exhumed. Such studies—and the change is significant—were henceforth made in oils and not exclusively, as had been the case with their forerunners, in watercolors (Jean-Pierre Houel, Jean-Jacques de Boissieu, Charles-Louis Clérisseau) or in sanguine (Fragonard, Hubert Robert).

The first landscape painter to be elected to the Institute (in 1813), Bidauld took advantage of his position as a jury member—a position he held for decades before he died at the age of nearly ninety—to exclude the work of the Romantics and the Barbizon masters from the Salon. A pupil of Joseph Vernet, whose two Roman pictures of 1745, *Castel Sant'Angelo* and *Ponte Rotto*, inaugurated the "Italian view" of the Corot type, Bidauld brought back from his youthful sojourn in Italy some studies suffused with luminous vibrations such as the *Nera Valley* (1787, Musée Duplessis, Carpentras) and a view of the wooded hills of Subiaco (1789, Louvre). But when he worked in his studio, his feeling for light was submerged by the painstaking precision of his drawing, with the result that we are reminded of the Italianizing Dutch landscapists of the seventeenth century (who, like him, are now enjoying a return to favor). After 1800, following in the footsteps of Jean-Jacques Rousseau, he roamed the countryside around Ermenonville and Montmorency, to the north of Paris. His contribution to the 1801 Salon was something of a surprise, consisting as it did of a single "study," thus described in the catalogue: "Mowing a field ending with a curtain of small trees." Landon, a painter and art reporter of the Salons of the First Empire, commended Bidauld's delicacy and accuracy of touch and described this "pretty trifle" as a complete success.

The sketches made by Valenciennes who, like his Swiss coeval Solomon Gessner (1730-1788) and the Austrian J. A. Koch (1768-1839), was a writer on art as well as a practising painter, are also very fine. His *pochades*, 128 in number, were assiduously collected by the Comte de l'Espine and, when presented to the Louvre in 1930 by his daughter, the Princesse de Croy, drew attention to his remarkable abilities. His first visit to Italy took place in 1769, when he was nineteen; he lived there from 1777 to 1782, and subsequently, at unspecified dates, made trips to the East, to England, Germany and Spain. Besides being a great traveler (as no doubt befitted a landscape painter born), Valenciennes was a well-read, if self-taught, man, with a wide knowledge of contemporary science and literature. He became a member of the Academy in 1787 and in 1800 published a voluminous work entitled *Eléments de perspective pratique à l'usage des artistes, suivis de Réflexions et conseils à un élève sur la peinture et particulièrement sur le genre du paysage*. A compendium of the neoclassical rules of landscape painting, this treatise was the *vade mecum* of beginners during the first three decades of the century (a second, enlarged edition was issued in 1820) and throws much light on the practices of Corot at the outset of his career. "The art of painting," Valenciennes categorically declared, "is one and indivisible and should concern only one genre—historical painting." However, he points out, landscape can attain the dignity of historical painting when it conforms to the principle of Ideal Beauty and includes antique, Biblical or mythological figures giving it an heroic quality. Though this process of sublimation takes place in the studio, it has to be preceded by direct studies of nature. He bids the young artist to start work just after a shower when lights and colors are brightest and to study "the movement of rivulets winding their way amid reeds and willows," and "tufts of water plants that cluster and interlace, with broad, colorful leaves floating on the surface of the water." Even more remarkable is the anticipation of Impressionism in his advice "to paint the same view at different hours of the day so as to observe the changes that the light produces in forms."

In his own work, the contradiction implicit in the counsels Valenciennes gave to the young is flagrant; indeed his "composite" landscapes (some of which can still be seen in the Louvre and the museums of Bourg-en-Bresse and Toulouse) do not seem to be by the same hand as the wonderfully sensitive sketches. These latter are the work of an artist who combines delicacy with boldness in his handling of color, and has made a scientific study of light; who is less concerned with buildings and natural objects than with subtle variations of the atmosphere around them; who often lingers over the humblest motifs, a tree trunk or a peasant's hut; who anticipated Constable in his study of the movement of clouds, and Turner in his rain and mist effects; who, like Millet, painted rainbows and, like Monet, recorded successive changes of light on a given spot. Strangely enough, this valiant champion of the "historical landscape" never included a figure in his finely balanced oil sketches. Most of them are variations on three motifs, which evidently had a special appeal for the painter: the Lake of Nemi, Villa Borghese and Villa Farnese. There are two versions of the *Two Poplars at the Villa Farnese*; the one reproduced here shows the trees punctuating a blue sky and telling out against the solid bulk of houses forcefully built up in contrasts of light and shade —a procedure Corot took over in his early phase. The importance of light, of cloud movements and of the sky as "a regulator of the color scheme" was even more strongly insisted on in the *Théorie du paysage* published in 1818 by one of Valenciennes' disciples, J. B. Deperthes.

In 1816 Valenciennes sponsored the creation of a Prix de Rome for historical landscape, which continued to be awarded until 1863 when the rise of naturalism made an end of conventional figuration and the distinction drawn between the sketch and the finished picture. The first (1817) prizeman was his most gifted pupil, A. E. Michallon (1796-1822), who died prematurely; some thirty of his excellent sketches from nature (also presented by the Comte de l'Espine) are now in the Louvre. His successor, J. V. Bertin (1775-1842), though an academically minded artist, shows real feeling for nature in some of his oil sketches. It was through Michallon and Bertin that Corot became acquainted with the doctrines of Valenciennes.

David painted only one landscape, but such is its technical perfection, such its clear-cut objectivity, that it constitutes a landmark in the history of French landscape art. Another remarkably successful work by his pupil Cochereau, whom we have already referred to, the *Boulevard des Capucines, Paris* (Chartres), shows the same direct, one might almost say timeless, approach. Ingres displayed a very real taste for landscape (always subjected to the classical disciplines) on several occasions. When in residence at the Villa Medici (1806-1810), he made some sketches of the view, one of the finest in Rome, from the San Gaetano pavilion (these delightful townscapes were published by Hans Naef in 1960), and he also painted the three scenes in tondo form, each a little masterpiece, flawlessly executed and wonderfully luminous, which are now at Montauban and in the Musée des Arts Décoratifs in Paris. They were made at the same time as the portrait of Granet (cf. page 37) whose finely molded head stands out so majestically against a stormy sky and a vista of greenery and houses worthy of Poussin. Wearing the cloak of a Provençal shepherd, billowing out in stately folds, the Aix painter is shown walking on the famous Palatine terrace overlooking the city and carrying the portfolio which contained "all Rome epitomized."

A pupil of J. A. Constantin (1756-1844), founder of the modern Provençal school of landscape painting, then of David, François-Marius Granet (1775-1849) was a close friend of Ingres during his first long stay in Rome, from 1802 to 1819. He made a name for himself in his lifetime with his monastery interiors and religious scenes, but meanwhile was producing more original, attractive works which never reached the public eye. Among them were landscapes and views of Italian edifices, bathed in a golden glow, such as *The Ognissanti Church* (Aix-en-Provence), which pointed the way to Corot and were doubtless seen by his fellow southerner, Cézanne; also some charming watercolors of Paris and the Seine banks, foreshadowing Jongkind and Impressionism. Some of these he bequeathed to the Louvre where he was curator before being appointed to Versailles (under Louis-Philippe). The bulk of his work he presented to the museum of Aix-en-Provence, his birthplace, along with several painted sketches by his friend N.D. Boguet (1755-1839), a neoclassical follower of Claude and Poussin, who went to Italy in 1783 and spent the rest of his life there. Chateaubriand, to whom we owe such eloquent descriptions of the Roman Campagna (oddly enough, the best descriptions and paintings of that region of Italy are the work of Frenchmen) and who was in Rome as secretary to Cardinal Fesch in 1803 and again as French ambassador in 1828, often accompanied him on his walks in the Roman countryside.

Like Vermeer and Chardin, with whom he has curious affinities despite the differences of period and themes, Corot is the picture-lover's delight and the Kunstforscher's despair. For the discrepancy between the basic principles of Corot's art and the works themselves is glaring and, when the miracle takes place, unhindered by any abstract speculation, the critic can but admit his bafflement. Corot accepted the neoclassical heritage, while disregarding the antinomies implicit in it, and in an age of divided purposes effortlessly achieved a perfect balance between style and truth, thought and visual experience, knowledge and spontaneity. He bridged the gap between Impressionism and Claude and Poussin (and even Fouquet), gave an instinctive welcome to the new art trends of his time, but without capitulating to their prejudices, and vindicated in his art the isolated ventures of such men as Joseph Vernet, Hubert Robert and Moreau the Elder. He was the purest representative of the art which is achieved as much by willpower as by talent and is so hard to persevere in: of that *natural vision* to which his age aspired but which was all too often blurred by moralism or virtuosity, as with Constable; by social preoccupations, as with Courbet; or by an insistence on the dramatic or emotive notes in landscape, as was the case with the Barbizon painters.

Jean-Baptiste Camille Corot was born in Paris on July 16, 1796. His parents' home was at the corner of the Rue du Bac and the river bank, where the rhythmic sequence of the Seine bridges is seen at its best, a vista of which he never tired, and the harmony of water,

stones and trees is at its most perfect. His parents, well-to-do milliners, wished him to enter the family business after he had finished his schooling at Rouen and Poissy, and with this in mind apprenticed him to a draper. Not until he was twenty-six did his father consent to his adopting the profession of art—his "mania" as he called it—but he was then provided with an allowance enabling him to live in reasonable comfort whether his pictures sold or not. Perhaps it was partly this late start that led him to elect for a relatively easy branch of the profession, landscape painting, but in any case he had an innate love of nature and there was then a growing interest in landscape art. He sought counsel of Michallon who was of the same age as himself, had already made his name and had just returned from Italy with portfolios full of sketches. "I did my first landscape from nature at Arcueil," he subsequently told Théophile Silvestre, "under the eyes of Michallon, who advised me to paint everything I saw in front of me with the utmost fidelity." When his friend died Corot enrolled in the studio of J. V. Bertin, but meanwhile he trained himself by conscientiously sketching in the neighborhood of Paris and Rouen and in the Forest of Fontainebleau.

In the autumn of 1825 he made, with his friend Behr, the usual pilgrimage to Italy, taking in Switzerland and the Alps on the way, and not reaching Rome until December. There he met Victor Schnetz (1786-1870), Léopold Robert (1794-1835) and Guillaume Bodinier (1795-1872), painters of Italian low-life and genre scenes. But his chief friends were two neo-classical landscape painters, Caruelle d'Aligny (1798-1871), a pupil of Regnault, and F. E. Bertin (1797-1871), a pupil of Girodet. The three friends formed an independent group, working together directly from nature. Bertin impressed on Corot the need for "sitting

Pierre-Henri de Valenciennes (1750-1819).

The Two Poplars at the Villa Farnese, Rome, about 1786. (10 × 14⅞") Louvre, Paris.

François-Marius Granet (1775-1849).
The Ognissanti Church, Rome, about 1807. (8⅜ × 11¼″) Musée Granet, Aix-en-Provence.

down in front of the motif" and d'Aligny was quick to recognize a master in the man who with his naïve application often gave the impression of a rather awkward amateur. Corot spent nearly three years in and around Rome. After visiting Naples and a brief detour by way of Venice he returned to Paris in September 1828. Robaut lists 150 studies made in the course of this first, decisive stay in Italy. Long neglected by connoisseurs, they rank today among his most admired works. They have a freedom and a forcefulness, due to that first fine rapture of discovery, which Corot was to recapture only in his last years. In their bold pictorial architecture of contrasting planes of light and shade, appropriate to open-air painting, in the artist's choice of subjects and in the unfailing accuracy of his responses, these studies mark the culminating point of the small picture painted directly from nature, and they also contain *in posse* the best of Impressionism. Here the topographical and picturesque allusions of the *veduta* give place to the poetry of contemplation, the vision of open space under a dome of light. The clarity and well-knit structure are not of the neoclassical order, but stem from the intrinsic qualities of the Roman countryside and are attuned to its spiritual essence.

After some tentative essays, two fully developed compositions (which the artist as in duty bound bequeathed to the Louvre) formed the real starting point of this sequence of early Roman works. Executed in March 1826, they represent the Colosseum and the Forum, seen from the Farnese gardens on the Palatine, and these views of famous monuments are

Camille Corot (1796-1875).
The Colosseum as seen from the Farnese Gardens, Rome, 1826. (11¾ × 19¼") Louvre, Paris.

transformed—by a supreme artistry calling for freshness of approach as well as technical proficiency—into masterpieces of inspired ingenuousness. By bringing the distant masses into the foreground, Corot overcomes the danger of dispersal inherent in a panoramic view, and transposes the basic stuff of reality on to the plane of creative art. The range of colors is limited. The azure sheen of the sky, the pink and lilac of the stones, the blue haze of the distant prospect, the brown and green of vegetation dappled with soft touches of yellow—all are held together by the iridescence of the atmosphere and a subtle handling of values, that is to say the exact rendering of light as it plays on the surfaces of volumes. Presumably the artist's rare, unerring feeling for values was a natural gift, due to something exceptional in his eyesight, but are we not justified in regarding it as due both to an "invincible awareness" (to use his own expression) of what his art demanded and to his famous "naïveté," a prerogative of the pure in heart, in which, when all is said and done, may lie the secret of his genius? As for technique, there are remarks in his notebooks describing his method of proceeding from strong to lighter values by gradual degrees. "We should always keep in mind the mass, the organic whole, that has caught our eye, and never lose the first impression which quickened our emotion. The design's the first thing to get; then the values—the relations of forms and values. These are the *points d'appui*. Next comes the color and, finally, the execution."

Abandoning the smooth enamel finish of his colleagues and the use of transparent glazes, he resorted to Chardin's vigorous and varied handling of the pigment, to his compact, granulated *matière*, and in the process of harmonizing values he modeled up the forms, simultaneously instilling (like Vermeer) light and substance into all the objects represented. A natural instinct led him to react against the customary use of highlights and translucent shadows and to invent a procedure accordant with his personal vision. Thus he added a little

white to all his colors, even to shadows, not only to clarify and lighten them but also to ensure the homogeneity of a texture at once dense and luminous. As remote from Davidian dryness as from the chiaroscuro and lushness of the Romantics, Corot's firm, full-bodied brushstrokes give eloquent expression to his feelings, but without ever lapsing into over-emphasis. Among the many admirable works produced during his first stay in Rome, of especial interest, by reason of its extraordinarily "cubist" crystallization, is the *Island of San Bartolommeo* (Boston).

The *Colosseum*, here reproduced, a canvas on which Corot set much store, was the first direct study from nature that he ventured to exhibit publicly—and this only in 1849 after the suppression of the Salon jury. In 1827 he sent from Rome, for the Paris Salon of that year, a landscape constructed on strictly neoclassical lines, the *Bridge of Narni* (Ottawa), a pale imitation of Claude Lorrain. This has often been contrasted with the corresponding study in the Louvre, for the two versions illustrate to perfection not the transition from a sketch to a finished picture, but the vital difference between a work born of a flash of inspiration and a studiously orthodox composition. Over a long period these divided aims had a baneful effect on Corot's art, since, to win admittance to the Salon, he had to produce historical pictures masking, not to say travestying, his authentic genius. Hence a series of such stereotyped canvases as the *Ford in the Forest of Fontainebleau* (1833, Washington), a genre scene in which we can see the influence, somewhat unusual in Corot's work, of Constable, victim before him of the same conventions; *Hagar in the Wilderness* (1835, Metropolitan Museum,

Camille Corot (1796-1875).
The Cabassud Houses at Ville-d'Avray, 1835-1840. (11 × 15¾″) Louvre, Paris.

New York), based on a Biblical theme justifying a setting of wild nature; *Silenus* (1838, J. J. Hill Collection, St. Paul, Minnesota), a Poussinesque, quite unconvincing mythological scene; *Homer and the Shepherds* (1845, Saint-Lô), a Virgilian theme, inspired by André Chénier, which, being more congenial, was his most successful work in this ambiguous domain. Yet even here the fusion between the mannered figures and the somewhat idealized landscape, the scenic layout of the picture elements, is incomplete. In compliance with the wishes of some friends, Corot tried his hand at mural decoration: for the Roberts at Mantes (c. 1840-1842; these murals are now in the Louvre); for the Bovy family at the Château de Gruyères in Switzerland (1854-1858) where he spent several holidays; for Decamps at Fontainebleau (c. 1858); and for Daubigny at Auvers-sur-Oise (1865-1868). He also painted some religious compositions: a *St Jerome* (1837) for the church of Ville-d'Avray; a *Flight into Egypt* (1839) for the church of Rosny; a *Baptism of Christ* (1847) for Saint-Nicolas du Chardonnet in Paris. Occasionally, too, he treated literary themes of a romantic type, such as *Macbeth and the Witches* (1859, Wallace Collection, London), but dramatic and monumental painting lay outside his range, he lacked inventive imagination and never felt quite at ease with subjects of this kind. It was in communing with nature that Corot's lyrical fervor found happiest expression—and, as with all intimists, in pictures of relatively small dimensions.

After his return from Italy in 1828 he traveled widely in France, adapting the style acquired in Rome to local atmospheric variations and giving it more flexibility. He showed his total mastery of his medium in a suave yet sublime view of *Chartres Cathedral* (1830, Louvre) and, with an eye as pure as Fouquet's, painted *Notre-Dame and the Quai des Orfèvres* (1833, Musée Carnavalet, Paris) in which we see, bathed in a soft golden light, this ancient quarter of the Cité punctuated by the staccato rhythm of the Seine bridges. To the same period belong the *Port of Honfleur* (c. 1830, Staub-Terlinden Collection, Männedorf) and the rustic landscapes traversed by the Gothic spires of *Rouen* (c. 1830, Wadsworth Atheneum, Hartford, Conn.) and *Soissons* (1833, Kröller-Müller Museum, Otterlo). Four very different parts of France provided him with subjects: Normandy, with which he had been familiar since childhood, a haunt of landscape painters from Bonington to Dufy; Auvergne and the Morvan region; and the Forest of Fontainebleau which, in the company of Bertin and d'Aligny, he discovered before the arrival of the Barbizon group.

In the summer of 1834 Corot returned to Italy, by way of Marseilles and the Riviera, and in Tuscany painted the ancient Etruscan citadel of Volterra. He made two versions (Louvre), bringing out the rugged grandeur and clean-cut forms of the old town with a truly Cézannesque handling of volumes and proportions. Here we see the compact style of the preliminary study enlarged to the dimensions of the easel picture. Towards the end of the summer he returned to France, visiting en route Venice and the North Italian lakes, where he was much taken by the fluidity of the atmosphere and the light mists hovering above the landscape (reminiscences of which can often be seen in his later works). In 1836 he traveled with Ravier in Auvergne and with Marilhat in Provence. In the course of this summer he made paintings of Avignon and the neighborhood (Louvre and Tate Gallery, London). Here solid pictorial construction and the delicate colors to which this much favored part of France owes its singular beauty were combined with the pink and grey tones that he so much admired in Enguerrand Charonton's *Coronation of the Virgin* in the hospice of Villeneuve, which he visited now and again in quest of motifs. Thus, in the middle period of his life, Corot achieved in pictures of moderate size and with a restricted palette of greens, browns and blues, mixed with grey, enlivened here and there with a note of red, a perfect balance and a fine serenity surely unique in the history of art. This can be seen to perfection in the landscapes made about 1840 in the Morvan region, in the countryside around Geneva and at Ville d'Avray, and several versions of the *Maisons Cabassud* (Louvre and Charles Lazard Collection, Paris) where he depicts the houses backed by a wooded hill which he saw from the family house, his haven of repose after his frequent travels, that his father had bought in 1817.

In 1843 Corot revisited the scenes of his youth, Rome and the Campagna, scanning them with a less ardent but more finely tempered gaze. The masterpiece of this later Italian sojourn, the *Gardens of the Villa d'Este at Tivoli* (Louvre), is one of his most harmonious compositions, bathed in a gold and silver sheen, a vibrant synthesis of the accurate observation of his earlier period and the emotive responses which were soon to carry the day. In 1846, at a time when he was still little known, Baudelaire and Champfleury called attention to his work and expressed their admiration for it. In the following year he met Dutilleux, his first patron, and the two men soon became friends. Delacroix paid him a visit (March 14, 1847) and acknowledged him to be "a true artist." Then Thoré discovered and admired his studies and Corot ventured to exhibit one of them, along with a larger canvas, at the 1849 Salon. In July 1851 he went to La Rochelle where he was enraptured by the sailing boats, the docks, the old houses and the pearly grey skies so well described by Fromentin, a native of La Rochelle, in his novel *Dominique*. There he painted some ten pictures, now among his most famous works. Like Vernet and Marquet, he was a born luminist and for him, too, seaports had a particular attraction. His views of Atlantic ports and Normandy beaches have an unfailing charm and the shimmering light and delicate colors exercise a magical appeal, midway between Vermeer and the Impressionists in their happiest moments. After adding some "picturesque" touches to his general view of the port of La Rochelle (Yale University Art Gallery, New Haven), as seen from a window on the quay, he exhibited it at the 1852 Salon —the first work done directly from nature to be deemed worthy of that honor. In later years Corot often admitted that this crystalline, translucent, perfectly constructed picture—and also his youthful *Colosseum*—numbered among his own favorites.

Camille Corot (1796-1875).

The Port of La Rochelle, 1851. (20 × 28¼″) Yale University Art Gallery, New Haven. Bequest of Stephen C. Clark.

But he now committed himself in the eyes of the public to another type of painting. At the 1851 Salon he had shown *Morning, the Dance of the Nymphs* (Louvre) which marks a turning point in his evolution, a lyrical prelude to his last phase. Compact, objective studies and neoclassical, Poussinesque compositions now give place to vaporous, romantic effusions, with sentimental undertones reminiscent of Claude and Watteau. While the new painting was all for realism and focused its attention on modern life, Corot sought refuge in a world of dreams and wistful imaginings. Employing landscapes transposed from Italy and the Ile-de-France and sketches of young actresses and ballerinas (he was an enthusiastic addict of the Paris Opera), he built up in his studio alluring pastorals and Arcadian idylls bearing such names as *Mortefontaine* (1864, Louvre), *Castel Gandolfo* (c. 1865, Louvre) or more simply "Souvenirs." The figures, diaphanous and deftly simplified—sylphs, goatherds playing flutes and so forth—and more fully integrated into the landscape, seem like emanations of the trance-bound countryside, of the lofty trees, their foliage ruffled by a gentle breeze, and the tranquil pools from which a dawn or evening mist is rising. Corot turned out a great many of these ethereal visions bathed in that silvery grey light for which he was renowned, but his success was based on a misapprehension, for though they genuinely reflect his poetic (or rather musical) temperament, they also flattered the taste of an undiscerning public hostile to the naturalism of Courbet and the Barbizon painters. "We prefer," wrote Paul de Saint-Victor in 1855, "the Sacred Grove peopled by fauns to the woodcutter's forest, and limpid springs where nymphs are bathing to Flemish ponds where ducks are paddling."

Meanwhile Corot continued painting directly from nature and produced during this period some of his most perfect works, such as the *Bridge at Mantes* (c. 1868-1870, Louvre) and the *Cathedral of Mantes*, its graceful spires seen from the river bank across a screen of trees, sometimes breadthwise, sometimes vertically (1865-1869, Rheims). Here contrasts give place to nuances and the dreamy poetic beauty of these scenes is largely due to the silver-grey veils mantling the landscape. Corot excelled in rendering the tremulous light of early morning and approaching dusk, and in recording its play on the delicate leafage of poplars and birches, obliquely mirrored in calm sheets of water closing a deep perspective vista (*Marissel*, 1866, Louvre). In his last pictures, the *Belfry of Douai* (1871, Louvre), the *Tanneries at Mantes* (1874, Louvre) and an interior of *Sens Cathedral* (1874, Louvre), he regained the vigor and vivacity of his early work, tempered with something of the serenity of the Dutch masters who had so deeply impressed him when he visited Holland in 1854. From 1852 on he was friendly with Daubigny and in 1862, after a brief stay in London, met Courbet in Saintonge.

In his treatise on landscape (1818) Deperthes observed that "only the presence of figures can bring to life this desert" (i.e. landscape). That Corot to some extent shared this view may have been due not so much to his neoclassical training as to his sociable temperament. In any case, after his return from Italy in 1828, he almost always felt a need to include human beings in his landscapes and in most of his views of the countryside we see tiny, yet essential figures represented in their leisure moments (not at work) but none the less reminding us of the intimate association of the peasant with the soil, whose costumes, touched by light, serve as *points de repère*, indicating spatial recession.

But Corot also painted, almost one would say *sub rosa*, a number of independent figures. The vast body of work produced by him—almost three thousand canvases—includes some three hundred figure paintings (only two of which he exhibited), and these followed the same line of evolution as his landscapes. Hence that intriguing charm, to which Hippolyte Flandrin was alluding when he said: "This devil of a man puts something into his figures that the specialists in that line have never put into theirs." Corot began with studies of Italian models in picturesque garments, handled with exceptional boldness. Then came portraits of his family and friends, made with a frankness and sobriety reminding us of Terborch (*Portrait of Sennegon*, 1842, São Paulo), or again of Clouet or even the Douanier Rousseau. Most

Camille Corot (1796-1875).

Interrupted Reading, about 1865-1870. (35¾ × 25¼″) The Potter Palmer Collection, The Art Institute of Chicago.

attractive, by reason of a sort of empathy we sense between the painter and his models, are those of young girls (*Claire Sennegon*, c. 1845, Louvre) and especially those of children (*Louis Robert* and *Maurice Robert*, 1843 and 1857, Louvre). After 1850 there are fewer of these delightfully appealing portraits; figures are larger, life-size or *petite nature*, and the sitters are professional models wearing exotic finery or stage costumes. But, though lacking in personality, they act as starting points for poetic reveries and provide admirable occasions for artistic tours de force. Often intenser than in the landscapes, the color is always subordinated to the light, which at once models form and sublimates it. Most of Corot's portraits are of women, but there are a few male figures, for example *Monks Reading* (c. 1850-1855, Louvre) in the Caravaggesque manner and *Knights in Armor* (1868, Louvre) in a romantic vein. Delacroix's influence can often be detected in this group of works. Corot's nudes, the finest of which is the study from life, *Marietta* (1843, Petit-Palais, Paris), may be described as Giorgionesque variations on the theme of the Reclining Nymph. She is depicted, for example, in a meadow (c. 1855, Geneva) and on the seashore (1865, Metropolitan Museum, New York). It was chiefly from 1860 on, when with advancing age he was less inclined to travel, that Corot made a practice of figure painting. There is no psychological intent in these figures, and they reveal the instinctive approach of the landscape painter used to working in the open air; thus we are justified in including them in a chapter reserved to landscape art.

In the series of five pictures named *The Artist's Studio* (c. 1868-1870, two versions in the Louvre, one each in the Musée des Beaux-Arts, Lyons, the Baltimore Museum of Art, and the National Gallery, Washington), Corot rings the changes on a traditional theme, showing a young woman holding a mandolin and pensively looking at a picture on an easel. He also made some delightful paintings, imbued with a wistful charm, on the theme of *Interrupted Reading*; the version in the Art Institute of Chicago (c. 1865-1870) is remarkable for its monumental grandeur. Here, as Lionello Venturi has pointed out, the structure is classical, the expression romantic, the intention realistic, and the execution almost impressionist; yet the picture holds together perfectly, there is no suggestion of any discrepancy of periods or styles, and the unique grace of Corot's art is everywhere apparent. The careful disposition of the planes, the balanced alternation of full and empty spaces, and the admirable cadence of the arms are worthy of Cézanne, but along with these we find the gentleness and suavity which are among Corot's most endearing qualities, and here they are enhanced by the delicacy of the colors: yellows, reds, brown and white broken with grey, and diversified in places with black and red accents. Nearly all his figure paintings are of isolated figures, as simple as they are grandiose. When, on occasion, he treats the theme of a mother and child, the composition is based on a schema of all-embracing, wonderfully graceful curves (1860-1870, Philadelphia). While the *Young Girl at her Toilet* (c. 1860-1865, Louvre) is pervaded by that strange enchantment of which Corot alone possessed the secret, others inevitably conjure up thoughts of Vermeer and Rembrandt: the *Woman with a Pearl* (1868-1870, Louvre) and the *Young Greek Girl* (1868-1870, Metropolitan Museum, New York), which have all those qualities of plenitude and poetic insight for which Corot's figure paintings are so justly renowned, and also the sublime works of 1874, with their undertone of melancholia due perhaps to the artist's awareness of his approaching end, the *Woman in Blue* (Louvre), the *Gipsy Woman with a Mandolin* (São Paulo), copied by Braque, and the *Monk with a Violincello* (Hamburg).

Made public only after his death, Corot's figure paintings fascinated Degas and after him the Cubists. Influences, psychological as much as technical, of his landscape art are plain to see in Impressionism (Pissarro and Berthe Morisot both went to him for advice), as in the works of several members of the Barbizon group. As might be expected they are still more in evidence in the work of two of his immediate disciples: Antoine Chintreuil (1814-1873), to whom we owe some fine views of the valley of the Bièvre and of vast plains (*Space*, 1869, Louvre), and Stanislas Lépine (1836-1892), who delineated with delicate precision scenes of the Seine banks, of river ports and byways of Paris (*La Rue de Norvins*, Glasgow).

From Romanticism
to the Barbizon Group

I F, as Fritz Novotny has remarked, the expression "neoclassical landscape" is a contradiction in terms, "romantic landscape" is almost a pleonasm, for the word "romantic" originally applied only to natural scenery, and indeed it is of the very essence of landscape to be romantic. Romanticism arose in opposition to the material limitations of the human body, on which the harmony of classical design was based, and the Romantics looked to nature, to its most elusive moods and aspects, for a visible expression of the infinite. Romantic art accordingly led to a kind of naturalistic mysticism, tending now towards the discipline imposed by a close delineation of nature, now towards the mystical rapture inspired by natural scenery. The landscape painters of the Barbizon school reflect this dual tendency.

Something has already been said about the international literary and philosophical sources of this new conception of nature—a conception particularly congenial to the Nordic mind. English and German artists here preceded and outclassed those of France, who were cramped by the humanistic disciplines imposed by David. Early nineteenth-century painting in France offers nothing comparable to the work of Constable (1776-1837), Turner (1775-1851) or Friedrich (1774-1840), all born a generation before Corot. The thoroughly Germanic art of Caspar-David Friedrich had no influence outside his own country, and the singular genius of Turner long went unrecognized. Constable on the other hand, and before him several other English landscapists, were known in France. They introduced and popularized a freer, more direct approach to nature, and a more fluid and luminous handling of paints which owed much to Flemish and Venetian influence, and also to the widespread practice of water-color painting in England. Watercolor is ideally suited to landscape painting—witness the unsurpassed examples of the Chinese masters (and of Dürer)—and in Europe, from Constable to Cézanne, it reached new heights. Though backgrounds of natural scenery played a major part in his great dramatic paintings, Delacroix produced scarcely any independent landscapes, apart from the famous *Seascape* of Dieppe (1852, Private Collection, Paris); he did, however, paint upwards of a thousand watercolors directly from nature.

Delacroix himself is one of the key figures in that long exchange of ideas between French and English artists which began in the eighteenth century, was speeded up by Géricault's stay in London, and culminated in the Salon of 1824. The two initiators in France and England of the new approach to nature, Joseph Vernet (1714-1789) and Richard Wilson (1714-1782), exact contemporaries, met in Italy and it was the encouragement he received from Vernet

that led Wilson, who had begun as a portrait painter, to devote himself exclusively to land-scape, a genre he transformed and revitalized. In 1771 the Alsatian painter P. J. de Louther-bourg (1740-1812), whose early work had attracted the attention of Diderot, settled in London where he designed stage scenery for Garrick. He specialized in genre scenes and dramatic seascapes fraught with storm and shipwreck (1793, Southampton Art Gallery), which owing to their subject matter rather than their interpretation, still artificial and theatrical, accelerated the evolution of Turner and the transition from static to dynamic landscape. In the autumn of 1801 and again in May 1802, a few months before his premature death, Thomas Girtin (1775-1802), who revolutionized landscape painting in watercolor, went over to Paris and made a series of views of the Seine wholly modern both in mood and handling. At Calais, then still an outpost of English life and culture, L. T. Francia (1772-1839), a friend of Girtin and Cotman, founded a school of landscape painting. It was here that young Richard Parkes Bonington (1801/1802-1828) was trained before going to Paris, where he became the principal intermediary between painters in France and England. Delacroix thought highly of Bonington and he was easily the most gifted of the English watercolorists who flocked to the Continent after the Restoration, enthusiastically painting the Channel beaches, the sites and monuments of Normandy, and the beauty spots of the Seine valley from Paris to Honfleur. Bonington contrived to impart to his watercolors the solidity of oil paints, while his small oils, views of the Channel beaches, of Versailles, Paris, Switzerland and Venice, have all the freshness and transparency of watercolors. Granet, Huet and Isabey came under his influence.

The influence of English landscape painting was above all of a technical order and was by no means confined to this special field. The brilliant renewal of French landscape at the end of the eighteenth century, interrupted by David and deflected into neoclassical channels, contained in embryo all future developments. The Free Salons of the Revolutionary era brought to the fore a whole group of racy landscape painters from the neighborhood of Paris and the rural areas of France, all uninfluenced by Italian traditions; many of these men deserve to be better known. A systematic inquiry into the origins of the modern landscape would reveal some surprising achievements and throw light on the various precursors of Corot (Joseph Vernet and his pupils), of Impressionism (Moreau the Elder), of the Barbizon painters. This latter school was anticipated by a strange artist who worked in isolation, S. M. Lantara (1729-1772), and was rediscovered about 1830; and by a trio of independents, Bruandet, Demarne and Michel, who led a Bohemian life, preferring the drab streets of the Paris suburbs to the majestic antiquities of Italy, and the unvarnished naturalism of the Dutch and Flemish masters to Claude and Poussin.

Something of a roisterer and a ne'er-do-well, condemned to death for having thrown his wife out of a window, Lazare Bruandet (1755-1804) lived and worked during the 1780s in Fontainebleau Forest, the Bois de Boulogne and the Bois de Vincennes, where his sketching trips were occasionally interrupted by the hue and cry of the royal stag hunts. During the Revolution he settled on the edge of Paris, in the region of Romainville and the Prés Saint-Gervais. The *Bassin d'Auteuil* (1795, Cherbourg) shows the accuracy of his vision and his naïve response to emotional stimuli. Less sincere, more finicking and affected, J. L. Demarne (1754-1829), a native of Brussels, fell back on landscape after failing to make his mark as a history painter. He too drifted from village to village on the outskirts of Paris. His favorite motif, taken up again by the Impressionists and also by Vlaminck, was the high road to Saint-Denis, extending into the distance in low, far-flung perspective.

Georges Michel (1763-1843), youngest of the group, was far superior to his elders, with whom he learned to paint. He formed his style by copying and restoring Dutch pictures, which he also bought and sold. He thus familiarized himself with Ruisdael and Hobbema and discovered Rembrandt. Thin and glassy to begin with, his texture became increasingly broad and vigorous. Like Bruandet, he traveled in Switzerland and Germany but his pictorial

Georges Michel (1763-1843).
The Storm, about 1820-1830. (18⅛ × 24¾") Musée des Beaux-Arts, Strasbourg.

horizon was deliberately limited to the plain of Saint-Denis (Besançon Museum), where he spent his childhood, and the hills around Paris overlooking wind-swept heaths and fields. "Any painter," he liked to say, "who can't work all his life over a four-league stretch of country is only a duffer." The first artist to settle in Montmartre (then a country village well outside the city), he painted the old church, the telegraph tower, the lime kilns and the windmills, dramatically silhouetted against a barren, hummocky landscape traversed by livid gleams of light (Louvre and Cailleux Collection, Paris). *The Storm* (Strasbourg) is an excellent example of his rich and surging brushwork, his sober, powerful style which galvanizes the essential movements of the ground under a lowering sky and intensely contrasting clouds. To the density of Géricault and the dynamic sweep of Ruisdael he adds a rugged vehemence of his own. Living in seclusion in his last years, catering for a single collector who bought all the pictures he cared to paint, Michel died completely forgotten in 1843 and was only brought to notice some years later, in 1846 in an article by Thoré, Rousseau's friend, and in 1872 in a study devoted to him by Sensier, Millet's biographer.

Paul Huet (1803-1869) is the most thoroughgoing exponent of Romantic landscape painting, which he was already practising on his own before the revelation of the English landscapists at the 1824 Salon. He specialized in natural cataclysms, storm-swept forests,

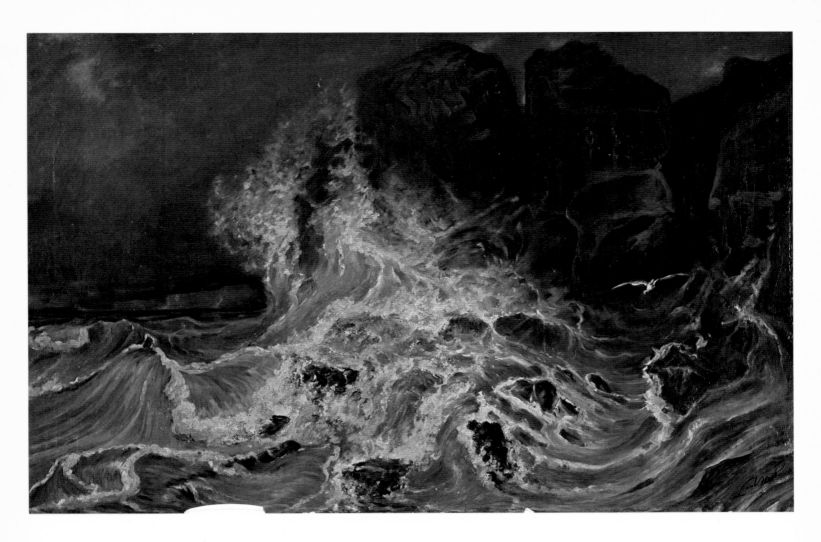

Paul Huet (1803-1869).
Breakers on the Promontory at Granville, 1853. (26¾ × 40½″) Louvre, Paris.

floods, whirlpools and yawning chasms, all of which Théophile Gautier described as "Shake-spearian," but which in fact was only a modern adaptation, in a different setting, of the "heroic landscape" of the past. He began by painting the great trees in the park of Saint-Cloud (1824, Petit-Palais, Paris; 1829, Louvre), a spot then much in vogue with painters, and indeed, as Louis Dimier has remarked, "before the Barbizon school one might almost enter a 'school of Saint-Cloud' in the annals of French painting." On friendly terms with Delacroix and Bonington, Huet was also intimate with such poets and writers as Victor Hugo and Michelet. Sainte-Beuve in his *Journal de Joseph Delorme* (1829), written at a time when he frequented the studios of his painter friends, voiced the conception of the Romantic landscape probably better than anyone else and in *Le Globe*, in October 1830, published an enthusiastic and pene-trating article on Huet. The latter's success was confirmed at the 1831 Salon where his desolate twilight landscapes, inscribed with some lines from Victor Hugo, attracted much attention. Dating from the same year (though later retouched) is one of his masterpieces, a *View of Rouen from the Mont aux Malades* (Rouen Museum), a vast lyrical panorama, freshly and luminously rendered, showing English influence and partaking of the rather spectacular effects of the peep-shows for which he was working at the time. Several journeys abroad, to England, Italy, Belgium and Holland, and long painting expeditions in the French provinces marked a prolific but erratic career dominated by the aspirations of his youth. He saw the sea for the first time at Honfleur in 1826 and thereafter found inexhaustible inspiration in the stormy seas and fantastically swirling waves for which he became famous (*Breakers on the Promontory at Granville*, 1853, Louvre). Far better than the large paintings by Huet to be seen in many French museums, often slackly composed or marred by facile decorative effects, the body

of watercolors and small panels in the Perret-Carnot Collection in Paris reveals his technical prowess and fine sense of poetry. Eugène Isabey (1803-1886), son of the famous miniaturist portrayed by Gérard (cf. p. 28), was in London with Delacroix and Bonington in 1825. His profuse and brilliant historical paintings are of far less interest today than the sincere, solidly constructed seascapes reminiscent now of Courbet, now of Boudin (*Port of Dieppe*, 1842, Nancy, and *Wave Effects*, Louvre).

Two highly gifted Romantic landscapists stand out in the field of graphic art: Charles Meryon (1821-1868) and, on a different plane, Victor Hugo (1802-1885). Endowed with a powerful visual imagination, adept at conjuring up the atmosphere of Rhine castles and medieval towns bathed in moonlight, Hugo was a master of pungent contrasts and, though admittedly an amateur, rivaled at times the greatest draughtsmen. "He excels," wrote Théophile Gautier, perhaps not without a pang of jealousy, "in mingling in his fierce and somber fantasies the chiaroscuro effects of Goya with the architectural terrors of Piranesi. He has a knack of lighting up the gloomy towers of a dismantled castle with a moonbeam or a flash of lightning, and darkly silhouetting a distant town, fretted with steeples and belfrys, against a livid shaft of sunlight." Son of an English doctor and a French dancer, color-blind and subject to hallucinations, Meryon was the visionary etcher of the effervescent Paris of

Narcisse Diaz (1807-1876).

Landscape. Undated. (38½ × 51⅜") By Courtesy of the Syndics of the Fitzwilliam Museum, Cambridge, England.

Théodore Rousseau (1812-1867).
Edge of the Forest at Fontainebleau, Sunset, about 1848. (56 × 77⅞″) Louvre, Paris.

Balzac, Nerval and Eugène Sue, of the epic splendors and terrors of the tentacular city whose streets and alleyways he peopled with the figments of his nightmares. His was a genius of the same order as that of Hercules Seghers—able, that is, to impart to topographical exactitude a visionary immensity.

There are two "Schools of Fontainebleau" in the history of French painting: that of the sumptuous decorators of the palace under Francis I (1515-1547), and that of the humble landscape painters of the forest in the mid-nineteenth century. The latter formed, however, not so much a school as an independent art colony established on the edge of the forest, in the tiny village of Barbizon. Hence the name "Barbizon School" by which they are usually designated, and which suits them better than "School of Fontainebleau," which had best be reserved for the brilliant sixteenth-century Mannerists, whose heir was Ingres. Besides Millet, the Barbizon group includes Théodore Rousseau, Dupré, Diaz and Daubigny, as well as some less important landscapists and several animal painters. Historically, they belong to the generation born in the last years of the Empire and cheated by the downfall of Napoleon of the heroic destiny to which they aspired. Socially, they had to contend with the implacable hostility of the bourgeoisie and convention-bound officialdom. Artistically, they inherited the restless yearnings of Romanticism, but weary of make-believe and all the tinsel of the romantic imagination, they turned towards nature and real life. Fontainebleau Forest, one of the oldest, most beautiful wooded tracts in France, "that vast region, somber, fantastic

and barren" (Michelet), where Obermann dreamed and brooded, where Flaubert and the Goncourts set the scenes of their novels, answered perfectly to their aesthetic and moral ideals and offered a haven for these sensitive souls enamored of the solitude of woods and fields. "Our art can only be moving by being sincere," declared their leader, Rousseau—a sincerity, however, too often wasted on the delineation of minute details and, while sometimes moving, too often lapsing into pathos and dramatization. In their approach to nature they by-passed the Italian tradition and followed the example of the Dutch landscape painters. Fromentin, after a masterly survey of the art of Ruisdael and Cuyp in the Dutch section of his *Maîtres d'autrefois* (1876), proceeds to examine their impact on the Barbizon group. These Dutch influences (by which Corot was unaffected) were superimposed on, and to some extent counteracted, the English influences previously undergone; they led back from color to tonal painting, from direct vision and an immediate response to the motif to the pantheistic celebration of nature in her timeless, eternal and static aspects. The Barbizon painters effected the transition from Romanticism to Naturalism and Impressionism. Today, after the freshness and spontaneity of the Impressionists, their work may strike us as dark and often artificial, and their efforts at realism seem hampered by the pressure of Romanticism and memories of museum art. But their will to grandeur goes far to redeem these shortcomings, and before belittling them we do well to remember what Van Gogh wrote to his brother Theo on June 25, 1889 (when his eyes had already been opened to color and light in the South of France): "I cannot forget all those fine Barbizon canvases, and as for doing better than that it seems to me unlikely and moreover unnecessary."

Théodore Rousseau (1812-1867).
The Little Fisherman, 1848-1849. (8 × 12″) Louvre, Paris.

Thoré, Silvestre and Sensier have all paid tribute to the fervor, integrity and exemplary courage of Théodore Rousseau (1812-1867), the moving spirit of the Barbizon group. With him ethic and aesthetic values tend to coincide, not for moralistic reasons but as the spontaneous overflow of a generous nature and deep religious sentiment. He was hardly more than a boy when he entered the studio of Lethière, a strict Davidian, then that of the landscapist Remond, successor of Michallon. In June 1830 he set out alone on a tour of France and went straight to Auvergne, to the heart of Celtic Gaul, a wild, volcanic region. He brought back a series of rugged, unpolished canvases, painted with a full brush regardless of presentation and layout; here the rude vigor of his temperament at once declared itself. He aspired to be "the painter of the countryside," to record its light, structure and daily life with the inquisitive eye of a naturalist, an ethnologist and a geologist. Next he went out to Normandy, pushing in 1832 to its farthest limit, the Mont Saint-Michel. There he fell in with the mystical-minded painter Charles Delaberge (1807-1842), who advised him to "work up from the small to the big," to "call forth from the earth a thousand forms of plant life and myriads of beings," to "search into the very soul of infusoria." He met with a certain success at the 1833 Salon with such pictures as *Environs of Granville* (Hermitage, Leningrad). He worked at Saint-Cloud, in Huet's preserve, then in the winter of 1832-1833, from November to February, in Fontainebleau Forest. There, for the time being, he produced only a few studies and drawings, but the place had made a decisive impression on him. After his discovery of the woodlands, came that of the mountains. In the autumn of 1833 he spent three months in the Jura, at the Col de la Faucille, overlooking the vast panorama of the Alps. He saw a mighty storm break in full fury over the Mont Blanc, and this incomparable spectacle inspired the great painting in Copenhagen (Ny Carlsberg Glyptotek), in which the elements are stirred to a frenzy with the breadth and sweep of Koninck and the dramatic energy of Seghers.

In 1834 he visited Nantes, the Loire estuary and the woodland district of Vendée known as the Bocage, exploring the marshes and peat-bogs and observing the aquatic plants which Valenciennes had called to the attention of painters. There he discovered a natural world of tremulous surfaces and hidden depths teeming with life, of glimmering waters and diffused light, which challenged his hand and eye and forced him to develop a suppler and subtler technique. The *Chestnut Avenue* (Louvre), the pillared trunks upholding a mighty vault of leafage, was painted at Souliers, near Bressuire in Poitou. But it was refused at the 1835 Salon. His work was again refused in 1836, and it became clear that he was to be systematically excluded from the Salon. Rousseau thereupon left Paris and, supported by a few friends, among them Théophile Thoré, the "French Ruskin," he settled in a cottage at Barbizon. There, between plain and forest, he found an austere and grandiose landscape after his own heart and drew from it inexhaustible inspiration. He seldom traveled now, though in 1842 he made an excursion along the river Creuse, in the home country of George Sand, and in 1844 accompanied Dupré as far as the Pyrenees by way of the Gascon moorlands and the Basque country. He recorded these vast, transparent distances in the *Plain in front of the Pyrenees* (1844, Louvre), and a *Marsh in the Landes* (1852, Louvre).

After the change of government in 1848, the tide began to turn. He was given an official commission and the resulting picture, the *Edge of the Forest at Fontainebleau* (Louvre), was exhibited at the Salon of 1850-1851. This, together with the famous *Oaks at Apremont* (1852, Louvre), is one of his most characteristic, most fully realized works. It combines his favorite motifs: a vault of trees and leafage, an opalescent pond, a romantic sunset, and a simple rustic setting magnified to cosmic dimensions. Under the majestic overhanging branches, and against the foil of the dark tree trunks rimming it round, the "hole" of open space in the center is pierced to infinite depths by the concentrated radiance of light. Scrupulous analysis of detail is united with the monumental breadth of the whole, a sturdy framework of forms with the aerial gradation of values. The sincerity of the execution and the harmonious coordination of parts attenuate whatever there is of deliberate theatricality in the composition.

Charles-François Daubigny (1817-1878).
Sunset on the River Oise, 1865. (15⅜ × 26⅜″) Louvre, Paris.

Scenic and picturesque effects are much less in evidence in the smaller canvases, *View of the Plain of Montmartre* (c. 1845-1848, Louvre) and the *Little Fisherman* (1848-1849, Louvre), which are handled more freely and naturally, with a lighter touch and brighter colors.

A measure of recognition came at last at the Paris World's Fair of 1855, where an entire room was set aside for him and Decamps. But this belated success made no change in the reserved and noble character of the faithful "hermit of Barbizon." In 1857 he worked in Picardy, in 1860 in Franche-Comté, Courbet's native province, and in Switzerland. In 1863 he returned to the Col de la Faucille, to see and sketch the Alps once again. In his last years he became a passionate admirer of Japanese prints. Unfortunately, as he grew older he took to retouching his canvases and by laboring over them often marred their original freshness. He left some admirable drawings which, with their precise and vibrant hatchings, enabled him to lay down what he called "the sinewy substructure" of his paintings.

Jules Dupré (1811-1889) worked in close fellowship with Rousseau from 1841 to 1849. A visit to England in 1834 opened his eyes to Constable, Morland and Gainsborough. The freshness of his palette, the breadth of his vision, and his lyrical sensibility bring to mind similar qualities in Huet and earned him the admiration of Delacroix. By working with Rousseau he was led to develop his style in the direction of realism. He was fond of riverside scenes, with tall trees setting up their dense screen of leafage against stormy or crepuscular skies calling for rich lighting and textural effects (*Sunset after the Storm*, 1851, Louvre, and *The Watering Place and the Tall Oak*, Louvre). All the Barbizon painters were, so to speak, tree worshippers, and the style of each may be distinguished by the way in which his trees are handled: majestically, like Celtic goddesses, by Rousseau; by Dupré, in heroic masses forming a single unit with the earth beneath them; more decoratively by Diaz, in richly colored masses of foliage; by Daubigny in graceful, lyrical clusters.

Son of a Spanish refugee, Narcisse Diaz de la Peña (1807-1876) made his debut at the 1831 Salon at the same time as Dupré, with whom he had served his apprenticeship at Sèvres as a porcelain painter. A lover of the forest, he was for years a familiar figure in and about Fontainebleau, suffusing his woodland landscapes with the romantic ardor of his southern temperament, though lapsing at times into a somewhat artificial virtuosity. The sun sparkles and dances on his patterned leafage (*The Heights of Jean de Paris*, 1867, Louvre), or again furtive gleams of sunlight steal through the brushwood. Occasionally he ventures out of the forest and paints a fantastic landscape beneath phosphorescent clouds (*Landscape*, Fitzwilliam Museum, Cambridge), banked up with a Baroque luxuriance anticipating Monticelli.

Not only a painter but a remarkable etcher, wood engraver and lithographer, whose work was pitched in a more peaceful and intimate key than that of his Barbizon friends, Charles-François Daubigny (1817-1878) played an important part in preparing the way for Impressionism. After an academic and neoclassical schooling under J. V. Bertin, Granet and Delaroche, he exhibited at the Salon from 1838 on and became a close friend of Corot's in 1852. From 1850 to 1860 he traveled throughout France, painting a long series of naturalistic landscapes that established his reputation. The most characteristic of these, with its serene, unerring mastery, is *The Lock at Optevoz* (1855, Rouen; replica of 1859 in the Louvre), painted in Dauphiné; the same motif was interpreted by Courbet from exactly the same spot (Neue Staatsgalerie, Munich). Appointed a member of the Salon jury, he courageously supported the younger artists in their struggle for recognition, Monet in particular, whom he strongly influenced and whom, in London in 1870, he introduced to the dealer Paul Durand-Ruel. To Daubigny goes the credit for being the first landscapist to work entirely out of doors. In 1857 he fitted up a studio on his houseboat, "Le Botin," from which he painted countless land- and waterscapes along the river Oise, whose lush green banks were his favorite theme; Monet later adopted the same method on the Seine at Argenteuil. In 1865, after working at Trouville with Courbet, Monet and Boudin, and painting such fresh and appealing river scenes as *The Barges* and *Sunset on the Oise* (both in the Louvre), he was singled out by one critic as "the leader of the school of impressions." He did away with the distinction hitherto made between sketch and finished picture (so that Théophile Gautier criticized his paintings for being mere "working sketches"), and though keeping to tonal painting, he used a brighter palette, was sensitive to light reflections, and struck a balance between the material structure of objects and the spontaneous play of sunlight.

The Dutch school, several centuries before, had raised animal themes to the level of a specialized branch of painting. So, too, the Barbizon school had its animal painters who, under the Second Empire, enjoyed widespread popularity. Charles Jacque (1813-1894), at first a romantic illustrator, turned realist in 1848 and specialized in farmyard scenes, with sheep and poultry. J. R. Brascassat (1814-1867), Rosa Bonheur (1822-1899) and Constant Troyon (1810-1865) were fond of painting cattle and, under the influence of Paulus Potter's famous *Bull*, sought to represent them on a vast scale, in the heroic vein, but without the corresponding verve and monumentality. Standing midway between Romanticism and Barbizon, the great animal sculptor Antoine-Louis Barye (1796-1875), a student of Gros's and a friend of Delacroix's, was also a gifted painter and, above all, watercolorist. He drew the caged animals in the Jardin des Plantes and, in imagination, set them roaming through the wildest thickets of Fontainebleau Forest.

After its triumph at the great exhibition held in conjunction with the Paris World's Fair of 1855, the Barbizon school began to exert an international influence. In France it affected the School of Lyons (Ravier, Carrand, Vernay) and many independent landscapists, L. Cabat (1812-1893), F. L. Français (1814-1897), Adolphe Hervier (1819-1879), and Henri Harpignies (1819-1916), an artist much admired round about 1900, whom Anatole France called "the Michelangelo of trees."

The Battle of Realism

Honoré Daumier (1808-1879).

The Burden. Undated. (58 × 37⅜″) Private Collection, Paris.

THE movement known as Realism bridged the interval between Romanticism and Impressionism and, in France, extended over two decades (1850-1870). In this urge to a realistic world-view, following the disruption of the time-honored ideologies, we have what was undoubtedly the most potent driving force of the mid-century. It was based on a belief in the autonomy of the outside world, in the possibility of understanding it and treating it objectively. The cult of nature and an inflexible faith in science led to a generalization of experimental methods and positivist dogma. Painting became, as Constable observed, a branch of natural philosophy and faithful observation of nature (meaning landscape, to begin with) developed into an aesthetic and moral duty involving a new awareness of the artist's social function. Just as there now were no "privileged" motifs, since everything in nature is equally beautiful to an understanding eye, so all men were held to have an equal right to a happy, well-filled life, and by the same token the highest merit was often to be found in the poorest class. Hence the latent connection between realism in art and socialism in politics. It was the 1848 revolution that led to a far-reaching change of heart in the three outstanding exponents of Realism in painting: Millet, Courbet and Daumier. Though held in control in the service of their art, their preoccupation with social problems and the generous humanism that pervades their work differentiate these artists militant from the earlier "painters of reality," whom they regarded as their forerunners and assiduously studied. Thoré, a friend of Rousseau and Millet, resuscitated Vermeer and the Dutch genre painters, while Champfleury, a friend of Courbet and the theorist of Realism, rediscovered the Le Nain brothers and, on another plane, explored the vast domain of folk art racy of the soil. And, finally, the collection of Louis-Philippe, on view in the Louvre from 1838 to 1848, revealed the Spanish golden age and its realistic scenes of everyday life.

In 1833 the two conflicting, yet complementary theses of art for art's sake and art in the service of man, i.e. with a social mission, made their appearance in the critic's vocabulary. In the same year Gustave Planche used the term Realism in connection with art for the first time, approvingly to begin with, but as the movement gained strength, with more and more hostility. After 1848, equating Realism with vulgarity, ugliness and downright anarchy, he vigorously trounced the Realists and all their works. When the battle of Realism took place under the Second Empire (1851-1870), the belligerents were less concerned with form than with the "outrageous" subject matter of the realist picture. The new school of painting rejected not only neoclassicism and its academic aftermath, but also romantic escapism and its cult of the exotic, and urged the artist to focus his attention on the realities of contemporary life. On the technical side the precise outlines of Ingres and Delacroix's lavish colors were replaced by tonal values and the atmospheric greyness which envelops the physical objects seen in daily life.

"For the term Realism to have any valid meaning," Delacroix protested, "we have to assume that all men have the same outlook and the same way of perceiving things." Fortunately Realism ranged far beyond its narrow definition and achieved a universal, archetypal grandeur, without hampering the personal élan on which the Romantics set such store. Thus Millet, Courbet and Daumier explored quite different fields of vision, rural or urban, material or moral, and each developed an individual manner, classical or Baroque, of "utilizing," as Millet put it, "the trivial for the expression of the sublime."

Jean-François Millet (1814-1875).
The Washerwoman, about 1861. (17¼ × 13¾″) Louvre, Paris.

Millet and the Soil

J EAN-FRANÇOIS MILLET (1814-1875) can be assigned to the Barbizon group on the strength of the best and largest part of his œuvre and of his career, and also in virtue of his close friendship with Théodore Rousseau. Like those of Vincent and Theo van Gogh at Auvers-sur-Oise, the graves of the two men lie side by side in the village churchyard at Barbizon. Actually, however, Millet went to live there only in 1849, a year after the 1848 crisis, which led him to part company with the romantic landscape painters whose style, already formed, was little affected by the upheaval of that eventful year. Rousseau was a dreamer lost in exclusive contemplation of the majesty of the natural world: "The soul of the artist can find fulfillment only in the boundless heart of Nature." Millet, however, stressed the human element in his evocations of scenes of nature: "When you paint a picture, whether of a house, a wood, the sea or the sky, always be mindful of man's presence." Turning his back on the forest in whose recesses his friends set up their easels, he gazed at the tilled fields and watched the gestures of the peasant, incarnation of the twofold faith of the age, in the People and in Nature. Though there had been others, he was the first artist faithfully and systematically to interpret the lot of the peasantry, depicting them at their daily tasks and at the same time investing them with a Biblical dignity, tinged with social implications. As the pioneer of a new type of painting, apart from other reasons, he ranks as one of the great pathfinders in the history of French art.

In the full-length studies by Sensier (1881) and Moreau-Nélaton (1921) the "legend" of the artist's life is set forth with admirable precision. His character and vocation were determined by the part of France he came from (which he never left until nearly twenty) and his home surroundings. Born in a farmhouse at Gruchy, near Gréville on the Channel coast, he worked in the fields with his father, plying the scythe and driving the plough. A great-uncle, a rustic curé living with the family, taught him Latin and had him recite his Virgil as he trudged along the furrows. His maternal grandmother, something of a Jansenist, had much influence on his religious and moral education. His father, who made a hobby of wood-carving, was struck by the boy's talent for drawing and took him to Cherbourg in 1833 to study art under Mouchel, a painter of the Davidian school. There were eight children and as the eldest son his sense of duty forced him to return to manage the farm on his father's sudden death. However, his mother and grandmother, feeling he had a "divine mission," persuaded him to return to Cherbourg in 1835. He continued studying under a pupil of Gros, Langlois de Chèvreville, who understood his temperament, encouraged him to persevere,

and procured a grant from the Municipality, enabling him to go to Paris in January 1837. There he entered the studio of Paul Delaroche, took no part in the academic competitions, and spent long hours in the Louvre, studying Mantegna, Giorgione, Lesueur and above all Michelangelo and Poussin. He made his first showing at the 1840 Salon, then went back to Cherbourg. Next year he married Pauline Ono and in 1842 the young couple moved to Paris, where they lived under miserable conditions. Pauline, always delicate, died of consumption in April 1844. Millet made touching portraits, exquisite in their quiet way, of her and her sister, Madame Lecourtois (Louvre and Cherbourg Museum). Meanwhile, to make ends meet, Millet had taken to painting the genre scenes in the Correggio or Boucher style belonging to his so-called "flowery manner" which lasted until 1848. The recherché color schemes and sometimes trivial grace of these works tend to conceal their solid pictorial qualities, which are fully apparent in the portraits. Those he made at Cherbourg and Le Havre (where he went to live after his wife's death) are particularly fine, for example the two half-length figures of naval officers in the museums of Rouen and Lyons. With their vigorous modeling, sober colors and studied objectivity, these portraits are in the lineage of Champaigne and Géricault.

In 1844 critics began to take notice of his mythological compositions, commenting on their supple, velvety texture, resembling that of Diaz and Tassaert, sometimes worked up with the palette knife in the manner of Decamps. The small *Offering to Pan* (1845, Montpellier), with its rich impasto, is one of the most significant. In December 1845 he returned to Paris with his second wife, Catherine Lemaire, by whom he was to have nine children, and in her found a devoted helpmate, ready to share the trials of a struggling painter's life. In 1846, employing a chiaroscuro resembling Prud'hon's, he made a number of small studies of nude figures, often shown in back view and built up in synthetic masses (Boston). In 1847 he met Sensier, who was to be his lifelong friend, and turned to a new range of subjects, countryfolk and workmen. At the 1848 Salon he exhibited *The Winnower*, a full-length figure in active movement, first of a series of world-famous pictures. The original perished in a fire in the United States, but two replicas are in the Louvre. In June 1849, on the advice of Charles Jacque, Millet moved with his family to a cottage at Barbizon; he had never liked city life and in that peaceful village found something of the atmosphere and surroundings of his childhood. From now on he never left Barbizon, except for a trip to Franche-Comté in September 1860 and two stays at his birthplace, from June to September of 1854 (after his mother's death) and from August 1870 to November 1871 (during the Franco-Prussian War and the Commune). Though he had no illusions about the rather unattractive mentality of the French peasantry, the glorification of peasant life on which he now embarked stemmed from the depth of his heart and his heredity, and it is to this that he largely owes his fame. "I was born a peasant and shall die a peasant. I have things to recount as I have seen them and I shall stick to my native soil, without budging a clog's length from it." True, it is going too far to say as some have done that before Millet the countryfolk had always been depicted as merely quaint or comical figures. The cathedral sculptors, Gothic illuminators, Bruegel and the Le Nain brothers had treated them seriously and sometimes shown them at their tasks. What distinguishes Millet is the exclusive, methodical nature of the program he set himself, whose political intent (sporadic at most) was by no means so subversive as his contemporaries professed to think. He never concerned himself with the social status of the peasants—in any case a highly conservative class and the mainstay of the Second Empire—or their individual oddities, but aimed at bodying forth the symbolic significance of the peasant and his immemorial gestures. Millet began with the closest possible observation, then proceeded to simplify and generalize.

His long sequence of pictures on peasant life includes both isolated figures and groups gravely absorbed in the immemorial toil of the farm and the fields. In a letter to Sensier of February 1862 he explained the expressive characterization and compact design that he had in mind. "I try to make things look as if they were not put together by chance or for a special

occasion, but as if there were an obligatory and indispensable connection between them. I should like the people I represent to appear dedicated to their way of life, so that it should be impossible for them to imagine any other." Thus *The Sower* (1850, Boston) and *The Washer-woman* (c. 1861, Louvre) form one with the bodily movements called for by their work and with the setting appropriate to it, out of doors in one case, indoors in the other. The implements of their labors have the same unvarnished roughness and epic breadth as the men and women who manipulate them. At the 1853 Salon he exhibited the *Harvesters Resting* (Boston; preparatory study, in reverse, in the Louvre), which he sub-titled "Ruth and Boaz." The sturdy figures of *The Gleaners* (1857, Louvre) stand out with monumental clarity against the sunny plain stretching behind them. The horizon line is placed unusually high so as to let the scene of work in the fields, at once compact and vibrant, speak for itself in all its ageless majesty. "A lofty soul, but is he a great painter?" asked Fromentin. Perhaps we may say that the artist in him is superior to the painter and as so often in such cases gives of his best in his drawings. Despite his monotonous tonality, his laborious execution, and the risks of schematization and sentimentality that he ran, his work retains, by its very sincerity, a certain grandeur and impressiveness. It profoundly affected the public of the late nineteenth century and influenced many artists, Liebermann in Germany, Segantini in Italy, Israels in Holland, and above all Van Gogh, who looked to Millet reverently as his spiritual and technical guide.

Jean-François Millet (1814-1875).
The Gleaners, 1857. (32⅞ × 43¾″) Louvre, Paris.

Gustave Courbet (1819-1877).

The Painter's Studio, detail: Portrait of the Artist, 1855. Louvre, Paris.

Courbet and the Majesty of Life

THE central figure of nineteenth-century French art, Courbet may be said to incarnate its ruling tendency, a concentration on the visible world, and its technical corollary, a brilliant handling of the painter's means. He forms the bridge between Géricault and Cézanne. Like a modern Caravaggio, carried away by his natural exuberance and passionate sympathy with the working classes, he converted painting into an aesthetic and social battle-field, and flung himself into the fray under the triple flag of Realism, Truth and Freedom. But he had no illusions about art theories and slogans. "The epithet Realist has been foisted on me just as that of Romantics was foisted on the men of 1830. Such names have never given, at any time, a true idea of the facts." To his mind, it was only the works, at once creative and informed with the spirit of the age, that counted; works that spoke for themselves and crystallized the revolutionary aims of the artist. All the same, though Courbet's art as a whole transcends any cut-and-dried definition, the epithet Realism can properly be applied to the masterpieces on which his reputation rests.

Jean-Désiré Gustave Courbet was born on June 10, 1819, at Ornans (Doubs), in that picturesque, strongly characterized region of France, spanning the Jura range, which, after its detachment from the Duchy of Burgundy, bore the name of Franche-Comté—a name that stressed its rugged independence. Already under the rule of Philip the Good (1419-1467), its inhabitants were famous for their "tall stature and jovial pride," and they have retained these traits. The small town of Ornans, which lies in the heart of Franche-Comté, that "free county" so mindful of its privileges, is situated in the valley of the Loue between steep crags and thickly wooded hills. In 1244 Ornans was given special rights permitting it to institute a local government on democratic lines, and in 1507 it was the only town in Europe granted that high honor, the "right of sanctuary." In view of their prestige and long tradition of freedom, the citizens of Ornans were known as *les glorieux*. Of purely autochthonous descent and endowed with the rude virtues of his native soil—forthrightness, unflagging energy, and pugnacity—Courbet could claim to be, in the fullest sense of the term, a *glorieux*. Ornans, for him, was the most favored spot in France and he deliberately set out to portray for all time and for all to see both its physical aspects and its way of life.

Courbet was the eldest child of a wealthy landowner, a talkative, impulsive man of restless energy, whose mind was always seething with fantastic schemes, and of a gentle, amiable, devoted mother. His three sisters, who shared their mother's taste for music, lavished affection

and admiration on their gifted brother. His maternal grandfather, a follower of Voltaire, had been a militant revolutionary in 1789; he instilled into the boy almost from the cradle his republican convictions and rule of life, "Shout loud and keep straight!" In 1831 Gustave began attending the small local school but he often played truant, much preferring to roam the countryside. The drawing classes, however, appealed to him and he never missed the open-air sketching parties which his teacher (who had studied under Gros) organized on fine days. In 1837 he was sent to the Collège Royal at Besançon, where he resented having to live in as a boarder and quickly realized that student life was not for him, there were other ways of getting knowledge. He protested vigorously and threatened to run away. "They're trying to put pressure on me," he said in a letter to his parents, "and all my life I've done nothing under pressure, it isn't in my nature." He had his way and after the Easter vacation took a room in a house where three painters-to-be were lodging: Arthaud, Baille and Jourdain.

From 1838 to 1840 he divided his time between Ornans and Besançon. When at Ornans during the holidays, he explored the neighboring country, alone or with friends whom he joined on their hunting and fishing expeditions. More and more enchanted with the local scenery he developed an almost pagan fervor for the beauties of nature. "The country," he told a friend, "gives me emotions just like love!" At Besançon he attended the art school, of which Flajoulot, one of David's disciples, was then in charge. At the Collège he renewed acquaintance with one of his schoolfellows from Ornans, who had meanwhile been studying at Fribourg. This was the poet Max Buchon (1818-1869), who became one of his closest friends. Courbet illustrated Buchon's first book, *Essais poétiques* (1839), with four lithographs. In his second volume of poems (1844) Buchon celebrated, in realistic terms, the works and days of the local peasants and villagers. He found in his native province an unfailing source of poetic inspiration, holding as he did that the creative impulse is stimulated to the highest degree by the life of "common folk." A great admirer of Courbet and the sociologist Proudhon (1809-1865), his two most eminent compatriots (both of them self-taught), Buchon stressed their points in common, "their stalwart, typically Franc-comtois build" and their splendid spontaneity. His political ideas led to his exile from France from 1851 to 1858. To him we owe a frank and reliable estimate of Courbet, an artist whose intentions have often been so grossly misinterpreted and whom perhaps he understood better than any other.

In November 1840 Courbet went to Paris, not to read for the bar as his father and his uncle Oudot, a professor at the Law School, had intended, but to make his way as a painter by dint of hard work. Instinct and temperamental obstinacy led him to steer clear of officialdom in all its forms and to train himself by copying in the Louvre and making studies from the living model in unofficial art schools. He went straight to the supreme exemplars, the Venetians (Veronese, Giorgione), the Spaniards (Ribera, Velazquez, Zurbaran), many of whose works were then on view in the collection of Louis-Philippe, and the Dutch masters (Frans Hals, Rembrandt). "I simply wanted," he said in 1855 (and the same remark might have been made by Manet or Matisse), "to elicit from a thorough knowledge of tradition a well-founded, independent sense of my own individuality." He made friends with François Bonvin (1817-1887), a painter of workmanlike, unpretentious genre scenes and still lifes, an intimist and luminist in the spirit of Chardin, whose very real merits have passed unnoticed. To start with, before meeting Bonvin, he was still unsure of the technique and subjects that suited him best and toyed with literary, sentimental, even Biblical themes, which he treated in broad volumes, tightly enveloped, however, in rigid outlines. The neoclassical conceptions with which he was indoctrinated at Besançon were long in dying and for years conflicted with his natural penchant for Realism, the result being a sort of Mannerism, traces of which can also be found in the work of Ingres and even more distinctly in that of Caravaggio, with whom Courbet has obvious affinities. By way of Delacroix, and on similar lines, he linked up with Gros and Géricault, whose influence he frankly admitted. He periodically revisited Ornans, feeling a need to "refresh his inspiration" (as later Cézanne was to return to Aix).

Courbet rapidly acquired proficiency, and during his formative period (1840-1848), except for some early, purely tentative compositions and a few landscapes, confined himself to nudes and portraits. The portraits are those of members of his family, of his friends, and of himself. Despite his need of money he refused to accept orders for portraits unless he felt a real link with the sitter. "The women want portraits without any shadows and the men insist on wearing their Sunday best—and there's no way out of it!" he complained (in January 1846). The likenesses of his father (c. 1844, Private Collection, Paris), of Juliette, his youngest and favorite sister (1844, Petit-Palais, Paris) and of a fellow student, Paul Ansout (1844, Dieppe) are forthright, carefully planned, confidently executed works which still abide by the classical tradition. In the numerous self-portraits, on the other hand, Courbet strikes romantic attitudes, employs a highly personal technique, and almost all are masterpieces of their kind. What they suggest is less a streak of narcissism than the artist's desire to know himself and to record and analyse to the full the fluctuations of his moods. "I have made a great many portraits of myself in my life, following the changes of my outlook on the world; in a word, I've written my biography." Courbet was a cynosure of contemporary criticism, often of a hostile kind, but all his critics agree that he was an exceptionally handsome man. In his youth he resembled Giorgione, as is evidenced by the small, curiously appealing portrait (c. 1841) in the Pontarlier Museum. This similarity is brought out yet more clearly, in all its splendid plenitude, in the self-portrait of 1846, the *Man with a Pipe* (Montpellier), where it is singularly apt, since the inspiration of this canvas, technically and psychologically, so obviously derives from the great Venetians. The *Self-Portrait with a Black Dog* (1842, Petit-Palais, Paris), his first successful work, opened to him the doors of the 1844 Salon. The *Wounded Man* (1844, Louvre) and the *Man with a Leather Belt* (c. 1845, Louvre) are also self-portraits. In the *Happy Lovers* (1844, Lyons) the man (Courbet again) is embracing his robust ladylove with evident delight, and the double profile might well seem ludicrous were it not for the superb artistry that so magically transfigures it.

Like Giorgione and Prud'hon, Courbet was fond of portraying women in the relaxed attitudes of sleep, when sensual appeal is merged into unconscious grace. In *The Hammock* (1844, Reinhart Collection, Winterthur) a girl is dozing in a woodland setting, and one divines the supple firmness of the young body under a dress rendered in the Ingres manner. The pictorial climate here is a new departure and the figure combines a curiously wraithlike charm with a realistic density. In the *Bather sleeping by a Brook* (1845, Reinhart Collection, Winterthur; another version in the Detroit Institute of Arts) the woman's gleaming body mingling with the stream—real flesh in a real landscape—illuminates the dark mass of surrounding leafage. It has the same theme as *La Source*, but without its mythological allusions. In 1846 he made a portrait of a Dutch art dealer, H. J. van Wisselingh (Gavin Astor Collection, London), the young man's expressive face crowned by a black velvet cap rendered with unusual fervor. Struck by the painter's talent, Van Wisselingh not only bought two pictures from him and commissioned this portrait but invited him to Holland. When Courbet went (in August 1847) he fell under the spell of Rembrandt, whom he already admired, and whom he now came to understand at a deeper level. "An experience like that," he said, "teaches you more than three years' work." Rembrandt's influence, added to what he had learnt from the Venetian and Spanish masters, promptly made itself felt in his portraits, which now became broader in handling and charged with a new psychological insight. *The 'Cellist* (1847, Stockholm) is a self-portrait of an unusual type, life-size and intensely compelling, and preceding Corot's figures of musicians by a good many years. Exhibited at the 1848 Salon, this was the first of his works to attract attention. Prosper Haussard, art critic of *Le National*, saw in it "a solid achievement both in style and manner; brushwork and chiaroscuro merit the highest praise and it reminds us of both Caravaggio and Rembrandt." In full control of his means, Courbet had at long last achieved his ambition of being a "master painter." And a year later the 1848 revolution gave the fillip needed to carry through a grandiose, consciously directed program.

Gustave Courbet (1819-1877).
A Funeral at Ornans (detail), 1849. Louvre, Paris.

Shortly before that momentous year he had moved from his studio in the Rue de la Harpe to another in the Rue Hautefeuille, next door to the Brasserie Andler, frequented by artists and the political avant-garde, where he soon became the moving spirit. The group included Buchon, his faithful friend and one of the champions of a realistic, popular type of art, the *chansonnier* Pierre Dupont (1821-1870), Champfleury (1821-1889), essayist and novelist, who headed and publicized the movement after Buchon went into exile. Their political convictions derived less from the socialist literature of the day, to which however they were drawn instinctively, than from a sincere devotion to the working class and all it stood for. They championed the simple, the natural, the naïve, both in life and in art, as against middle-class respectability and the academic tradition. Champfleury not only wrote a number of works dealing with music, literature and folk art (to which he assigned a special value), but was also keenly interested in the popular imagery which has always flourished in France. The relation between Courbet's painting and popular imagery is the subject of a remarkable study by Meyer Schapiro, which also demonstrates the aesthetic and social significance of the nineteenth-century vogue for the popular arts associated with the peasantry and, ultimately, with traditional values. This concern for peasant art was, at bottom, a reaction

Gustave Courbet (1819-1877).
A Funeral at Ornans (detail), 1849. Louvre, Paris.

against the essentially modern trend towards a realism centering on city life, and a manifestation of that romantic cult of the primitive which later—Gauguin is a case in point—was to run counter to both Realism and its outcome, Impressionism.

The proletarian uprising of 1848 lasted only a few months and was ruthlessly suppressed. But it had sufficed to change the climate of opinion, to open men's eyes to the stern realities of life and to engender a new, virile type of humanism. Though he did not personally take part in the revolutionary movement, Courbet was horrified by the savage reprisals that ensued. In February he made a vignette representing the barricades for *Le Salut Public*, a paper edited by Baudelaire and Champfleury. It was at this time that Baudelaire came in closest touch with Courbet, who, when the poet was homeless, put him up in his studio and painted his portrait (Montpellier). Fascinated though he was by Delacroix and the glamour of exoticism, Baudelaire felt drawn in spite of himself to Courbet. For while temperamentally the two men, the hard-headed peasant and the sophisticated dandy, were poles apart, they sensed a community of feeling on a higher plane and in their dealings with each other antipathy was tinctured with respect. Baudelaire, who loathed what he called "positive triviality," was also

Gustave Courbet (1819-1877).
A Funeral at Ornans, 1849. (123¾ × 261″) Louvre, Paris.

a harbinger of that modernity of which Courbet was the first exponent. And now that the works of both can be seen in their true light, without regard to the theories that masked them, we realize how much the poet and painter had in common and the truly Baudelairian magic of some of Courbet's canvases. Even had he been aware of this, Baudelaire could not have admitted it. However, in 1862 when a new star was rising—Manet—whom he viewed with the same ambivalence, Baudelaire observed: "In justice to Courbet we can but recognize that he did much to revive a taste for simplicity and frankness, and also the disinterested love of painting for its own sake." And on both counts not only Impressionism but all modern art owes a debt to Courbet.

Until 1848 he had confined himself almost exclusively to portraits and single figures of small dimensions, treated in a neoclassical or romantic vein. The revolution led to radical and rapid changes both in his style and his subjects. From 1848 to 1855, in pursuance of his "realistic" program, he produced large compositions whose themes and technique startled and often shocked the public. During this crucial phase he was influenced by Géricault, a painter after his own heart, to whom Michelet drew attention in 1848 in one of his lectures in the Collège de France, and four of whose pictures were acquired by the Louvre in 1849 and three more in 1851. At the 1849 Salon Courbet exhibited a "trial" picture on these lines, *After Dinner at Ornans* (Lille) in which we see, grouped round the family table, the painter himself (still invested with a romantic aura), his father and two of his boyhood friends: Adolphe Marlet, in back view, lighting his pipe, and Alphonse Promayet playing the violin. This is in effect a genre scene rendered (unlike those of Bonvin and Decamps) life-size and thus promoted to the rank of the history picture, while the figures are not generalized types, as with Millet, but real individuals—hence its singular power. Francis Wey, a connoisseur and writer on art who came from the same part of France as Courbet and had recently made his acquaintance, has recorded the remarks made by Delacroix and Ingres on the opening day, voicing the staggering effect produced on them by this unlooked-for masterpiece which challenged the aesthetic of both alike and was to act as the link between the Le Nains' peasants and Cézanne's.

Courbet's picture was awarded the second gold medal and purchased officially by the government. In October he made a triumphal return to Ornans and converted a garret in his father's house into a studio. Before the year was out he had completed two still bolder canvases, *The Stone Breakers* (Dresden) and *A Funeral at Ornans* (Louvre). Proudhon, whose friendship for Courbet seems to have begun about this time, acclaimed *The Stone Breakers* as the first truly socialist painting. Characteristically enough, he described it as "a Gospel parable, morality in action," adding that the inhabitants of Ornans desired to place it on the altar of the local church. Courbet, however, as his letters show, had no didactic or political intention; he had merely been moved to compassion (and a sudden sense of the pictorial possibilities of the scene) by a chance encounter on a road near Ornans with two roadmenders in rags, a young man and an old, intent on their back-breaking task. "This compassion," he subsequently told Henri d'Ideville, his biographer, "stemmed from a realization of the injustice of their lot and that is why, though without any such intention and simply with a view to painting what I saw, I drew attention to what they call a social problem." Naturally enough a true-to-life picture on a monumental scale of poverty-stricken workers was regarded by the well-to-do middle class as a piece of revolutionary propaganda. The two men, one lifting his basket of stones and the other plying his hammer, "tell out against the side of a great mountain which fills the canvas and over which cloud shadows skim." The fully plastic, synthesized forms of the two men, brought well forward, harmonize dramatically with the chiaroscuro of the landscape. The singular perfection of this work transcends both the anecdotal style of the genre scene and the limitations of the social message. The subject was not a new one; as early as 1837 the Leleux brothers had embarked on a series of works on the theme, then in fashion, of *Les Métiers* and at the 1844 Salon Adolphe Leleux had exhibited his *Roadmenders*, which Théophile Gautier had hailed as a "masterpiece of the realistic school." But the small scale and sentimentality of these works relegate them to a lower plane, despite their merits. Views of factories and pictures of blacksmiths had been painted by Auguste Jeanron from 1836 on, by François Bonhommé in 1838 and 1840, with a sincere plebeian fervor, but they lacked the breadth of treatment needed to make such themes strike home. From Millet and Courbet to Van Gogh the life of the peasantry was given pride of place. But no artist of genius directed his gaze to the lot of the workers in the industrial towns (which Marx denounced so bitterly), where men are reduced to the state of robots.

Marquet described *A Funeral at Ornans* as the finest work in the Louvre. And indeed the execution is worthy of the greatest Spanish masters, emotions are expressed with the candor and veracity of the Primitives, and if the layout has the simplicity of a popular color-print, this is because, as Champfleury observed, "highly expert art carries the same accent as naïve art." Around the gaping hole into which the bearers are about to lower the coffin a group of villagers has gathered for a last farewell. The cliffs of Le Mont and the Founièche, which overlook the graveyard and close the far horizon with their gaunt anatomy under a lowering sky, reiterate and consolidate the alignment of the mourners. The rather cramped studio where Courbet worked and the lack of backing space obliged him, as he put it, "to paint blind"; hence the frieze-like composition. To this he has imparted a monumental grandeur and a dramatic concentration seconded by a somber, low-pitched color scheme appropriate to the subject, solemn harmonies broken here and there by passages of white. On the right, behind two veterans of 1793, is the famous group of weeping women—among whom are the artist's mother and sisters—in deep mourning, wearing large white bonnets. Between the priest and the gravedigger, two vergers with somewhat grotesque faces, wearing surplices and ribbed caps in black and scarlet—they might have stepped out of a Rouault canvas—strike the only note of vivid color in this austere composition. Even the most solidly organized group portraits, if we compare them with this grandiose work (described by Paul Mantz as "the Pillars of Hercules of Realism"), seem arbitrary and unconvincing. The entire population of a village has gathered on its native soil and a collective bereavement has welded its diverse units into an organic whole.

Gustave
The Painter's Studio,

9-1877).

235½") Louvre, Paris.

In the spring of 1850 Courbet made a third large picture on a rural theme, in which he also demonstrated his gifts as a painter of animals. The *Peasants of Flagey returning from the Fair* (Besançon) was described by Proudhon as a living image of rural France and a "happy compromise" between realism and imagination. Since the opening of the Salon had been delayed by the unrest prevailing in the capital, Courbet resorted to one-man shows in the provinces, at Besançon and Dijon. "In our ultra-civilized society," he wrote in a letter to Francis Wey, "I'm forced to play the lone wolf and, what's more, refuse to kowtow to the powers-that-be. That's why I have just elected for the footloose, independent life of the Bohemian." But his Bohemianism differed from that of the Romantics, whose fading glories he had shared before 1848; it was to make of him an apostle of "free art" when so many others were flinging themselves heart and soul into religious or social missions. On his return to Paris he was able, thanks to Wey's good offices, to make his *Portrait of Berlioz* (Louvre), whose genius was still unrecognized. To the Salon which opened belatedly on December 30, 1850, he sent two landscapes, four portraits and his three outsize canvases, which raised a storm of fury and accusations of willful ugliness and subversion. At Brussels, which he visited in the autumn, his pictures had a measure of success. He began another large composition, one of his rare incursions into city life: *The Fire* (Petit-Palais, Paris). Deliberately left unfinished after the *coup d'état* of December 2, 1851, this picture has an epic sweep and superb light effects in the spirit of Caravaggio and Rembrandt. He went back to Ornans in November and, with a view to "throwing dust in his critics' eyes," chose for his next Salon picture (1852) an "innocuous" subject, the *Village Maidens* (Metropolitan Museum, New York), showing his three sisters in their summer finery in a green landscape. But this charming scene of country life, despite the blandishment of its color harmonies, failed to produce the desired effect and was even taxed with vulgarity! However, before the opening day, it was bought by the Duc de Morny, one of the foremost personalities in the régime of Napoleon III. An ardent art lover and collector, the Duke henceforth did all he could for Courbet, behind the scenes. Undaunted by the hostility of critics and public, the artist contributed to the 1853 Salon a deliberately provocative set piece, *Women Bathing* (Montpellier). This represents two buxom young peasants on the banks of the Loue; one of them, seated, has just drawn on her petticoat, the other, standing, has just stepped out of the water and is hurrying to a thicket. Shown in back view and displaying ample buttocks, this figure so much disgusted the Emperor that he flicked her posterior with his riding whip as if they were the hind parts of a mare. Though Mérimée and Gautier scoffed at the picture, and even Mantz and Champfleury were at a loss how to defend it, Alfred Bruyas, the most discriminating collector of the period, was enthusiastic and promptly had his portrait painted simultaneously by Delacroix and Courbet. In 1854 Courbet produced a sequel to *The Stone Breakers*. This was the *Women sifting Wheat* (Nantes), an interior in which women's forms, bathed in a pale golden glow, are rendered in broad, smoothly flowing rhythms. From May to September he was at Montpellier staying with Bruyas, with whom he now struck up a lifelong friendship and who much enjoyed the company of his jovial; exuberant guest. There he made what is perhaps the best of his self-portraits (Montpellier), also his first seascapes and that famous tour de force, *The Meeting* (Montpellier), with its three magnificently posed figures, of which his alone casts a shadow. The vast scene is flooded with the light of southern France, which he now experienced for the first time and learnt to handle with as much assurance as the discreeter light of his Jura homeland. After visiting Max Buchon in Switzerland he worked from November to April on the canvas he was preparing for the 1855 World's Fair. This, *The Painter's Studio* (Louvre), might be described as his Declaration of Faith, and in it he renewed and enlarged the scope of a stock theme, traditional since the seventeenth century.

Delacroix at once hailed as a masterpiece this strange picture which so greatly puzzled his contemporaries, and called it "one of the most unusual works of modern times." The somewhat prolix title originally given it by the painter ran as follows: *Interior of my Studio, a Real Allegory covering a seven-year Phase of my Life as an Artist*. Courbet was well aware

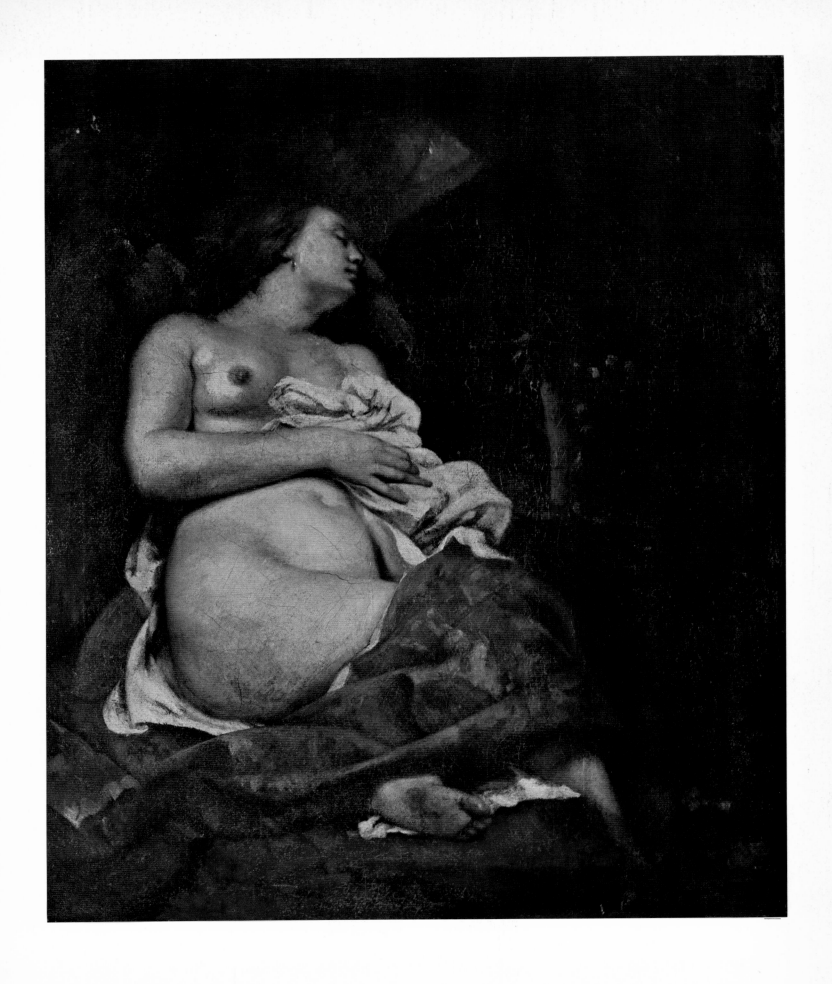

Gustave Courbet (1819-1877).

Sleeping Woman, 1857. (25½ × 20⅞″) Madame Georges Duthuit Collection, Paris.

that since the pivotal year of 1848 (of which the picture's title is a discreet reminder) he had been passing through the climactic period of his career, and in this autobiographical summing-up he portrayed the social climate of the mid-century by giving a universal significance to his personal experience. It was easy enough for Proudhon and Champfleury to demonstrate that "real allegory" was a contradiction in terms. Yet in effect there could have been no better formulation of what was the crucial problem of the age, the quest of sublimation without transcendence, and of its solution: a visionary contemplation of reality.

His letters to Bruyas and Champfleury record the gradual stages by which the artist built up *The Studio*, which covers a picture surface of over twenty square yards and contains thirty life-size figures, all brushed in directly, without any preliminary sketches. The fundamental letter is the one Courbet wrote in January 1855 to Champfleury, in which he gives a full description of the work in progress, naming the figures and pointing out the individual significance attaching to each. Many modifications were made before Courbet gave the final touch to the composition which, despite its air of incoherence, conforms to the classical structure of a triptych with clearly marked divisions, its focal point and nucleus being the painter's palette on which are mustered the five basic colors: brown, green, white, vermilion and carmine. Courbet shows himself seated, in a grandly rendered attitude, in the center of his studio, engaged in painting from memory (as always) one of his characteristic landscapes. "To paint a bit of country one has to know it. I know my countryside and I paint it. That woodland's near my home, that river is the Loue. Go and look at them and you'll see my picture." Supporting figures are the child gazing in delighted wonder at the picture taking form and the radiant figure of the naked woman behind the artist, bending over his work with loving comprehension. More than the Muse, the model or the helpmate, so comely without idealization, this woman (one of the finest of all nudes) is the image of Truth, the essence of Womanhood, the majesty of Life. Painter, woman and child compose the human triad, linking up with the generative urge of the natural world. Leitmotiv of so much modern painting, the landscape, placed here on the easel as upon an altar, is also a symbol of the religion of today, the universal, democratic cult of Nature. Little wonder that Delacroix could remark that "it looks like a *real sky* there in the middle of the picture," for such indeed was its function, that of a luminous reality amidst the ghostly shadows of the studio. The easel holding this painting within the painting separates, physically and morally, the two figure groups distributed on either side of it like the Blessed and the Damned in a Last Judgment. On the right stand or sit "the people who live on life"; that is to say, as Courbet himself explained, "the people who serve me, who champion my ideas and share in my action." They include some of his closest friends, Promayet, Bruyas, Proudhon, Cuénot and Buchon, all standing; between Baudelaire and Champfleury, both seated, are the couple representing free love untrammeled by conventions (in the embrasure of the window) and the couple of fashionable art lovers (in the foreground). The two women in profile lean back slightly in a fine symmetrical movement, one of them (destined to inspire Monet) wearing a light blue dress with dark blue stripes, the other (to be remembered by Renoir) magnificently draped in a colorful Indian shawl. Massed on the left is a confused and disparate crowd of "people who live on death"—who live, that is to say, outside the world of art, slaves to passions and material needs. Here can be distinguished, roughly grouped in threes, the Jew, the priest and the veteran of 1793, the poacher, the hunter and the mower, the merchant, the strong man and the clown, the worker, the prostitute and the undertaker's mute; then, apart and to the fore, the Irishwoman in rags suckling her babe and the booted hunter with his dogs. At the feet of this hunter (who was added as an afterthought to balance the figure of Champfleury), a still life of "romantic accessories," feathered hat, dagger and guitar, balances the beautiful still life formed by the crumpled pink robe of the nude model. Behind the seated Irishwoman, a skull lying on the *Journal des Débats* and a kind of crucified mannequin are meant to ridicule bourgeois thought and academic routine. An Angora cat and a boy drawing on his knees complete the picture. Though the grouping of the figures follows no particular

Gustave Courbet (1819-1877).

The Trellis, or Girl arranging Flowers, 1863. (43¼ × 53¼″) The Toledo Museum of Art, Gift of Edward Drummond Libbey.

system, each element has its pictorial necessity and its symbolic value. The back wall, with draperies and a medallion hanging on it, together with what look like landscape panels, is made deliberately dim, painted in brown, russet and green of infinite delicacy, so as not to impair the mild penumbra of the room or detract from the clarity of the central group, illuminated by a shaft of light from the window. Apart from the poet absorbed in his book, the two children (one drawing, the other gazing at the picture) and the two lovers whispering to each other, all the figures are inert and shadowy. With his head thrown back and his outstretched arm disengaging his pure "Assyrian" profile (Botta's excavations at Khorsabad had made Assyria fashionable), the painter alone is active, galvanized into life. Firm, sturdy, plastic and timeless, he stands out hieratically like "a Persepolis relief" (Sir Kenneth Clark) amidst the ephemeral crowd of figures around him, conjured up from memory. Thus this "fairly mysterious" picture (as its author admitted it to be), which brings together in a single grandiose composition a whole series of portraits (including a self-portrait), a landscape, a nude, still lifes and animals, all handled with equal power; which is at once an autobiographical document, a historical cross-section of Second Empire society, and a complete cycle of human

life from birth to death, including the metamorphoses of womanhood; which sets out the relations between the sexes, age groups and classes; which explores the enigma of the individual condition and the collective destiny—this picture is, first and foremost, a glorification of the creative act as the true foundation of reality. Every detail is a stunning piece of painting in its own right, and the evenly diffused light bathing the entire room and ensuring pictorial unity has the magic effulgence of Velazquez.

The exhibition jury of the 1855 World's Fair rejected *A Funeral at Ornans* and *The Painter's Studio*, his two masterworks. Courbet's answer to this was to exhibit his pictures in a private booth, built at his own expense, thus by-passing the official bureaucracy and affirming the artist's independence. There he presented himself to the public under the banner of Realism and summed up his program as follows: "To convey the ideas, way of life and aspect of my time, as I see them, and to be not only a painter but a man." This manifestation brought to a close the heroic period of his struggle for recognition. Thereafter social implications gradually disappeared from his work and it developed without a break, undergoing a slow, organic evolution. He gave up genre scenes in favor of figures and nudes, landscapes and still lifes. His visualization of space changed as his themes changed and became increasingly interiorized. His pictures were no longer built up in terms of lateral planes tightly interlocking, but in terms of fluid volumes and open pulsations cleaving to the continuous movement of nature and its atmospheric respiration. Hence Courbet's supple, homogeneous technique, proceeding from dark to light by tonal gradations, discarding glazes for thick, transparent touches of paint, laid on with the finger, the palette knife or the brush.

At the 1857 Salon he exhibited *Girls on the Banks of the Seine* (Petit-Palais, Paris), a landmark on the road to Impressionism, an open-air composition almost Bruegelian in its directness and power, inimitably blending nature and womanhood; and his first great hunting picture, *Hind forced down in the Snow* (Collection of the Vicomtesse de Douville-Maillefeu, Paris), a theme of his own invention enabling him to exploit the pictorial possibilities of snow (neglected by Corot and the Barbizon masters). From the same year dates the *Blonde endormie* or *Sleeping Woman* (Duthuit Collection, Paris), once owned by Matisse, one of his most perfect nudes, matchless in its detached sensuality and rhythmic concentration. From September 1858 to February 1859 Courbet was at Frankfort indulging in the hunting exploits which he bragged about to his new friend and champion, Castagnary. The results of this experience were shown at the 1861 Salon in three unusual paintings, including the *Stag at Bay* (Marseilles), the monumental form of the bewildered animal seen against the light, modeled by the last rays of the setting sun. From May 1862 to March 1863 he was in Saintonge, where he painted a luminous series of landscapes and flower pieces. The *Girl arranging Flowers* or *The Trellis* (1863, Toledo Museum of Art), combining a figure and a still life, is the distillation of a happy moment, full of freshness and poetry. Her face outlined against the sky, her figure placed entirely to one side as in similar pictures by Degas, a girl in a summer dress reaches for the full-blown flowers with loving fingers. "In the fingers," said Courbet, "lies refinement."

More powerful than the corresponding pictures of Rousseau, and a greater work than any of the Barbizon school, the *Great Oak of Ornans* (1864, Pennsylvania Academy of the Fine Arts, Philadelphia) consecrates the alliance between the painter and his native soil, now to inspire some of his finest works. In the *Stream in the Forest* (1865, Louvre) his mastery reaches its highest pitch of perfection. A limited range of colors, running from blue-green to grey-brown, suffices to convey the secret of stone, the spongy softness of moss, the luxuriant foliage and the unruffled stillness of the water, thanks to rich effects of transparency and depth, to the powdery texture of the paints and the focus of light. In 1866 Courbet made a replica of this picture on a smaller scale (Montpellier) and sent it to Bruyas with the following words: "A superb landscape of profound solitude, which I painted deep in the vales of my own country. It is perhaps the finest one I've made. The Loue can be seen deeply embanked

between vast blocks of moss-covered stone, with thick sunny branches in the background." The many female nudes painted between 1865 and 1870 partake of the same spirit of religious contemplation, and their glowing sensuality seems to issue naturally from the convergence of the cosmic elements amid which they live and have their being (Louvre and Petit-Palais, Paris; Metropolitan Museum, New York). During the same period his hunting pictures and snowscapes were interspersed with incomparable seascapes, stormy (Louvre) or calm (Caen), which he painted in summer on the Channel beaches, where young Monet joined him. A final series of seascapes at Etretat dates from 1869 (Cleveland and Birmingham). Meanwhile he went on painting portraits whose accuracy and penetration are greater than is usually realized, for they reveal a deep sense of the gravity, mystery or grace of human beings. Outstanding are those, all in different veins, of *Jules Vallès* (c. 1861, Musée Carnavalet, Paris), *Madame Boreau* (1863, Private Collection, Paris), *Madame Proudhon* (1865, Private Collection, Paris) and the *Woman with a Mirror* (1866, Stockholm). At Munich in 1869 he enjoyed his last triumph and in the Alte Pinakothek, with the naïve veneration of a beginner, happily unconscious of the trials in store for him, he copied Rembrandt, Frans Hals and Velazquez, the supreme masters with whom he is not unworthy of comparison. Held responsible for the destruction of the column in the Place Vendôme during the Commune uprising in 1871, he was imprisoned in Sainte-Pélagie. In his cell he painted some magnificent still lifes of fruit, midway between those of Chardin and Cézanne. Persecuted by the government and condemned to pay for the reconstruction of the Vendôme column, he went into voluntary exile in Switzerland in 1873 and died there on December 31, 1877.

Gustave Courbet (1819-1877).
The Stream in the Forest, 1865. (37 × 53⅛″) Louvre, Paris.

Honoré Daumier (1808-1879).
Girls Bathing. Undated. (13 × 9⅜″) Pierre Lévy Collection, Troyes.

Humanity of Daumier

W ITH the temperament of a Romantic and the approach of a Realist, Daumier belongs to the Barbizon generation, except that his domain was the human figure and not landscape. He did not really devote himself to painting until after 1848, but did so then with a freedom of style more modern than that of any other artist of his time; hence his chronological position in this chapter. As against the realism of Courbet, racy of the soil and savoring of the outdoor life, he represents the realism of the city streets and the moral sphere. "The people of the present day: straight out of Michelangelo and Goya," noted Delacroix in his *Journal* (April 7, 1824). It was left to Daumier to give life and body to this astonishing formula, which indeed sums up the grandeur and searching truthfulness of his vision.

Born at Marseilles, near the docks of the old port, on February 26, 1808, Honoré Daumier was the son of a glazier who wrote poetry on the side, and who moved with his family to Paris in 1816, where he hoped to make a name in literature. He brought out a volume of verse and in 1819 an amateur troupe put on one of his plays, a tragedy. The boy probably attended the performance, and his lifelong love of the theater may well date from this time. In the following year, though he was only twelve years old, he had to begin earning his own living, first as the office boy of a *huissier*, then as a bookseller's clerk at the Palais-Royal, at that time the hub of Parisian life. Here he sharpened his powers of observation and developed an aptitude for drawing. In 1822 he was accepted as a pupil by the painter Alexandre Lenoir, founder of the Musée des Monuments Français, who taught him the rudiments of art and communicated to him his own love of sculpture and his veneration of Rubens and Titian; it may have been Lenoir who gave Daumier the casts of Trajan's Column which were still in his studio when he died. He frequented the Académie Suisse, where he drew from the model and where one of his fellow students was Auguste Raffet (1804-1860), rival of Charlet's and illustrator of the Napoleonic legend. He took up lithography, a new process invented in Germany in 1798 and widely practised in France in the years following the Restoration as a result of the vogue for illustrated journals. Its expressive possibilities at once attracted the younger artists and Goya, Géricault and Delacroix all experimented with it. Daumier completely mastered the technique of lithography, which was particularly well suited to his gifts and reached new heights in his hands from 1825 to 1830, when he was employed by the printer Belliard. Half the prints published at that time were caricatures, hitherto an English specialty but now tending to become a French one. Baudelaire has demonstrated once for all the artistic value of this genre centered on the human face and traced its historical

justification. Caricature implies both a fidelity to visual reality and a radical transposition of it, and the caricaturist's implacable accuracy of observation often goes hand in hand with a deep sense of justice and even, in Daumier's case, with genuine benevolence and kindliness. Hence Forain's exclamation: "Oh, Daumier, that was something else again, *he* was generous."

His first signed prints did not appear until after the 1830 revolution, and as the new régime of Louis-Philippe proved to be increasingly reactionary, he put his talents in the service of the liberal movement. He contributed to *La Silhouette* (1829-1839), the first illustrated satirical weekly to appear in France, edited by Ricourt. Daumier's work stood out unmistakably from that of the Romantic illustrators, like Achille Devéria (1800-1857) and Tony Johannot (1803-1852). Ricourt was impressed and told him, "You know how to hit off a gesture all right!"—by which he meant the power of summing up the expression of character in a synthetic attitude embracing the whole body (and not just the face). When Philipon, himself a painter (he had studied under Gros) and the leading journalist of the Opposition, launched *La Caricature* in 1830, he invited Daumier to join the staff, which included Balzac as literary editor. When the budding novelist saw Daumier's satirical portraits, in the form of both sculptures and lithographs, he exclaimed (1832), "Why, this fellow's got Michelangelo in the blood!"—a prophetic judgment, confirmed by Daubigny's outcry upon entering the Sistine Chapel for the first time: "But this is pure Daumier!" And Daumier does in fact resemble Michelangelo in his moral passion and his magisterial creation of a whole world of living and suffering figures. His kinship with Balzac is also self-evident and the four thousand lithographs catalogued by Delteil give us a picture of the age no less vivid and comprehensive than that contained in the *Comédie humaine*. For a caricature of Louis-Philippe as "Gargantua" he was sentenced to six months' imprisonment at Sainte-Pélagie (from August 31, 1832, to February 14, 1833), where he met the militant revolutionaries of the period, Blanqui, Barbès, Raspail and others.

On his release he settled in the Rue Saint-Denis in an artists' phalanstery where many of his friends lived, including the painters Diaz, Huet and Jeanron and the sculptor A. Préault (1809-1879). Aspiring to a career as a painter and sculptor, Daumier tried again and again to make his mark, but the systematic hostility of the official jurys to what Courbet called "living art" and the necessity of earning his daily bread compelled him to fall back on lithography, which completely absorbed his time and energies. In 1834 he published four vengeful lithographs which created a great stir: *Le ventre législatif*, *Rue Transnonain*, *Enfoncé Lafayette*, and *Ne vous y frottez pas*. The first two are perhaps his masterpieces in the field of political satire, one for its scathing pungency and plastic condensation, the other for its tragic poignancy and arresting foreshortenings and chiaroscuro. In 1835 the stringent laws for the muzzling of the press led to the suppression of *La Caricature*, many issues of which had been seized by the police. Philipon also controlled another paper, *Le Charivari*, founded in 1832, whose accent now shifted from political caricature to social satire. Here was the germ of the realist movement and, for Daumier, a field of action wider and more fruitful than any hitherto open to him. At exactly the same time as Balzac, and years before Flaubert (who took inspiration from him), he embarked on a searching study and criticism—a complete anatomy—of the French bourgeoisie and in 1836 created the famous type figure, Robert Macaire, who surpassed in intensity the Joseph Prudhomme of Henri Monnier (1805-1877). As a chronicler of the age, in competition with such clever artists as Grandville (1803-1847) and Gavarni (1804-1866), Daumier alone attained the universal scope and classic simplicity of Molière, his favorite author. About 1845 he moved into a studio on the Quai d'Anjou, on the Ile Saint-Louis, located between two famous town houses, the Hôtel Lambert where Chopin played the piano for Princess Czartoryska, and the Hôtel Lauzun where Baudelaire lived until 1847 (he now became a close friend of Daumier's) and where he frequented the art circle of Boissard de Boisdenier. Here he executed the masterly series of *Gens de Justice* (1845-1848) and developed a less plastic, more open and luminous vision.

Honoré Daumier (1808-1879).
The Painter at his Easel. Undated. (13⅛ × 10¼″) The Phillips Collection, Washington, D.C.

The 1848 revolution brought his friends temporarily to power and gave him at last an opportunity of concentrating his energies on painting. Daumier was largely self-taught; he trained himself in the Louvre by studying and copying Rubens, Rembrandt and the Spanish masterpieces in the collection of Louis-Philippe. Courbet and Bonvin now persuaded him to take part in the competition for the allegorical figure of the Republic. He submitted a sketch (Louvre), praised and championed by Champfleury, but never finished the actual painting. The problem of finish, or rather lack of finish, which had already been raised by Michelangelo and Leonardo and again came to the fore in the nineteenth century, was a crucial one for Daumier, owing to the extreme freedom of his style and his impetuous dynamism. On February 5, 1849, Baudelaire called on Delacroix, who noted down in his *Journal*: "He spoke to me of the difficulties Daumier has in finishing his work." He was then struggling with a vast composition, of which there exist three sketches and several studies of details, intended to commemorate the 1848 revolution, a kind of heroic counterpart of Delacroix's *Liberty leading the People*. At the 1849 Salon, which marked his first public appearance as a painter, he exhibited a little known subject from La Fontaine, *The Miller, his Son and the Ass* (Glasgow). The obvious influence of Rubens and the same type of exuberant volumes wrapped in shadows and lights reappeared in *Two Nymphs pursued by Satyrs* (Montreal), which he sent in to the Salon of 1850-1851. In 1849 he received a commission from the State, but for a religious picture—which showed the veering policy of the republican government. It was no doubt in connection with this commission that he was led to paint such works as the *Mary Magdalen* (Private Collection), *Jesus and his Disciples* (Rijksmuseum, Amsterdam), *The Good Samaritan* (Glasgow) and the moving sketch in grisaille *We Want Barabbas!* (Folkwang Museum, Essen). Finally in 1863, instead of a religious painting, the State purchased a drawing touched up with gouache, Rubensian in inspiration, the *Drunkenness of Silenus* (Calais).

Honoré Daumier (1808-1879).

The Refugees. (15 ¼ × 27″) The Minneapolis Institute of Arts. Ethel Morrison Van Derlip Fund, 1954.

Honoré Daumier (1808-1879).

Don Quixote and Sancho Panza. (39⅜ × 31⅞″) Courtauld Institute of Art, London.

It was probably the events of 1848 (as Jean Adhémar has pointed out), the expulsions and deportations *en masse* following the stern repressive measures of General Cavaignac, that led Daumier to treat the grandiose theme of *Emigrants* (also known as *Refugees* or *Prisoners*) in a poignant bas-relief standing midway between Géricault and Rodin, and in a series of paintings spanning a period of several years. Men, women, children and horses, bending under the withering blasts of fate, wend their way in a single concerted movement across the entire composition, moving off to the left (Reinhart Collection, Winterthur) or the right, huddled together (Minneapolis) or scattered and straggling (Montreal). The tragic power of these scenes, rising above contingencies of time and place, reflects a universal drama, a universal fatality.

Daumier reverted to lithography after the *coup d'état* of Napoleon III, whom he held up to ridicule in a virulent piece of sculpture, *Ratapoil* (1850). Michelet admired his courageous art and wrote to him, "This is pure Tacitus, terrible and sublime." He went on painting intermittently, producing both interiors of shops and theaters with their artificial lighting effects, and open-air scenes of daily life on the Seine banks, like the *Girls Bathing* (Lévy Collection, Troyes), a wooden panel with colors reminiscent of Millet, whose charm is unique in his work. The two contemporary painters to whom Daumier owed most were Decamps and Millet. After 1855 he moved increasingly closer to Corot and the Barbizon masters, Millet, Rousseau and Daubigny. In October 1857 Baudelaire published a masterly study of his graphic work but made no mention of his paintings, which at that time were still few in number. After a serious illness in 1858 he grew weary of journalistic work and was dismissed from the staff of *Le Charivari* in March 1860—only to be re-engaged in December 1863. It was presumably during this period of comparative leisure that he produced many of the paintings which, both in technique and subject matter, form a group quite distinct from the earlier paintings of 1849-1851. From a sculpturesque vision combining Michelangelo and Rubens, Daumier had now arrived at a pictorial vision in which volumes are absorbed by chiaroscuro, with the Baroque élan of Tintoretto and the suggestive depths of Rembrandt. Vibrant blues, diluted violets and purplish highlights quicken a muted color scheme, toned down by his contacts with the Barbizon painters, while moving lights set up strong contrasts or subside into tender modulations. Discarding subjects drawn from history, mythology, religion and literature, Daumier turned, even before Manet, to contemporary themes and pictured the daily life of the lower-class Parisian, at work and at play. Formidably broad and sweeping in style, nearly all his paintings, whether on canvas or wood, are nevertheless very small in size, except for two studies on an exceptional theme, *The Man on the Rope* (Boston and Ottawa) and the monumental version (cf. page 124) of a theme, steeped in warm humanity, which often attracted him, *The Washerwoman* or *The Burden* (Private Collection, Paris). *The Third-Class Carriage* (Baltimore, New York, Ottawa) is an extraordinary social and psychological synthesis, an indictment of modern life in which the crowd swallows up the individual. On a theme then much in vogue, *The Print Fancier*, he made some admirable variations (Paris, Glasgow, Rotterdam, Mannheim). *The Painter at his Easel* (Phillips Collection, Washington) is a marvel of concentration, luminous energy and certitude. "As an artist, what distinguishes Daumier," wrote Baudelaire, "is certitude." Besides the *Tumblers* in watercolor (Louvre and Petit-Palais, Paris, and Hartford), the theme with which he most completely identified himself, and in which he carried expression to a higher pitch than any painter of the century, is Don Quixote, which first appeared about 1850 and was magisterially developed in his last years. As against the romantic myth of Hamlet illustrated by Delacroix, Daumier conjured up and imposed the two figures of Don Quixote and Sancho Panza (Courtauld Institute, London) as the very image of the human condition forever alternating between dream and reality, hope and despair, the sublime and the grotesque. In 1865 he withdrew to the village of Valmondois, near Auvers-sur-Oise, where he died, very poor and nearly blind, on February 11, 1879, in a cottage discreetly placed at his disposal by his friend Corot, the only contemporary artist of as pure and free a spirit as himself.

Monticelli and Provincial Painting
Fantin-Latour

THE official painting of the Second Empire, academic through and through, is of interest today only as an episode in the history of taste. A pupil of Gros and Paul Delaroche, Thomas Couture (1815-1879) was the leading exponent of eclecticism, which has always been the bane of art and a sure recipe for success. At the 1847 Salon, from which the best artists of the day were excluded, he scored the triumph of the century with his *Romans of the Decadence* (Louvre), a vast orgy picture artificially combining Veronese and Tiepolo; it is the very archetype of the bogus history painting based on highly skilled imitation and not on direct experience. In his portraits, nudes and studies of heads, however, Couture proved himself to be a bold and unaffected executant. As a teacher he exerted a widespread influence, notably on Manet and the German painter Feuerbach. Emulator of the Dutch little masters, of Gerard Dou in particular, Ernest Meissonier (1815-1891) was in his lifetime the most famous of all French painters and his pictures fetched the highest prices. He delineated the campaigns of Napoleon with microscopic precision, and in his genre pictures, which inaugurate or vulgarize many themes taken over by Daumier (but in a style the reverse of Daumier's), we find the same insistence on minute detail. However, *The Barricade* (Louvre), an evocation of June 1848, deserves special mention both for its subject and its fine pictorial qualities. The eighteenth-century tradition of French genre painting was continued during the First Empire by Louis-Léopold Boilly (1761-1845), under the July Monarchy by Eugène Lami (1800-1890) and under the Second Empire by Constantin Guys (1802-1892). Lami and Guys were familiar with English life and specialized in watercolor painting. A cosmopolitan dandy with a keen eye for outward appearances, but devoid of moral passion and psychological insight, Guys is in every respect the opposite of Daumier. But his thematic repertory, in which society women and courtesans predominate (Musée Carnavalet, Paris; Courtauld Institute, London), is immense and he transcribes what he sees with wit and brio. He was perhaps overpraised by Baudelaire, but as a chronicler of "modern life" he sowed the seeds that bore such brilliant fruit in Manet and Lautrec.

Far from the glitter of Parisian life, several artists or groups of artists of marked originality developed independently in the provinces, in Burgundy, in Alsace, and above all at Marseilles and Lyons. One of the most promising of them all, the Dijon painter Félix Trutat (1824-1848) died at the age of twenty-four. His vigorous and arresting portraits and his splendid *Recumbent Nude* (Dijon) reveal a nature as sensitive as that of his fellow Burgundian, Prud'hon, and a breadth of vision harking back to Géricault. From the time of Martin Drolling

Adolphe Monticelli (1824-1886).
Portrait of Madame René, 1871. (25⅜ × 21¼″) Musée des Beaux-Arts, Lyons.

(1753-1813) Alsace is notable for its little masters in the intimist vein, and from Gustave Brion (1824-1877) to Gustave Doré (1832-1883), the last and most famous of them all, produced a long line of Romantic illustrators.

Lyons was not only a center of mystical painters akin to the Pre-Raphaelites and Ingresque decorators chiefly remarkable for their cold, austere technique. Three landscapists, Ravier, Carrand and Vernay, alike in their melancholy ardor and their love of rich texture and rare values, go to form a curious regional school. All three made the trip to Italy and knew Corot and the Barbizon painters, but lived and worked in solitude, cultivating an unobtrusive lyricism of their own. In 1836 the eldest, F. A. Ravier (1814-1895), whose lively sense of color brings him closest to the Romantics, met Corot in Auvergne and found valuable support in his friendship. In 1840 he went to Italy, where his Roman period was marked by dense, solidly constructed pictures (*Garden of a Roman Villa*, Louvre). After several painting trips in France, he settled near Lyons, first at Crémieu, then at Morestel, where Daubigny, Corot and Courbet paid him visits. His oils, with their impasto of pure colors over a dark underpainting, and his watercolors, as visionary as those of Turner, record the fiery glow of sunset on quiet pools of water. Louis Carrand (1821-1899), who chose the humblest motifs, orchards, autumn boughs, muddy lanes and lonely river banks, was the elegiac poet of the late seasons of the year and early morning mists, and his silvery greys have a dainty charm

recalling Corot and Boudin. Vernay (1821-1896) was at his best in his quiet, well-integrated landscapes and his sensuous, accurately rendered still lifes of flowers and fruit. Lyons also had its painters of rustic interiors and household still lifes, Antoine Bail (1830-1918) and above all Antoine Vollon (1833-1900) who, following Bonvin, combined a Spanish rigor of execution with a northern presentation of the subject.

Daumier worked all his life in Paris, but in background and temperament he belongs to that current of Provençal Baroque which goes back to Puget and Fragonard and, by way of Monticelli, reaches its climax in Cézanne. Marseilles is, with Lyons, the most active and best characterized of the regional art centers. Its founder was the Aix painter Emile Loubon (1809-1863), whom Granet took with him to Italy in 1829. After spending two years there, Loubon went to Paris where he was on friendly terms with Delacroix, Corot, Decamps and the Barbizon painters. In 1849 he settled at Marseilles and struck out on a path of his own as the interpreter of his native soil, in all its stern grandeur and strongly marked structure. He trained or encouraged a whole group of local landscape painters, Auguste Aiguier (1814-1865), M. Engalière (1824-1857), Prosper Gresy (1804-1874), and an artist of outstanding gifts, Paul Guigou (1834-1871), who did for Provence what Lépine did for Normandy and the Seine valley. "He made," wrote Mistral, "a faithful and eternal portrait of his little homeland," of the scrub country of inner Provence, between the Rhone and Durance, and the waste lands around Marseilles, as pictured in the *Route de la Gineste* (Louvre) and the *Collines d'Allauch* (Marseilles). With his dense texture and taut design Guigou admirably conveyed the rugged landscape, majestic architecture and crystalline light of his native province. From 1860 to his premature death in 1871 he lived in Paris, painting the banks of the Seine and the Marne, and (before Sisley) even those of the Loing, but made regular trips back to Provence. He was a close friend of Adolphe Monticelli (1824-1886), the strangest phenomenon of the school of Marseilles and the last great Romantic painter of the nineteenth century. A natural child of Italian origin, reared on the high plateaux of the Durance, at Ganagobie, Monticelli returned there in 1849 after an initial stay of three years in Paris. From 1851 to 1862 he drifted to and fro between Paris and Provence, leading a Bohemian existence, painting and selling his pictures wherever he happened to be, as the need arose. Fascinated by Delacroix, he came under the direct influence of Diaz, whom he met in 1856, and among the Old Masters especially delighted in Veronese, Rembrandt and Watteau. From 1862 to 1870 he lived uninterruptedly in Paris or its suburbs. Uprooted again by the war, he returned to Marseilles in May 1871, where he remained for the rest of his life, and where the young Cézanne paid him several visits. His last period was his most original and productive. He distilled the experiences of a lifetime, gave vent in solitude to his lyrical powers of expression, and worked out his prodigious alchemy of colors. He painted at times from imagination, love scenes and serenades, but usually from nature, landscapes, still lifes, portraits, fairs and side-shows. His copious output, the upsurge of an ebullient temperament, is necessarily uneven, but it contains some gems of the painter's art, for example the *Parade des Saltimbanques* (1877, Musée Grobet-Labadié, Marseilles), the *White Pitcher* (1878-1880, Louvre) and the *Portrait of Madame René* (1871, Lyons), an intense and sensitive face, built up in terms of flickering lights. Both Cézanne and Van Gogh owed Monticelli a real debt. "Sometimes," declared Van Gogh, "I really believe I'm continuing what he began, only mine is not the amorous color that his is."

Nearly all these provincial painters have the raciness and technical audacities of the self-taught artist. An outstanding teacher, H. Lecoq de Boisbaudran (1802-1897) reacted vigorously against academic routine. In addition to the sculptor Rodin, he numbered some excellent painters among his pupils, Guillaume Régamey (1837-1875), Alphonse Legros (1837-1911) and Henri Fantin-Latour (1836-1904). A portraitist and religious painter (*The Ex-voto*, 1861, Dijon), Legros found inspiration in Holbein and Courbet. After making his name, he settled in England and devoted himself to teaching. He was a fervent admirer of the Spanish masters (like most of the painters of his generation) and influenced Théodule Ribot

(1823-1891) and Henri Regnault (1843-1871). After receiving a thorough grounding from Lecoq, Fantin-Latour completed his schooling by making some admirable copies in the Louvre. In 1859 he was invited to London by Whistler. In 1863 he exhibited at the Salon des Refusés and met Manet and his circle. Though a friend of the Impressionists, he never shared their way of seeing. Steeped in music and literature, he practised, gracefully and discreetly, a kind of romantic intimism and intellectual realism. Oscillating between Courbet and Whistler, he enveloped his volumes in wispy shadows and delicate colors without attempting a pictorial fusion; hence the rather photographic aspect of his paintings, despite the emotion sustaining them. His work includes paintings and lithographs of musical inspiration which tend towards the symbolism of Odilon Redon and Gustave Moreau; still lifes of flowers and fruit, "a kind of feminine edition of those of Courbet" (Charles Sterling), whose atmosphere of nostalgic reverie has always appealed to English and American collectors; and many portraits, of himself, his family and his friends (*Portrait of Manet*, 1867, Chicago), and some fine group portraits, fervent tokens of his friendships and sympathies. In the Louvre are four of these collective portraits, in which he paid admiring tribute to a group of painters (*Homage to Delacroix*, 1864, and *The Batignolles Studio*, 1870), a group of poets (*A Corner of a Table*, 1872) and a group of musicians (*Around the Piano*, 1885). We reproduce the fine sketch for *The Batignolles Studio*, showing Zola, Astruc, Bazille, Renoir and Monet, the Impressionists and their defenders, silent and grave as conspirators, grouped around Manet seated at his easel.

Henri Fantin-Latour (1836-1904).
The Batignolles Studio, 1870. Sketch. (11⅜ × 15⅝″) Louvre, Paris.

The Impressionist Revolution

Claude Monet (1840-1926).
Boulevard des Capucines, Paris, 1873. (31½ × 23½″) Marshall Field Collection, New York.

THE origins of Impressionism are well known. A group of young painters, including Monet, Renoir, Pissarrro, Sisley, Cézanne, Degas, Guillaumin and Berthe Morisot, weary of being systematically excluded from the official Salon, organized an independent exhibition of their work, from April 15 to May 15, 1874, in the studios that had just been vacated by the photographer Nadar, on the Boulevard des Capucines, in the heart of Paris. It unleashed an unprecedented storm of abuse and ridicule. In the April 25 number of *Le Charivari*, a satirical weekly, the journalist Leroy mockingly coined the term "impressionist" to describe the group, after a canvas by Monet entitled *Impression, Sunrise* (1872, Musée Marmottan, Paris). The word at once gained currency and, though originally derisive, is now the honored name of the greatest art revolution of the nineteenth century.

Impressionism was born of the chance encounter of a group of young painters of genius, whose combined efforts created an incomparably fruitful and many-sided movement. After a preparatory phase (1860-1870) and the period of full maturity (1870-1880), it began to break up after 1880; this internal crisis and its significance for the future will be studied in the conclusion to this volume. More than any previous movement, Impressionism involved revolutionary changes in both technique and vision, which reacted on science, literature, music, and the whole sensibility of the age.

Impressionism was the outcome of the effort to obtain ever greater naturalism in painting, devoid of social or sentimental implications, and to render purely optical sensations. Unity of texture and light, so perfectly achieved on different planes by Corot and Courbet, gave place to unity of light and color, as under the impact of light objects disintegrated into patches of color swimming in the radiance of the surrounding atmosphere. Light came to be adopted as a general stylistic principle because it is the one element of the real world to which the flux of visual appearances can be reduced. Impressionism is thus the ultimate form of illusionism and bore within itself the seeds of its own destruction. For in order to render the vibration of light, it depended on bright colors and the divided brushstroke, means which in fact are anti-naturalistic and which, subsequently developed into autonomous vehicles of expression, opened the way to modern painting. "Treating the subject for its tones and not for the subject itself, this is what distinguishes the Impressionists from other painters," wrote in 1877 the most clairvoyant of their friends, Georges Rivière, thereby stressing their sensitive response to color.

But even Rivière, at that very time, could describe Renoir's *Moulin de la Galette* as a "history painting" in the contemporary sense. The conquest of pure painting and purely pictorial form necessarily involved a whole new way of seeing and an extraordinary extension of the painter's range of subject matter. The Impressionists were delighted and faithful observers of the life of their time. They were the first, after Manet, to discover the poetry of Paris and modern life, the first to give expression in painting to the "modernity" called for by Baudelaire, which in their hands was not so much the attribute as the substance of painting and from now on merged with its autonomy.

Edouard Manet (1832-1883).
Portrait of Emile Zola, 1868. (57½ × 43¾″) Louvre, Paris.

Manet and the Modern Way
of Seeing

DIDEROT, in his *Pensées détachées sur la peinture*, advised artists to refrain from painting the drab street clothes of their contemporaries. Manet was still a schoolboy when he first read this stricture, but he jotted down the following comment in the margin of the book: "An artist has got to move with the times and paint what he sees." These words exactly describe the program he set himself. For it is with Manet, rather than Courbet, that modern painting really begins, delivered from the anecdote and bogus conventions, attuned to the new rhythms of life and embodying its own justification and its own autonomy. "He was the first," as Matisse put it, "to react directly to what he saw and thereby to simplify the painter's craft... expressing only what impinged directly on his senses." With Manet there was no intermediate step from eye to hand, from sensation to transcription, no dallying over the picturesque or sentimental. It was to him that the impressionist movement, to which he gave a vital impulse but to which he never wholeheartedly adhered, owed its technical emancipation and its guiding principles: the cult of nature, freedom of expression, modernity of subject matter, unattenuated lighting, frankness and spontaneity of vision. Never, however, was an artist less of a revolutionary than Manet, a man of the world, elegant and sociable, a believer in tradition, whose one thought was to gain official recognition and the honors of the Salon. It was very much against his will that he aroused a storm of protests and alienated the public—results that both surprised and pained him. He was perfectly sincere in what he did, was sure of his powers and his painterly instincts, but in an age when the bourgeoisie reigned supreme nothing was more disconcerting than spontaneity. "The effect of sincerity," as Manet himself modestly and apologetically explained, "is to turn one's works into a kind of challenge, whereas the painter only intended to render his impression, sought simply to be himself and no one else."

Edouard Manet was born in Paris, at 5 Rue des Petits-Augustins (today Rue Bonaparte), on January 23, 1832, of an old, well-to-do family of the upper middle class. His father, a stern and exacting man, was a magistrate. His mother, more romantic and imaginative, was the daughter of a French diplomat in Sweden and god-daughter of Marshal Bernadotte, later King of Sweden; a talented musician, she played and sang for her own pleasure. In October 1844 he became a boarder at the Collège Rollin, near the Panthéon, where he formed a close friendship with his fellow student Antonin Proust, future Minister of Fine Arts, who later gave him some much-needed encouragement and left a volume of reminiscences which give us the most vivid and reliable picture we have of Manet. A mediocre student, he took little

Edouard Manet (1832-1883).
Concert at the Tuileries, 1862. (30 × 46½″) By Courtesy of the Trustees, National Gallery, London.

interest in his lessons, apart from gymnastics and drawing. His uncle and god-father, Edmond-Edouard Fournier, encouraged him to follow a special course in drawing and on holidays took him and Antonin Proust to visit the museums and exhibitions. He showed an aptitude for art, but his father had set his heart on sending the boy to Law School; as an alternative he was allowed to enter the Navy. In 1847 he failed the entrance examinations to the Naval Training School and on December 9, 1848, went to sea as an apprentice aboard the transport ship "Le Havre et Guadeloupe" bound for Rio de Janeiro. Upon his return to France in June 1849, with sheaves of drawings in his bags, his father gave in at last and consented to his studying art. In January 1850 he entered the studio of Thomas Couture and about the same time fell in love with the Dutch pianist Suzanne Leenhoff, whom he was to marry in 1863. Though master and pupil were continually at odds, Manet remained with Couture for six years, acquiring from him a solid technical grounding. This he rounded off and completed by regular visits to the Louvre, two study trips to Italy (1853 and 1856), and a tour of the great museums of Holland, Germany and Austria (1856). He copied Old Masters like Titian, Rembrandt and Velazquez, and the best of the moderns, Goya, Delacroix, Courbet, Daumier. "You'll never be anything but the Daumier of your time," was Couture's scornful comment when Manet left him in 1856 to begin his own career. Thereafter his biography merges with his work, and the true story of his life is that of his pictures and their far-reaching repercussions.

Critics have often pointed out the paradox of his art, radically new yet full of borrowings, and the duality of his nature, a subversive ardor mingling with all the instincts of a gentleman. A witty talker, a man of cultivated tastes, a music lover, well read, as much at ease in the

drawing rooms of society as in Bohemian circles, Manet was a close friend of the two greatest French poets of his time: of Baudelaire in his early years (whom he met in 1858 at the home of Commandant Lejosne), of Mallarmé at the end of his life (whom he saw almost daily from 1873 to his death in 1883).

His originality asserted itself as early as 1859 by way of many influences well and profitably assimilated. The *Absinthe Drinker* (Ny Carlsberg Glyptotek, Copenhagen), his first realistic picture, powerfully handled and rigorously simplified, Baudelairian in spirit though slightly melodramatic, was rejected outright by the jury of the 1859 Salon, Delacroix alone (to whom Manet had paid a visit in 1857) voting in favor of it. On the other hand, the dazzling *Spanish Guitar Player* (Osborn Collection, New York) was awarded a medal at the 1861 Salon, and its picaresque subject earned it the warm commendation of Théophile Gautier—whose enthusiasm, however, was soon to be damped. The real novelty of the picture, and one that was to prove decisive for the evolution of Manet in particular and modern painting in general, lay in eliminating the half-tones dear to Delacroix and the traditional chiaroscuro governed

Edouard Manet (1832-1883).
Ball at the Opera, 1873. (23¾ × 29″) Mrs Horace Havemeyer Collection, New York.

by a dominant value and replacing them with bold contrasts of color. Encouraged by his success, by the approbation and friendship of Degas and the admiration of the younger artists (among them Legros and Fantin-Latour), Manet produced in 1862 an ambitious series of works. Victorine Meurent, an authentic *gamine de Paris*, now saucy and alluring, now docile and ingratiating, for years his favorite model, posed first for the *Street Singer* (Boston), then for *Mademoiselle V. in the Costume of an Espada* (Metropolitan Museum, New York), i.e. a matador about to dispatch the bull. The marriage of Napoleon III in 1853 with Madame de Montijo, a Spanish beauty, revived that cult of Spain and all things Spanish which, originally sponsored by Romanticism and Realism, now became the rage in France, pervading the literature of the day and bringing to Paris an influx of Spanish singers, dancers, musicians and toreros. Manet, always sensitive to changing fashions, made the most of this one, which is reflected not only in the themes of his pictures but in his very technique. After several preparatory studies made in the course of actual performances, he brought together in the spacious studio of his friend Stevens the troupe of the *Spanish Ballet* (Phillips Collection, Washington), which was then scoring a triumph at the Hippodrome. The presentation is vivid and racy, but the figures, each remarkable in itself, are disproportioned and unconnected. Owing to "the fury with which he flung himself at the bare canvas, pell-mell, as if he had never painted before" (Mallarmé), Manet was an uneven painter, despite his virtuosity, and compositions with several figures never came easy to him. He was much more successful in individual portraits and *Lola de Valence* (Louvre), star dancer of the same Spanish Ballet, stands out superbly, the "*bijou rose et noir*" of Baudelaire's great poem. Manet's infatuation with things Spanish, which died out in 1863, then was revived by a trip to Spain in 1865, would be of merely documentary interest, had it not been sustained by a real knowledge of the Spanish masters. As a young man he must have visited the famous collections of Louis-Philippe and Maréchal Soult before they were dispersed, and during his trip to Vienna in 1856 he undoubtedly saw the masterpieces by Velazquez in the Habsburg collections. He often took inspiration, moreover, from Goya's prints, a series of which had been published in 1859. It was his interest in Spanish painting, joined to the fluid brushwork of the Venetians, that helped to shape Manet's personal style and goes far to account for its directness and simplifications.

From the same year, 1862, dates a major work, the *Concert at the Tuileries* (National Gallery, London), the first real picture of contemporary city life, painted without any transposition, jotted down directly and tellingly from the actual scene itself in the gardens of the Tuileries. Manet was the first to have eyes for the hitherto unrecorded sights and scenes of mid-nineteenth-century Paris, for its shifting and suggestive concourse of forms and lights, to which Baudelaire had been pointing for years as an untapped source of themes—and Baudelaire himself, as it so happens, figures in this picture, with many other of the painter's friends. "With Manet," wrote Antonin Proust, "the eye played so great a part that Paris has never had a stroller in her streets on whom so little was lost. He noted down in his sketchbook the merest trifle, a profile, a hat, in a word the most fleeting impression." Costumes and faces were caught with all the grace of a casual encounter made in passing, and committed to canvas with an unerring hand in bright and vivid colors.

After holding a one-man show at the Galerie Martinet in March and April 1863, Manet created a sensation in May with his *Déjeuner sur l'herbe* (Louvre), the main attraction at the famous Salon des Refusés of that year and a work which excited the admiration of the younger, independent-minded painters in revolt against academicism. It was considered indecent by the public, yet it was only a restatement of a classical theme treated by Giorgione and Raphael, but presented now "in the transparency of the atmosphere," frankly modern and lifelike, and no longer mythological. In 1864, with a series of still lifes, flowers, fruit and fish, and above all a series of peonies incomparably rich and sensuous in texture, he won over a small group of enlightened collectors, but the general hostility reached its height when, at the 1865 Salon, he exhibited *Olympia* (1863, Louvre). Thoroughly shocked by the subject, the public took

it for a deliberate outrage against the moral order, while critics damned the picture for its absence of shadows and modeling, for its bright colors and the uncompromising novelty of its style. It is precisely this work, so scathingly condemned when it first appeared, that Manet himself regarded as his masterpiece and that we today regard as one of the marvels of painting. And it has lost none of its power to startle. How arresting it still is, with the unashamed frankness of the pose, its taut and wiry firmness of outline, the serenity and brilliance of the colors. "There's only one way of going about it," said Manet. "Put down what you see, straight off." The painter's means have been simplified in the extreme, plastic and expressive values reduced to the magic of the obvious, to an unadorned grandeur of style. Crystallized in all her provocative nudity, abstract, yet very much alive, throbbing with the life that style confers on the loftiest creations of art, Olympia sits up and asserts her unabashed presence, her sovereign indifference, and the colorful bouquet held out by the Negro maid-servant contains all Fauvism in embryo.

Chafing at the incomprehension and ill-will he had met with, Manet went to Spain for a brief holiday (August 1865), where he fell in with Théodore Duret, the future historian of Impressionism. He stayed only ten days in Madrid, just time enough to develop a taste for bull-fighting and to realize that Velazquez was "the painter of painters." Upon his return to Paris, he deserted the fashionable Café de Bade and Tortoni's for the Café Guerbois, in the new Batignolles district, where the younger artists and writers gathered round him in the evenings. In 1865-1866, after some rather too literal interpretations of Velazquez (for example the *Tragedian*, Vanderbilt Collection, New York), he painted three magnificent versions of *The Bull Fight* (Art Institute of Chicago; Matsukata Museum, Tokyo; Goldschmidt-Rothschild Collection, Paris) and *The Fifer* (Louvre), a dazzling display of technical prowess, his most popular and most representative canvas, in which the boy's figure, built up in broad tracts of flat color ("like playing cards," observed Daumier), stands out against an abstract background of unrelieved grey. Both half-tones and modeling have disappeared; forms are outlined in a deep, vibrant black that enlivens the silhouette without blurring or softening it. The picture is a bold, highly personal synthesis of influences stemming, on the one hand, from Spanish painting and, on the other, from Japanese prints. The latter, discovered by Manet's generation, were to have a very different effect on the artists of the next generation, Gauguin, Van Gogh, Lautrec and the Nabis; for him the charm of Japanese art lay in its decorative spontaneity, its rhythmic linear patterns, its simplified handling of space, its rapidly shifting contrasts of brighter and darker values. Photography (which he, like Degas, took up and practised) also contributed to the complex formation of his style, cemented and vivified by his natural gifts.

Excluded from the official exhibitions held at the Paris World's Fair of 1867, Manet had a wooden pavilion erected at his own expense on the Place de l'Alma, opposite Courbet's private pavilion, and exhibited there. The public laughed at his works but the Impressionists-to-be came and admired them. In 1868, in token of his gratitude, he painted the *Portrait of Zola* (Louvre), who had been warmly defending his work since April 1866. The writer, shown in profile from close at hand, is seated with ease and assurance beside a rather untidy writing desk, above which, pinned to the wall, are a Utamaro print and a reproduction of *Olympia*. In this portrait Manet boldly combined the humanist tradition of the West, and the renewal of interest in accessories and still life (the figure itself being treated like a still life, but in the manner of Vermeer), with the flat, decorative patterning of the Far East. Though hostile to historical painting and blaming Delacroix for having indulged in it, he himself was several times inspired by contemporary events which appealed to his generous, liberal sentiments. Thus in 1867, appalled at the fate of Maximilian, the Habsburg prince who had become Emperor of Mexico, he painted his *Execution of Maximilian* (Kunsthalle, Mannheim). In 1868, while summering at Boulogne, where in the following year he painted several beach scenes, he began his *Déjeuner dans l'Atelier* (Neue Staatsgalerie, Munich), his most harmonious and

Edouard Manet (1832-1883).
A Bar at the Folies-Bergère, 1882. (37¾ × 51⅛")
Courtauld Institute of Art, London.

unconstrained composition. It was accepted at the 1869 Salon along with *The Balcony* (Louvre), a theme taken from Goya, which concluded his Spanish period and brought him to the threshold of his Impressionist phase. The color scheme is extremely bold, with its clash of metallic greens against those light greys which are Manet's hallmark, but the central background of the painting remains indistinct in the shadows and each of the three models lives a life of its own. Leaning on the railing in the foreground, her large dark eyes gazing into the distance, is the stately figure of Berthe Morisot, who often posed for the artist before marrying his brother Eugène in 1874. Four portraits of her date from the summer of 1872 alone, including the one in a black hat (Madame Ernest Rouart Collection, Paris) which Paul Valéry singled out as his finest work.

After the Franco-Prussian War of 1870, in which he served as a lieutenant in a National Guard regiment commanded by Meissonier, Manet rejoined his family in the Pyrenees, where they had taken refuge, and returned to Paris by easy stages along the Atlantic coast, painting a number of fluid, broadly handled seascapes on the way, finest of which is the *Port of Bordeaux* (Bührle Collection, Zurich). From 1869 on, no doubt under the influence of Berthe Morisot, Manet turned increasingly to open-air painting. After a holiday at Berck-sur-Mer, he brought back with him in September 1873 a whole batch of oils and watercolors painted entirely out of doors, aglow with bright colors and effects of transparency and vibration. In the limpid, mellow light of late summer in Paris, his new manner came to fruition in figure compositions. Manet's favorite model, Victorine Meurent, who had posed for *Olympia* and had just reappeared in Paris after a mysterious escapade in America, posed now for his *Railroad* (National Gallery, Washington), a brilliant canvas brushed in a single afternoon in the small garden behind the studio of his friend Hirsch, also a painter. In the *Game of Croquet* (Städelsches Kunstinstitut, Frankfort), painted about the same time in the garden of the painter Stevens, the fusion of figures and bright daylight is even more complete. Dancing lights and shadows sweep over the scene, yet make no breach in the firm bulwark of contour lines encasing figures, one of the enduring traits of Manet's art, which sets it apart from the characteristic evanescence of Impressionism. In 1873 he painted another picture of contemporary manners, based on a gamut of blacks, in the same spirit as the *Concert at the Tuileries* but a kind of nocturnal counterpart of it: the *Ball at the Opera* (Mrs Horace Havemeyer Collection, New York), "a work of capital importance in the painter's output, something of a culmination summing up many an earlier effort" (Mallarmé).

Intent on making his mark at the official Salon, Manet refused to take part in the first group exhibition of the Impressionists in 1874, but he spent the summer in his country house at Gennevilliers, just across the Seine from Argenteuil where Monet was working, and he now came under the latter's influence, but without adopting all his principles, for he practised neither pure landscape painting nor the prismatic division of tones. Nevertheless the impressionist pictures he painted there in August 1874, texturally richer and more luminous than anything he had done before, say much for the rapidity with which he mastered the new style. They include several pictures of Monet painting in his garden and on the houseboat which he had fitted up as a studio, two landscapes of the Seine banks and two large boating compositions bursting with space and sunlight. The same picturesque couple in variegated clothes posed in close-up for both: in front view, stiff and motionless in *Argenteuil* (Musée des Beaux-Arts, Tournai), in profile in *Boating* (Metropolitan Museum, New York), in which outlines are sharper and more vivid, and the vision more dynamic and unitary. Though tersely, vigorously drawn, and quite flat, as the silhouettes of *The Fifer* and *Olympia* had been, figures here are born of color alone and, unchecked by their contours, share in the effervescent radiance of the atmosphere. With easy mastery Manet effects the all but impossible synthesis between image and light. From a brief trip to Venice in September 1875 he brought back two canvases in which his mature personal style is wedded to a brilliant display of impressionist effects heightened by the pageantry of the Grand Canal.

The output of his last years was more abundant but more unequal than that of his youth. His technical skill remained unrivaled, but the boldness and unity of his vision faltered occasionally as a result of divided interests and the momentary attractions of naturalism on the one hand and society life on the other. But when he kept within the firm lines of his own style and drew on his unfailing source of inspiration as a chronicler not of passing fashions but of contemporary life, he could still produce such genuine masterpieces as the three characteristic canvases of 1877, *The Plum* (Arthur Sachs Collection, New York), *Skating* (Mrs Wertheim Collection, New York) and *Nana* (Kunsthalle, Hamburg) and two dazzling compositions of 1879, *In the Greenhouse* (Staatliche Museen, Berlin) and *Chez le père Lathuille* (Musée des Beaux-Arts, Tournai), delightful genre scenes in which the sensation of the moment is transmuted into pure poetry. In the summer of 1878, before vacating his studio in the Rue de Saint-Pétersbourg, he set to work on a view of the Rue Mosnier (now Rue de Berne) as seen from his windows, a view he had looked out on almost daily for six years. In the end he made five successive versions of it, with different details; these rank among his finest townscapes, and also among his best works in the impressionist style. That same summer, immediately after this series, he began a sequence of paintings (and drawings) devoted to the large cafés and café-concerts, whose popularity was then rapidly increasing. Several of them were painted

Edouard Manet (1832-1883).

The House at Rueil, 1882. (28¾ × 36¼") Staatliche Museen, Berlin.

in the Brasserie Reichshoffen, in the Boulevard Rochechouart, including the *Servante de Bocks* or *The Waitress* (National Gallery, London), her buxom figure standing out in a black jacket and white apron against a patchwork of gorgeous colors and transparent lights.

In 1879 he felt the first symptoms of the illness that was to prove fatal four years later. He turned now to pastel painting, a suppler medium, easier to handle, whose stylistic and technical resources both he and Degas, at the same time, explored and expanded. He made pastel portraits of Parisian celebrities and of the pretty young women who flocked to his new studio in the Rue d'Amsterdam. The vivacity of the brushwork and the brilliance of the color by no means impair the serene depths and monumentality of these portraits. He spent the summer each year in the country outside Paris, at Bellevue, Versailles and Rueil, where in gardens and greenery, in spite of increasing paralysis and pain, he went on painting with feverish eagerness. Early in 1881 he conceived the idea of painting four figures of women symbolizing the seasons, but only two were actually executed: *Autumn* (Nancy), posed for by Méry Laurent, and *Spring* (Mr and Mrs Harry Payne Bingham Collection, New York), personified by the young actress Jeanne de Marsy. The latter, one of Manet's most radiant and delightful portraits, earned him, for the first time, an unqualified success at the 1882 Salon. Also exhibited there was his last large-scale composition, *Un Bar aux Folies-Bergère* (Courtauld Institute, London), which concentrates the splendor of his palette and, in the large mirror behind the bar, stretching across the full length of the canvas, conjures up a scintillating, phantasmagorical picture of Parisian night life in the eighties. There exist a number of preliminary studies for various details of this limpid and mysterious masterpiece which, with its enlargements of space and its vibrations of light, divides and unites a double reality, tangible and intangible, exterior and interior, and evokes in its purest terms that "absent presence" (Valéry) characteristic of modern life. "When I came back to Paris in January 1882," wrote Jeanniot (in *La Grande Revue*, August 1907), "the first call I paid was on Manet. He was then painting the *Bar at the Folies-Bergère* and the model, a very pretty girl, was posing behind a table laden with food and bottles... Although he painted his pictures from the model, Manet by no means copied nature; I realized how masterly his simplifications were... He abridged everything; tones were brighter, colors more vivid, values closer to one another. All this as a whole went to form a tender, light-colored harmony... Manet left off painting and sat down on the sofa. Among other things he had this to say: 'Concision in art is a necessity and a means to elegance... In a figure, concentrate on full light and full shadow; the rest will follow naturally.' "

He dreamed of decorating the Hôtel de Ville with a vast fresco glorifying Paris and the modern world, but he was bed-ridden and had only strength enough to paint the dainty bouquets of roses and lilacs sent to him by his women friends. He died on April 30, 1883. "He was greater than we thought," Degas was heard to say as he left the little cemetery at Passy where Manet was buried, and where for a long time after his death the beautiful Méry Laurent came each week to lay flowers on his grave. Though he was not one of the giants of painting, Manet, like Giorgione and Caravaggio, marks a decisive turning point, for with him one world came to an end and another was born.

Monet and Light

THE term Impressionist in the strict sense applies only to three painters who devoted themselves essentially to open-air landscape painting: Monet, Pissarro and Sisley. Monet was the impressionist painter *par excellence* and his art is one long hymn of praise to light and its life-giving vitality. "When I see a canvas by Monet," said Berthe Morisot, "I know exactly which way to tilt my sunshade." From dawn to twilight, from season to season, his eye observed unerringly, and his brush recorded to perfection, the manifold, ever-varying aspects of the scene before him. Monet once confessed to a young painter that he almost wished he had been born blind and suddenly endowed with sight, so that he could look at things with a virgin eye. At a time when philosophers were debating whether the sense of touch or that of sight takes precedence in our apprehension of the phenomenal world, Monet instinctively championed the autonomy and priority of sight. Hence Cézanne's famous remark (which echoes what Ingres said of Courbet) voicing an admiration that he made haste to qualify: "Monet is only an eye, but what an eye!"

Claude-Oscar Monet was born in Paris on November 14, 1840. He was the eldest son of a grocer who moved with his family to Le Havre in 1845. A naturally unruly child, he spent much of his boyhood roaming the seashore under the luminous, ever-changing skies of the Channel coast. Like Courbet, a "child of nature" with little taste for study, he was always playing truant from school, which he regarded as a prison, scrambling over cliffs and running down to the sea, which was to hold a fascination for him all his life. "I'd like to be always facing it or above it," he said in later life, "and, when I die, to be buried in a buoy." When only fifteen he made a name for himself locally with his caricatures which he exhibited in the shop window of the one and only frame-maker at Le Havre. This shop, where stationery was also sold, had been opened by Eugène Boudin (1824-1898), son of a sailor from Honfleur, who also exhibited sketches of his own on the premises. Encouraged by sales to his customers, among whom were Millet and Troyon, he had sold his business and set up as a painter. In 1850 Boudin had received a municipal grant enabling him to study in Paris for three years. When he came back he announced that "the Romantics have had their day and we now must turn our attention to the simple beauties of nature." Struck by young Monet's talent, he gradually won him over to his views and in 1858 persuaded him to try his hand at sketching from nature. "It came in a flash, as if a veil had been torn from my eyes," Monet told a friend. "I understood at last what painting really means, and the example of this painter, passionately devoted to art and personal independence, made me realize once for all my true vocation."

Eugène Boudin (1824-1898).

The Empress Eugénie at Trouville, 1863. (13⅝ × 22½″) The Burrell Collection, Glasgow Art Gallery and Museum.

In May 1859, on the advice and with the aid of Boudin, Monet went to Paris. Visiting the Salon, he admired the work of Corot, Daubigny and Troyon. He took to dropping in regularly at the Brasserie des Martyrs, then a favorite haunt of Courbet and the Realists, and instead of studying under Couture (as Troyon advised him to do) he attended the free classes at the Académie Suisse, where he met Pissarro. In June 1859, on a visit to Le Havre, Courbet in turn discovered Boudin, who took him out to Honfleur where Baudelaire, then staying with his mother, joined them. Courbet's self-assurance and dashing brushwork had a tonic effect on Boudin, and Baudelaire was enraptured by Boudin's pastels, made on the spot, in the open air, rendering sky and sea effects "according to the time of year, the hour of the day and the set of the wind." He enthusiastically praised these "meteorological beauties" in his review of the 1859 Salon.

Monet spent April 1860 painting at Champigny-sur-Marne, perhaps in Pissarro's company. Called up for his military service in the autumn, he elected for an Algerian regiment. "The impressions of light and color that I got in Africa were to be sorted out only later, but the seeds of my future work were planted while I was there." In 1861, at Troyon's invitation, Boudin made a trip to Paris, where he saw Courbet again and met Corot, who hailed him as "the monarch of the skies," a designation particularly apt in Boudin's case. For if the sky is in a sense the "pivot" of every landscape scene, this applies especially to the skies of Normandy, strewn with moving clouds and mirrored everywhere in the vast sea spaces. In 1862 Boudin moved to Honfleur, lodging at the Ferme Saint-Siméon, a small inn patronized by fishermen, located on the cliffs just outside the town, with a magnificent view over the Seine estuary. There he became the leading figure of the group known as the School of Saint-Siméon, true begetters of Impressionism. Sea bathing was becoming fashionable and

Johann Barthold Jongkind (1819-1891).
Rue des Francs-Bourgeois, Paris, 1868. (13⅜ × 16½") Gemeentemuseum, The Hague.

thanks to the railway the beaches of Normandy were now within easy reach of Paris. The Duc de Morny launched those two famous seaside resorts, Deauville and Trouville, and the colorful crowd of summer visitors, especially the elegant ladies in crinolines, provided Boudin with subjects after his own heart. "One feels a bit ashamed," he admitted, "of painting all these idlers," but he justified himself by adding that "since our peasants have their dedicated painters, why shouldn't the well-dressed men and women who promenade the sea-front on fine afternoons have the right to figure on my canvases, and be brought into the light?" By which he meant that light absorbs and purifies everything, strips the subject of its social implications and transforms it into a "motif." And what better motif could a painter wish for than the ballet of vagrant gleams and colors presented by the Empress Eugénie and her suite on the beach at Trouville (1863, Glasgow)? Figures and costumes come to vivid life, rendered with the wit and precision of a Constantin Guys. A few slender verticals, masts, flagposts and a street lamp—"picturesque trifles," as he called them—link the successive horizontal planes of earth, sea and sky. Naturally the sky is the vastest, most delicately modulated of the three, a tremulous expanse of azure blue and lilac, dappled with fleecy white and pearl-grey clouds. Despite its modern tonalities, Boudin's subtle, dainty, exquisitely wrought canvas conjures up reminiscences of the Dutch little masters and even of Guardi.

No sooner had Monet returned from Algeria, early in 1862, than he hastened to Le Havre and started work again. It was at this time that he met the Dutch artist Jongkind (1819-1891) who, after leading a dissipated, Bohemian life in Montmartre from 1845 on, had been cured in the nick of time, in 1860, of the drinking habits which had reduced him to total destitution and brought him to the brink of madness. Jongkind was already familiar with the region of the Lower Seine, having worked there off and on from 1847 to 1852 with Isabey, and soon after his return Monet made his acquaintance. "He asked to see my sketches, invited me to come out and work with him, explained to me the why and wherefore of his way of painting and so added the crowning touch to the encouragement Boudin had already given me." Monet introduced him to Boudin and the three artists went out together on painting expeditions and thoroughly enjoyed each other's company. In 1863, Jongkind who, now that he had recovered his health and his zest for painting, was in fine form, stayed part of the year at Honfleur, where he returned in 1864 and 1865. "In his art," wrote Castagnary in 1863, "the impression is everything." The singular perfection of his watercolors, their forthrightness and clarity, their combination of extreme precision with complete freedom (so finely analysed by Signac), should not cause the oil paintings of his best period to be overlooked. Vibrant with light and tense with concentrated energy, these seascapes and above all the views of Paris and the Seine banks struck a new note. For Jongkind discovered, before the Impressionists, the pink-and-white charm of the old streets of Paris, the picturesque appeal of the working-class districts and the semi-countrified suburbs, and even the house-breakers' yards (*Rue des Francs-Bourgeois*, 1868, Gemeentemuseum, The Hague). "A thing that has struck me," Edmond de Goncourt noted in his *Journal* (May 4, 1871), "is Jongkind's influence. Every worthwhile landscape that's turned out today derives from this painter, borrows his skies, his atmosphere, even his terrains. That's plain to see—but no one says it!" Monet, however, admitted his debt, while Boudin, whose sedater art contrasted with his young friend's bold experimentalism, observed in retrospect: "I, too, came in by the door he had flung open."

In November 1862 Monet returned to Paris and, to please his parents, enrolled in the Ecole des Beaux-Arts, where he studied under Gleyre, Delaroche's successor. But after his experience of open-air painting, it went against the grain to bow to academic disciplines. Fortunately, however, he found congenial companions; Bazille, Sisley and Renoir entered Gleyre's studio at exactly the same time as he and the four young men became firm friends. They had much in common, notably a taste for independence and for striking out in new directions, and in the spring of 1863 they shared in the exciting experience of discovering Manet, first at the Galerie Martinet and then at the famous Salon des Refusés, where his *Déjeuner sur l'herbe* created a sensation. In July 1864 Frédéric Bazille (1841-1870) went with Monet to Normandy, but had to hurry back to his home at Montpellier after a short stay. From the Ferme Saint-Siméon, where he stayed until winter set in, Monet sent Bazille an enthusiastic letter. "We're in full force just now, Boudin and Jongkind are here and we get on together famously. A great pity you're not here; in such company one can learn such heaps of things." In December Monet went back to Paris, but he had quarreled with his parents and they now cut off supplies. In January 1865 Bazille, better off than his friends, gave him shelter in his studio on the Place de Furstenberg, where Courbet, Cézanne and Pissarro visited them. For the first time Monet exhibited at the Salon, scoring a notable success with two seascapes, one of which, *The Honfleur Jetty* (Jöhr Collection, Zurich), inspired by a picture by Jongkind, he had painted the previous summer. The critic Paul Mantz praised his "harmonious colors" and his "bold way of seeing things and forcing the spectator's attention."

Monet's apprenticeship was completed (1858-1864) not in the schools, but in direct contact with the best painters of the day. With an extraordinary sureness of hand he worked out a style of his own, a naturalistic style distinct from the realism of his precedessors. From 1865 to 1871, during an intensive phase of experimentation, he perfected his approach and his means, moving rapidly towards what was soon to be known as Impressionism. Eluding the

pitfalls of mannerism that lie in wait for studio painters, he worked directly from nature, following an organic evolution which may have depended on the subjects chosen or may have determined them, it is hard to say which. In the spring of 1863 and again in 1864 after Gleyre's studio was closed down, Monet induced his friends to join him in Fontainebleau Forest where they painted landscapes in the spirit of the Barbizon masters. He was there again in April 1865 with his mistress Camille Doncieux, whom he married in 1870 and who died in 1879. He now decided to execute a large figure composition, a *Déjeuner sur l'herbe* even bigger and bolder than Manet's, free of studio conventions, representing a picnic in a clearing of the forest. He threw himself into the work with all the passionate intensity of his temperament. "I think of nothing but my picture," he wrote to Bazille, begging him to come out and pose for him (he came in August), "and if I thought it was doomed to failure, I believe I'd go mad." The canvas was too big (20 feet wide) for all of it to be painted out of doors, but it was based entirely on studies made in the open air. Intrigued by this bold venture Courbet came out to see how it was getting on and suggested some changes which Monet soon keenly regretted. So much so that he abandoned the picture by which he had set so much store, leaving it with his innkeeper as security for his unpaid bill. When he retrieved it later, damp and mold had eaten away the sides, particularly at the top and on the right. These he slit off with a knife, and only the lefthand figure group (Louvre) and the central fragment (Private Collection, Paris) now remain, broadly handled and astonishingly fresh and natural. Light and shadows sweep over the leafage, the figures and the still life, treated in terms of flat surfaces enhanced with lively accents of color. Exquisitely graceful are the movements of the standing girl in blue, raising her arms to doff her hat, and her seated companion in the center, with her flowing white dress spread out around her, who is holding out her plate at arm's length as if to offer the spectator a tidbit. The complete version (Moscow), a sketch post-dated 1866, or rather a replica on a smaller scale, reveals the truly heroic aspiration of the young artist: to vie with Courbet and Manet on their own ground, to establish once for all the validity of open-air painting and contemporary themes as the basis of his new aesthetic.

In the autumn of 1865 he worked at Trouville, on the Channel coast, with Daubigny, Boudin, Courbet and the latter's pupil (for so he declared himself to be at that time) Whistler. Just before the opening of the 1866 Salon he dashed off in four days' time a masterly portrait of Camille, known as *The Woman in the Green Dress* (Bremen), and sent it in as a substitute for his *Déjeuner*. Highly praised by Zola and Thoré, it was purchased shortly afterwards by the writer Arsène Houssaye. Seen from above and behind, about to pass by, she turns and lingers for a moment, as the light plays over the folds of her striped skirt. Monet and Manet now met for the first time, introduced to each other by Zacharie Astruc. In the early summer, from the balconies of the Louvre, along a plunging line of sight, Monet painted three views of Paris: the *Church of Saint-Germain-l'Auxerrois* (Berlin), the *Jardin de l'Infante* (Oberlin, Ohio) and the *Quai du Louvre* (The Hague), contemporary with the first snapshots and aerial photographs of the city. Strollers and passing hansoms are brushed in with all the sketchlike vivacity of Jongkind, while the light, dancing through the leaves and shattered into a thousand brilliant, knife-sharp points, clashes with the local color of the lawns and the lusterless immobility of houses. Atmospheric vibration is as yet only partially obtained, but the sunny vigor of each brushstroke lends a quivering tension to the whole. Nascent Impressionism found in Paris, then in the throes of drastic changes, its finest landscape. Monet rented a house at Ville-d'Avray, just outside Paris, where Corot often worked, and there embarked on another large-scale composition, *Women in the Garden* (Louvre), which this time he was determined to paint entirely out of doors. So as to reach the top of it with his brush, he had a trench dug in the garden into which, by means of a pulley and ropes, he could lower his canvas at will, to the utter amazement of Courbet, who stood by watching these unheard-of operations. Executed from start to finish in the open air, its revolutionary character was so pronounced that it was rejected outright at the 1867 Salon. Yet Monet got the idea for the picture from a photograph, and Camille posed for each of the four figures successively, smelling or plucking

Claude Monet (1840-1926).

Le Déjeuner sur l'herbe, 1864. (94½ × 85½") Private Collection, Paris.

Frédéric Bazille (1841-1870).
The Family Reunion, 1867-1869. (60 × 90½″) Louvre, Paris.

flowers. Here Monet inaugurated a new theme, that of garden spots in springtime, the quiet pleasures of a bourgeois afternoon, and in this atmosphere blossomed the Impressionists' finest works, which sealed the doom of traditional conceptions of form and color, here dissociated by the play of sunlight. Blue and violet shadows, diffused by the sunshade, flicker over the face of the seated girl. Despite this close observation of nature, the composition keeps to a decorative pattern of flat, stylized silhouettes and the tapering, corolla-shaped dresses are carefully grouped round the slender treetrunk in the center.

Bazille did his best to interest the collector Alfred Bruyas in Monet's work, but it was no use. He himself bought the *Women in the Garden*, paying for it in monthly instalments. Bazille was killed in action in the Franco-Prussian War and his own work covers a period of only six or seven years, the best of it painted in and around Montpellier, where he was born. It includes landscapes, still lifes and portraits. Of these by far the most significant are the figures painted in the open air, integrated into the surrounding atmosphere, yet conceived as a portrait. In the *Pink Dress* (1864, Louvre) and the *View of a Village* (1868, Montpellier) a single figure seen in close-up stands out against the sunny landscape of Languedoc. When it came to representing a group of figures, the difficulties were substantially increased, but Bazille solved them in his masterpiece, the *Family Reunion* (1867-1869, Louvre), showing all the members of his family on the terrace of their estate at Méric, near Montpellier. All the figures are quite motionless, several leaning tensely forward as if waiting for the click of the camera, and one feels sure that each is a faithful likeness. On the far left, only partially visible, is the tall figure of the painter himself, standing behind his uncle. Seated in the left foreground,

Auguste Renoir (1841-1919).
La Grenouillère, 1869. (23¼ × 31½″) Hermitage, Leningrad (on deposit at Moscow).

on a green bench, are his father (the only figure shown in profile) and his mother in a dark blue gown with a black lace shawl drawn round her waist. Seated at the small garden table are his maternal aunt and his sister Thérèse. Standing behind them, under the chestnut tree, are his cousin Pauline and her husband. On the right, forming a group apart on the edge of the terrace, are the artist's brother Marc and his wife, and his cousin Camille. The two girls, Camille and Thérèse, wearing pale blue muslin dresses, sit in the luminous zone of the picture, telling out against the deep greens of the landscape. On the garden table is one still life, a wicker basket and skeins of colored wool; in the foreground is another, a bouquet, a sunshade and a straw hat, added as an afterthought when Bazille retouched the painting in 1869. It is closely akin to Monet's *Women in the Garden* in the accuracy and brightness of the open-air atmosphere and the elegance of the young women's dresses, but very different from it in the sharpness and clarity of the southern light, the clean-cut volumes of each form, the impression of unbending austerity that emanates from this silent, compact family group, bourgeois and Protestant, solidly united, yet each member of which is pursuing in secret, one feels, his own train of thought. Owing to his moral reserve and classical stability, Bazille diverges from the main stream of Impressionism. Preceding Cézanne, Renoir and Seurat, he studied the nude in the open air and painted a composition of bathers, *Summer Scene* (1869, Fogg Art Museum, Harvard), combining the full glow of sunlight with the plastic rhythm of the human body.

In the autumn of 1866 Monet painted his *Terrace at the Seaside* (Reverend Theodore Pitcairn Collection, Bryn Athyn, Pa.), skillfully blending the garden landscape, figures out of doors and the seascape. From the summer of 1867 date some dazzling seascapes, notably the *Beach at Sainte-Adresse* (Art Institute of Chicago), a marvel of truthfulness, spontaneity and luminous transparency. In 1868 he was saved from want by a timely commission for the *Portrait of Madame Gaudibert* (Louvre), ordered by a rich industrialist of Le Havre; this picture and *The Meal* (Frankfort), an interior, a glimpse of home life at a happy moment, prove that he might have become a great figure painter, had it not been for the opposition of the Salon and the irresistible appeal of nature. In 1868 appeared the theme that was to bulk so large in the formation of the impressionist style: views of the Seine banks. In the summer of 1869 Monet settled at Bougival, where he was often joined by Renoir, then living with his mother at nearby Ville-d'Avray. They spent days on end painting side by side at La Grenouillère (the "froggery"), a popular bathing spot on the Seine where, a few years later, Maupassant was to locate several of his short stories: "Round about the Grenouillère a throng of strollers wound among the giant trees that make this end of the island the most delightful spot in the world." Monet and Renoir each made at least three versions of this theme, bright with sunlight and the gaily dressed figures of trippers. We illustrate the boldest and least

Claude Monet (1840-1926).

La Grenouillère, 1869. (29⅜ × 39⅛") Private Collection, Oxford.

known of Monet's three pictures (Private Collection, Oxford) and the Renoir version in Moscow, more complex and less familiar than those in Stockholm and the Reinhart Collection. An attentive study of the light reflections decomposing objects into flickering patches of color led them to employ dabs of pure color applied in "comma" brushstrokes. Monet applies his colors in dense, flat, contrasting strokes of the brush. He introduces only a few figures in order to build up space to its full intensity; the boats in the foreground, oval forms characteristic of Monet, break up the breadthwise layout stressed by the foot-bridge running across the entire canvas. With Renoir, in spite of strong accents, the brushstrokes merge into a tender sheen of light enveloping the picturesque throng of figures and the composition develops spiralwise. Monet looks down from above, Renoir catches the scene along a low angle of vision and savors every detail of it.

If Monet was fascinated by the mirage of rippling water in sunlight, Camille Pissarro (1830-1903), who represents the other aspect of Impressionism, was the fervent poet of the soil and the open countryside. "He, of all painters," said Cézanne, "approached most closely to nature." Born on the island of St Thomas in the West Indies, of a French father and a Creole mother, he came to Paris to study art in 1855. Arriving a few days before the World's Fair closed its doors, he wandered through the galleries devoted to Ingres and Delacroix, lingered in the Barbizon rooms and was impressed by Daubigny. But when he saw Corot's landscapes he stopped short. Here was the master of his choice, to whom he was drawn by deep affinities of temperament and vision. He ventured to call on Corot, who received him with open-hearted kindliness, gave him a drawing and impressed on him two principles which Pissarro was never to forget: form and values, i.e. structural solidity and accurate lighting. He made his debut at the 1859 Salon, and in 1861 at the Académie Suisse met Cézanne and Guillaumin, with whom he formed a group quite distinct from the group at Gleyre's studio centering on Monet. Castagnary noticed the work he sent in to the Salon des Refusés in 1863 and warned him against a docile surrender to Corot, "a good master but one above all others whom it is dangerous to imitate." He also shows the influence of Courbet, in his textural effects of dense, contrasting pigments spread with the palette knife. By 1866 his personality had asserted itself and he attracted the attention of Zola: "A grave, austere brand of painting, an extreme concern for truth and accuracy. A man of strong, undaunted willpower." That same year he settled at Pontoise, where the hill overlooking the river, with its trees, houses and winding lanes, offered the compact, vibrant masses answering in every way to the structural coherence of his style and the subdued vitality of his palette. Most of his pre-1870 canvases were destroyed in the Franco-Prussian War, but there remain a few important landmarks of his early evolution, like the *Côte du Jallais at Pontoise* (Metropolitan Museum, New York), dated 1867. His colors have brightened up and the tremor of light runs through the solid courses of planes and volumes. Although friendly with Monet since 1859, Pissarro never joined in his expeditions to the Channel coast; for one thing, he now had a family to support and in 1868 was so poor that he had to paint window-blinds to make ends meet; for another, the endless flux of the sea and the boundless horizons would have interfered with the order and stability he craved. In 1869 he moved to Louveciennes and, following the example of Monet and Renoir, studied the play of sunlight on the Seine.

In 1870 he painted a series of masterpieces on the theme of a road running across the countryside—a theme taken over from Hobbema, the Barbizon painters and above all Corot. But to the plunging perspective of Corot's roads, disappearing into hazy distances, Pissarro preferred roads that wind away in perspective or slew off to one side (*The Louveciennes Road* and *The Louveciennes Diligence*, Louvre), which better concentrate space, organize the crisscrossing of shadows and lights, and focus the eye on the middle distance. A larger, more intricate canvas, *The Versailles Road at Louveciennes* (Bührle Collection, Zurich), which also dates from 1870 and partakes at the same time of the genre picture and the portrait, sums up Pissarro's initial phase. In the small front garden of his house on the side of the road (which

Camille Pissarro (1830-1903).

The Versailles Road at Louveciennes, 1870. (39¾ × 32¼") E. G. Bührle Collection, Zurich.

Claude Monet (1840-1926).
The Bridge at Argenteuil, 1874. (23⅝ × 33⅞″) Louvre, Paris.

in part explains his predilection for the theme) stand the artist's wife, the maid-servant and his little girl, Jeanne, aged five. Three figures in their Sunday best, treated on a much smaller scale, are passing on the road and re-echo those in the foreground. Though perfectly natural, the composition is governed by a subtle geometry which intensifies and distributes light. Flowers and leafage stand out brilliantly against local tones still pitched in a low key.

In the summer of 1870 Monet was at Trouville with Boudin. There he painted some beach scenes (London, Hartford, Budapest) which, with their broad yet intimate approach, surpass even those of his master. After the outbreak of war both Monet and Pissarro took refuge in London, and there in 1871 Daubigny introduced them to the dealer Paul Durand-Ruel, who from now on gave them much-needed support and encouragement. Undue importance has often been attached to this stay in England, but the truth is that it brought about no real change in their style. The evanescent atmosphere of London, with its water, fog and smoke, and their study of the Dutch and English landscapists in the London museums only went to confirm an evolution already well under way. In the autumn of 1872, after two trips to Holland, where he discovered and bought a sheaf of Japanese prints, Monet settled down at Argenteuil, at that time an unspoilt village and a haunt of canoers and boating parties

on the Seine. His five years there correspond to the most glorious, most homogeneous period of Impressionism. Whereas Manet had led the way in the sixties, and before him Courbet, the leading role now unquestionably fell to Monet. He became friendly with a young engineer passionately fond of painting, Gustave Caillebotte, who bought his pictures; fitted up an old houseboat as a floating studio, following the example of Daubigny; and soon gathered round him Renoir, Sisley and Manet himself, now at last won over to open-air painting. Working daily in friendly rivalry with his companions, Monet surpassed himself. While he did not altogether abandon either figure paintings or interiors, he found in boating scenes and riverside views the themes most congenial to him. The freshness of his vision gave a matchless, almost magical beauty to the new style. The *Bridge at Argenteuil* (1874, Louvre) is often considered the most perfect, most representative work of the impressionist school. Contrary to what is commonly supposed, no single, set technique presides over the organization of the picture. Colors—rarely pure colors—are now juxtaposed, now blended. The rhythm, form and density of the brushstroke change continually, always being adapted to differences of texture and nuances of light. The painting owes its unity to the even vibration of the atmosphere. Thanks to the setting of natural scenery interwoven with mobile elements, the boats and their rigging—aerial architecture between sky and water—this "instantaneous" vision is as well organized as a classical composition, and has the same serenity.

Alfred Sisley (1839-1899).
The Flood at Port-Marly, 1876. (23⅝ × 31⅞") Louvre, Paris.

Before 1870 Alfred Sisley (1839-1899) painted simply as a dilettante, but by 1872 he was producing works which are marvels of tonal accuracy and refinement within the limited range of the subdued palette favored by Corot. Before settling at Moret on the banks of the Loing, he worked in the immediate environs of Paris, at Louveciennes, Marly, Bougival and Argenteuil, sometimes leaning in the direction of Pissarro, more often in that of Monet. Exclusively a landscape painter, Sisley was the purest Impressionist of them all and, though of English origin, the subtlest interpreter of the Ile-de-France, of its light and skies, conveying them as well in paints as Gérard de Nerval had conveyed them in words several decades before him. He did not invent his technique but adapted Monet's methods to his own sensibility, refined his palette and entered into closer communion with his motifs, which are more varied than is usually realized and to which he responded with naïve and graceful spontaneity. After 1880 his style became a little mannered. His finest pictures date from the Argenteuil period and the most famous of them, on a typically impressionist theme (but one already treated by Huet), is *The Flood at Port-Marly* (1876, Louvre). Subdued light plays over the pale water in which the winter sky is reflected. The subtle simplicity of the composition, the delicacy of the colors, with their wintry limpidity reminiscent of certain English watercolors, and alternately vibrant or well-blended shadings turn the very melancholy of the scene into a delight for the eye. This humble, rather bleak view of the Paris suburbs takes on all the enchantment of a Venetian scene, and the house with its pallid tones and the geometry of its windows brings to mind Vermeer. But all is handled with a quiet delicacy and refinement of touch that is inimitably his own.

In 1872, while Monet was settling down at Argenteuil, Pissarro moved back to Pontoise, where he had already lived in the sixties and where he was now to remain for the next ten years. Argenteuil was at the gates of Paris, with all the animation of the Seine, its boating parties and holiday makers, its pleasure gardens with music and dancing, and the endless play of light effects between sky and water in which Monet reveled. Pontoise, a small rustic town overlooking the valley of the Oise, lay farther out from Paris, in the open countryside of the Vexin, breathing both the calm and the sterling vigor of the earth, with meadows, orchards and houses dotted over the hillsides, the dependable regularity of seasons and days, and the bucolic simplicity so congenial to Pissarro. Around him, enamored of the same rustic ideal bound up with the soil and the same constructive values, he gathered a group quite distinct from that at Argenteuil, made up of Cézanne, Guillaumin and several minor painters like Victor Vignon (1847-1909) and Frédéric Cordey (1854-1911). Senior member of the impressionist group, as kindly and indulgent towards others as he was exacting with himself, Pissarro was looked up to by all both as a moral conscience and an artistic guide. Cézanne, who worked with him from 1872 to 1874 and again in 1877, deeply admired him and owed to him his decisive change of style. Pissarro in turn benefited from the companionship of a man whose powers he divined long before anyone else recognized them, and from whom his own work gained in force and monumentality. In December 1873 the critic Théodore Duret wrote to Pissarro: "You have neither Sisley's decorative flair nor Monet's fantastic eye, but you have what they lack, a deep, intimate feeling for nature that makes a fine canvas by you absolutely foursquare and sound." And as his forms grew surer and sounder, his colors grew richer and denser. By 1875, in *The Little Bridge* (Mannheim), without any prejudice to his natural qualities and his freshness of vision, he had achieved an order and plenitude that can only be described as Cézannesque. In 1876 he paid a visit to his painter friend Piette at Montfoucault (Mayenne) where he painted a canvas remarkable for its constructive power and resplendent colors, the *Harvest at Montfoucault* (Louvre). In 1877 he painted a series of masterpieces on a theme familiar to him since 1868, variously interpreted according to the time of year: country houses, with red or blue roofs, clinging to the hillside, seen through a curtain of trees that disseminate light and set it vibrating. Structural solidity, fortified by contact with Cézanne, is here joined to a new vitality of light inspired by Monet. Among these works are the *Red Roofs* (Louvre), a winter scene with leafless branches standing out against the clean-cut articulation of planes;

the *Côte des Bœufs at Pontoise* (National Gallery, London), with a vertical layout on more decorative lines, tinged with the melancholy grace of autumn; and the *Garden with Trees in Blossom* (Louvre), an image of spring almost Dionysian in its exultation. "I doubt if there is any other painting," writes Lionello Venturi of the last, "which better conveys the joy, the freshness and the pleasurable sense of rebirth awakened by spring." Pigments are thick and richly worked, while the massive, pyramidal composition rises up, stage on stage, and leaves only a narrow strip of sky at the top. Already painted by Daubigny, the exuberant colors of orchards in bloom inspired Van Gogh upon his arrival in Provence.

In one of his finest paintings, *Snow at Louveciennes* (1874, Phillips Collection, Washington), Sisley combines, in his usual key of gentle melancholy, two motifs characteristic of Pissarro: a lane seen in perspective and volumetric houses standing among trees. The scene as a whole, with the tiny figure exquisitely poised in the center, lies under a blanket of snow, streaked with delicate tints of grey and pink. For the Impressionists studied not only the play of light on water, but the play of light on snow, which gave them a unique opportunity to observe and analyse colored shadows, one of the fundamental principles of their style. They realized

Camille Pissarro (1830-1903).
Garden with Trees in Blossom, Pontoise, 1877. (25¾ × 31⅞") Louvre, Paris.

Alfred Sisley (1839-1899).

Snow at Louveciennes, 1874. (22 × 18″) The Phillips Collection, Washington, D.C.

that pure colors, though less brilliant than white, actually give a truer idea of the luminous intensity of snow than white itself, and that the shadows cast on snow are not black but colored. Monet's first snow scenes were painted at Honfleur about 1865-1867 (*The Cart*, Louvre). They are still close to Courbet and Jongkind and make no attempt to analyse reflections, though beneath a veneer of realism we feel the first delicate stirrings of atmospheric light. During their stay in London in the winter of 1870-1871, prompted by the climate and their keen interest in problems of technique, Monet, Pissarro and Sisley painted whole sets of snow-scapes handled in accordance with their new conception of color. Thereafter they continually reverted to snow effects which, they found, lent themselves to an inexhaustible range of chromatic variations. Monet's most remarkable series of snowscapes are those painted at Argenteuil in 1874-1875 and at Vétheuil in 1878-1881, the latter reflecting his loneliness and grief during the final illness of his wife (who died in September 1879). *Snow Effect at Vétheuil* (c. 1878, Louvre), showing the village under snow with the frozen river in the foreground, was painted either from an island in the Seine or from his floating studio. Of all his river views, this is one of the smallest but, as William C. Seitz has written, surely one of the finest. Delicate and well-blended in the sky, the brushwork on the river is broken up into sharp, separate strokes, vibrant and spirited, highly varied under a monochrome appearance, which convey

Claude Monet (1840-1926).
Snow Effect at Vétheuil, about 1878. (20½ × 28″) Louvre, Paris.

Claude Monet (1840-1926).
La Gare Saint-Lazare, Paris, 1877. (32¼ × 39¾″) Courtesy of the Fogg Art Museum, Harvard University,
Maurice Wertheim Collection.

the bleak silence of winter and catch the light differently according to the surface texture of water, ice and snow. The composition consists of a broad, horizontal foreground, with an angle of vision perpendicular to the course of the river, and a background dominated by the verticals of houses, the church steeple, the man in blue and treetrunks, the only warm and somber notes in the cold tonality of the whole. Very important technically, the Vétheuil interlude marks the transition between the instinctive, lyrical works of the Argenteuil period and the more systematic, more deliberate works of the later years at Giverny (1883-1926).

Throughout the seventies, during the Argenteuil period, Renoir never strayed far from Paris, where Manet and Degas, old Parisians both, lived almost uninterruptedly, where Monet, Sisley and Pissarro turned up periodically, and where even Cézanne lived and worked for long periods. Paris remained not only the rallying point of the Impressionists (the Café de la Nouvelle Athènes having now replaced the Café Guerbois) and the scene of their group exhibitions, but also one of their themes of predilection. Impressionism may have been born in the countryside and on the seashore, but it grew up in part in the city streets, where Monet and his

friends found both a marvelous landscape in its own right and a stimulating incentive to paint modern life as it really is. Just as we turn to Watteau for a picture—transfigured but authentic—of early eighteenth-century Paris in the Regency Period, that "legendary translation" (Baudelaire) of reality which in the last analysis is truer than history, so in the paintings of Manet, Degas, Renoir and Monet we rediscover, far better than in the pages of contemporary writers, the poetry and period atmosphere of late nineteenth-century Paris. Never has the Ville Lumière, the city of light, been better painted than by the painters of light.

The first masterpiece of Berthe Morisot (1841-1895), painted in 1866, was a *View of Paris from the Heights of the Trocadéro* (J. T. Ryerson Collection, Chicago). She had by then assimilated the lesson of Corot and her very original sensibility, at once bold and refined, was asserting itself. This work, with its exquisite colors and firm structure, was shown at the 1867 Salon, where Manet was so much struck with it that he made a painting on much the same theme (National Gallery, Oslo), but with the temporary buildings of the World's Fair in the background. In the following year, 1868, Berthe Morisot not only met both Degas and Manet, but became for a time the latter's favorite model, undergoing his influence and in turn reacting on him. Her particular contribution to Impressionism is a wholly feminine note of charm and delicate feeling, quite free of sentimentality or affectation. "She never betrayed her true self," writes Louis Rouart, "never attempted to drape herself in false colors, but remained a woman, simply and genuinely feminine." She excelled in discreet and graceful scenes of home life, animated by the presence of children (*The Cradle*, 1873, Louvre). Her canvases are painted with a deft and easy touch, "as if she were plucking off the petals of flowers" (Théodore Duret).

Armand Guillaumin (1841-1927), backed and encouraged by Cézanne and Pissarro (his work was less appreciated by Monet and Degas), was unable to devote himself entirely to painting until after 1892. His most characteristic canvases of the impressionist period are his suburban landscapes (*Sunset at Ivry*, 1873, Louvre), notable for their high-pitched colors at times anticipating Fauvism. Guillaumin exerted a certain influence on Van Gogh.

While Degas restlessly and inquisitively explored the secret life of the city, behind the façades, Monet, like Renoir, was the genial landscapist of its outward setting, of the picturesque bustle of the boulevards. In 1873 he set out to catch the atmosphere of carnival time. From the studios of his friend Nadar, the photographer, he painted the Boulevard des Capucines along a plunging line of sight, showing the surging crowds and long lines of carriages under the bare trees. This revolutionary canvas (Marshall Field Collection, New York), reproduced here (page 158) as the frontispiece to the chapter on Impressionism, figured in the first group exhibition held the following year in the same premises and was the object of particularly violent attacks. Yet the picture is a miracle of tonal accuracy and atmospheric verisimilitude, as visitors to the exhibition might have discovered for themselves simply by looking out of the window. In June 1878 the streets of the city were decked out with flags and bunting for the opening of the World's Fair—a sight that Manet and Monet each recorded in two canvases, Monet from his own windows, Manet in the crowded popular quarters of the Rue Saint-Denis (Lindon Collection, Paris) and the Rue Montorgueil (Rouen). And the impressionist technique gave a marvelous visionary picture of this phantasmagoric atmosphere, this dynamic chaos of forms and colors. Van Gogh and the Fauves later revived this theme, but with a different conception of the picture surface and color, without the corpuscular tremor that spellbinds and vitalizes everything it touches. From 1876 to 1878 Monet painted eight or ten views of the Gare Saint-Lazare, with unprecedented effects of sun, smoke and steam; at least seven of these canvases figured in the third group exhibition in 1877. A revolutionary technical achievement on a pre-eminently modern theme, they constitute the first of the "series" of pictures of which Monet was to paint so many in later years, and in which the true motif was always light and its infinite variations.

Auguste Renoir (1841-1919).

The Box at the Theater, 1874. (31½ × 25⅛″) Courtauld Institute of Art, London.

Paradise of Renoir

THE Impressionists struggled for years against poverty and the hostility of public and critics alike. Yet no painting so much as theirs breathes sunny optimism, humanity and confidence in people and things, no painting better incarnates the pleasures of life and generous, democratic aspirations. Renoir's work in particular is a hymn to joy, a re-creation of the earthly paradise. As with Giorgione, the nostalgic myth of the golden age comes alive under his brush, and through his ingenuously pagan eyes we see it as he saw it, a contemporary reality. His ability to enjoy life to the full and express his enjoyment in paint-ing is probably unexampled in the history of art, and illustrates both the simplicity and the vitality of his nature. He shared the cult of light to which Monet in the end completely surrendered, but with Renoir it was accompanied by an equally strong love of form. Asso-ciating form and light, saturating figures in the full radiance of sunlight, and stepping up colors to their highest pitch, he brought Impressionism to a rapturous conclusion.

Son of a small tailor, Pierre-Auguste Renoir was born at Limoges, the great French center of porcelain manufacture and enameling, on February 15, 1841. In 1845 the family moved to Paris. Gounod, his music teacher at school, is said to have tried to orient him towards music, for which he showed considerable aptitude. Renoir did not follow this path, but his painting is musical through and through, often bringing to mind Haydn or Mozart. His parents apprenticed him at thirteen to a porcelain painter. Here he acquired a respect for tradition and sound craftsmanship, and acquired too his lifelong taste for fluid, limpid colors played off one against another. He drew from the antique in the Louvre and in strolling through the streets of Paris discovered the nymphs of the Fontaine des Innocents, carved by Jean Goujon, the purest French offshoot of Greek art and the source of his lifelong love of the softly rounded forms of the female body. For a time he earned a living painting fans, copying the *scènes galantes* of Watteau, Lancret, Boucher, Fragonard and the eighteenth-century painters of whom he was always particularly fond, and of whom in many ways he was the heir and continuator. Next he painted blinds intended to do duty as stained-glass windows for missionary preachers. Finally, in the autumn of 1862, having saved a small sum of money, he enrolled in Gleyre's studio, where he met Monet, Bazille and Sisley. Meanwhile he continued to pay regular visits to the Louvre, often accompanied by Fantin-Latour. His views on museum art were the very reverse of Monet's. "A painter has got to move with the times. But it's in the museums that one acquires a taste for painting which nature alone can never give you. It isn't a pretty view that makes one want to be a painter, it's a picture."

Renoir is thought to have destroyed a great many of the pictures he painted before 1866. Two notable early works remain, however, both dated 1864: a flower piece, *Arum and Hothouse Plants* (Reinhart Collection, Winterthur), and the portrait of a little girl, *Mademoiselle Romaine Lancaux* (Cleveland). These already reveal his flair for graceful decorative effects and his iridescent colors. About this time he made the acquaintance of Diaz, who encouraged him and urged him to use brighter colors. He worked in Fontainebleau Forest but did not follow his friends to the Normandy beaches. The most ambitious composition of his early period, *The Inn of Mother Anthony* (1866, Stockholm), an evocation of the free and easy Bohemian life of the art colony at Barbizon in those days, testifies to the strong influence of Courbet, equally evident in his *Diana* (Washington), which was refused at the 1867 Salon. Accepted and admired at the 1868 Salon, *Lise with a Sunshade* (1867, Essen) is a study of light filtering through leafage. Instead of treating the figure in flat colors and reducing it to a silhouette, as Monet was doing (following in Manet's footsteps), Renoir preserved the well-rounded volumes, handled lightly in vaporous, well-blended colors. Faintly suggestive, despite its dark color scheme, of the great nudes of his last years, the *Bather with a Dog* (1870, São Paulo) is an attempt to combine the warm appeal of real life with the stylized pose of the Cnidian Aphrodite. Renoir also painted some portraits: *Bazille at his Easel* (1867, Louvre), showing his friend in informal attire, hard at work in his studio, and *Sisley and his Wife* (1868, Cologne), seen against a green background of lawn and leafage, almost like a Courbet with a touch of Watteau. In addition to a few views of Paris, he painted some ice-skating scenes in the Bois de Boulogne (1868, Baron von Hirsch Collection, Basel), one of his rare attempts to render winter effects. "Perhaps the only great painter who never painted a sad picture," observed Octave Mirbeau, and in fact Renoir hated winter when, as he said, "nature went into mourning," and took no interest in the snow effects that so much delighted Monet and Sisley. In the summer of 1869 he joined Monet at La Grenouillère, where he rejoiced as much in the glittering play of light on the river as he did in the colorful crowds of holiday-makers who gathered there, and whom he interpreted with an almost Baroque exuberance.

On the outbreak of war in 1870 he was called up and stationed first at Bordeaux, then at Tarbes. When the war ended, he returned to Paris and divided his time between his lodgings in the Rue du Dragon and his mother's home at Louveciennes. In 1871 he worked at Louveciennes and Bougival with Sisley. In 1872 he executed some sunny views of Paris and the increasing animation of the streets, for example the *Pont-Neuf* (Marshall Field Collection, New York). In 1873, with Durand-Ruel now buying his pictures, he moved into a large studio in Montmartre and laughingly declared that he had "arrived." And it was true in the sense that he had fully assimilated the influences he had undergone—the influence of Courbet in the sensuality of his volumes, of Manet in the arrangement of the picture and the modernity of his themes, of Diaz and Delacroix in his handling of color, of Monet in his approach and vision, of the eighteenth-century French masters in the spirit and craftsmanship of his work. Again he joined Monet, this time at Argenteuil, and with him painted *The Duck Pond* (1873, Emery Reeves Collection, New York) and *The Seine at Argenteuil* (1873-1874, Portland Art Museum). While Monet was painting his own garden with its beds of full-blown flowers, Renoir stood a little way off and painted his friend standing at his easel, his brush in his outstretched hand, his eye darting a glance at the motif, certainly one of the most striking pictures we have of an artist at work (1873, Mrs Josiah Titzell Collection, Georgetown, Conn.). His *Portrait of Madame Monet on a Divan* (c. 1874, Washington), taken by surprise as she lifts her eyes from a book, has all the distinction and vivacity of a sketch by Manet. The whole canvas is handled as lightly and deftly as a watercolor. "When I was a beginner," he remarked late in life, "I put on my green and yellow very thickly, in the belief that I was getting stronger values. Then one day I noticed that with a light scumble Rubens outdid all my impasto." The half-length *Portrait of Monet* (1875, Louvre), seen in close-up, is like a tribute of admiration and friendship for the intrepid leader of the Impressionists, who by his selfless example spurred on all his friends. "Without him," confessed Renoir, "I would have given up."

When the Impressionists held their first group exhibition in the spring of 1874, in Nadar's studios, Renoir supervised the work of the hanging committee, the walls on which the pictures were hung being draped with red-brown cloth. He himself exhibited six paintings, including two gems, *The Dancer* (Washington), an adolescent girl gracefully poised in a color scheme of pearly greys tinged with blue and pink, and *The Box at the Theater* (Courtauld Institute, London), generally held to be Renoir's masterpiece, and a work fraught with all the rather showy splendor implied by such a term. Yet the easy naturalness of the composition goes far to absorb and chasten its brilliance. The cardinal features of the color scheme and layout have often been analysed: the well-defined lozenge pattern formed by the two figures, the man discreetly leaning back to give full prominence to the dazzling beauty and finery of his companion, the contrasting rhythms of the diagonals, the gradations and transitions of tones between light and shade. Brought together here, not as a demonstration of skill but casually, almost instinctively, are superb details which Renoir admired in some of the world's finest paintings: the diamond necklaces of Goya's portraits, the rose in the hair of one of the figures in Delacroix's *Algerian Women*, the little pink ribbon in Velazquez' *Portrait of the Infanta Margarita*. But the most amazing feature of this picture, painted at the very time when Impressionism was at its brightest and most colorful, is Renoir's masterly use of black, flowing here unchecked, this way and that, in the broad stripes of the woman's gown and casting dark shadows over the man's shirt-front. The contemporary *Portrait of Madame Hartmann* (1874, Louvre), full-length and life-size, is again built up around black, which Renoir declared to be the queen of colors. The face and the dainty hand hanging down against the dress emerge from the somber depths of satin with—it has been said—the strange, appealing whiteness of winter roses. After making the acquaintance, in 1876, of the publisher Charpentier, whose wife presided over one of the most brilliant salons in Paris, he embarked on a whole series of portraits of women, notably *Madame Henriot* (c. 1876, Dr and Mrs David M. Levy Collection, New York), *Jeanne Samary* (1877, Moscow) and *Madame Georges Charpentier* (c. 1876-1877, Louvre). Uninhibited by social prejudice of any kind, he approached society women in all their luxurious finery with the same simplicity as he approached the shop-girls whom he invited to pose for him, for all in his hands were molded into a new type of feminine beauty invented by his poetic imagination. "Renoir," declared Cézanne, not without a shade of envy, "has painted the woman of Paris," from the working girl of the suburbs to the opulent woman of fashion, and Proust himself fell under the spell and wrote nostalgically of "women passing in the street, women different from those of the past, for they are Renoirs, the very Renoirs in whom, not long ago, we failed to recognize real women."

Even more varied than Monet's, Renoir's brushwork records the most fleeting gleams and evanescent effects of light. After 1875 his assimilation of the impressionist style enabled him to treat figures with the same freedom as landscapes and to achieve a fusion between them. "I struggle with my figures until they make one with their landscape background." In this he was equally successful in both his nudes and his genre pictures. Anna, a professional model whose "skin does not repulse light," posed both for the *Bust of a Woman in Sunlight* (c. 1875-1876, Louvre) and the splendid *Nude in an Interior* (1876, Moscow), whose radiant harmony of forms and colors can stand comparison with the finest Titians. In 1876 Renoir worked in the mornings on *The Swing* (Louvre) in the garden behind his studio in the Rue Cortot, and in the afternoons on *Le Moulin de la Galette* (Louvre), having the large canvas carried out each day to the grounds of the Moulin. In the latter the unity of lighting and atmosphere is complete, being achieved not by the specifically impressionist technique of clotted or flickering brush-strokes, which he was then using in his open-air landscapes, but by means of the smoothly blended colors laid on in thin successive layers which he was so adept at handling, and which suggest masses by enveloping them in a luminous halo. His colors melt into each other like drifting clouds and leave behind them, all over the picture surface, tinted pools of light filtering through the leafage. Georges Rivière has given a detailed account of the execution of this painting, including even the names of the people figuring in it. He realized at once its

Auguste Renoir (1841-1919).
Le Moulin de la Galette, 1876. (51¼ × 69″) Louvre, Paris.

artistic and historical value, describing it as "a page of history, a document of Parisian life, and strictly accurate." For here Renoir immortalized the spirit of youth as he saw it embodied in the happy, carefree couples dancing under the trees, in the days when Montmartre was still a straggling village dotted with windmills on the outskirts of Paris, and so perfect is the illusion he gives us of that scene of long ago that one almost listens for the strains of the music and the shuffling of the dancers' feet. "To paint in joyful colors works from which everything literary was carefully banished"—such was his ambition. Despite the inexhaustible fascination of details, the fragments of still lifes, the delicate features of pretty girls, the aerial lightness and variety of the setting, no anecdotal element breaks the spell cast by the light and movement of the whole. All the figures were painted from actual models, but while the men are fairly well differentiated, the women, varied only in their garments, all partake of the same ideal type of womanhood. The figures of the dancers, deliberately elongated, and the slender shafts of the lamp-posts create a network of verticals within the rippling succession of overlapping curves engendered by the rhythm of the dance. The fading of the lakes mixed with white, which Renoir himself noticed towards the end of his life, has accentuated the blue dominant of the canvas, whose original coloring was somewhat warmer in tone. A contemporary picture, the *Woman Reading* (Louvre), treated in another technique, in a phosphorescent impasto thinned out here and there, without any glazing, shows Renoir's sumptuous palette intact—a palette whose evolution goes from the cold harmonies of his early work, blues and

Auguste Renoir (1841-1919).

Place Clichy, about 1880. (24¾ × 21¼″) Butler Collection, Halstead, Essex.

pinks, blues and violet, to the glowing reds of the last years at Cagnes. When first produced, the *Moulin de la Galette* was written off as "unsaleable" by all who saw it. It was finally purchased by Renoir's friend Caillebotte, who bequeathed it to the Louvre. The sketch (now in the Whitney Museum, New York) was bought by that most modest and discriminating of collectors, Victor Chocquet, whose portrait Renoir and Cézanne made at the same time. Renoir's natural gifts and his wonderful skill in composition, in which he so well combined invention and tradition, are seen at their best in his masterpieces of the late seventies, *Confiding* (1878, Reinhart Collection, Winterthur), *On the Terrace* (1879, Chicago), *The End of the Meal* (1879, Frankfort) and the *Oarsmen at Chatou* (1879, Washington). In the summer of 1881, after an excursion to Algeria and just before a trip to Italy that was to mark a turning point in his evolution, he finished the *Luncheon of the Boating Party* (Phillips Collection, Washington), a transposition in popular and modern terms of the princely feasts of Veronese, and the glorious conclusion of his impressionist period. On the sunny terrace of a *guinguette* on the banks of the Seine, he brought together for the last time the Bohemian friends of his youth and his favorite models, including his wife-to-be, Aline Charigot. In a small canvas painted shortly before, *Place Clichy* (c. 1880, Butler Collection, Halstead, Essex), the head and shoulders of a pretty girl loom up in the immediate foreground, cutting across a view of the hurrying crowds of the open street, with a horse-drawn omnibus in the background—an authentic glimpse of nineteenth-century Paris. The off-center composition, with the street receding at an angle, brings to mind Degas, though the spirit of the picture is altogether different.

Edgar Degas (1834-1917).

Café-Concert at "Les Ambassadeurs," 1876-1877. (14¼ × 10½″) Pastel on Monotype. Musée des Beaux-Arts, Lyons.

Complexity of Degas

RENOIR's love of painting was happily wedded to a genial love of life. Degas, misanthropic by nature and a confirmed introvert, held that the painter should devote himself exclusively to his vocation. "There's love and there's the job to do, and we have only one heart." And since one cannot serve two masters, he opted for solitude and work, shut himself up in his studio, and concealed his sensitivity, his rankling unrest, under a mask of aloofness and disdain. The touching letter he wrote, on October 26, 1890, to his old friend Evariste de Valernes, reveals, if with studied reticence, that he was acutely conscious of this inner conflict and dissatisfaction with himself. "I was, or seemed to be, surly with everybody. I had a sort of urge to be brutal, due to my unsureness of myself and my bad temper. I felt so ill made, so ill equipped, so ineffectual, and yet it seemed to me that my approach to art was the right one. I nursed a grievance against everyone and against myself. I beg you to forgive me if sometimes, because of this confounded art of mine, I have wounded your lofty, so wonderfully understanding mind, even perhaps your heart as well."

Born in Paris on July 19, 1834, Edgar Degas was the eldest son of a banker with Italian connections and a Creole lady who died when he was thirteen. He was educated at the Lycée Louis-le-Grand, where he struck up a friendship with Henri Rouart. A highly cultivated man, with a keen interest in art and music and a wide circle of friends who shared his tastes, Degas's father took him at an early age to the Louvre and made him acquainted while still in his teens with the leading collectors and connoisseurs in Paris: Lacaze, Marcille, Soutzo (who taught him etching) and Valpinçon, owner of the large *Odalisque* and a fervent admirer of Ingres. Thus his initiation into the world of art took place under the best conditions. In 1852 he converted a spare room in his father's apartment in the Rue Mondovi into a studio, overlooking the Place de la Concorde and the Tuileries. In the following year he enrolled in the classes of the painter F. J. Barrias, at the same time studying and copying the prints by Dürer, Mantegna, Rembrandt and Goya in the Cabinet des Estampes, where Achille Devéria was then curator. In 1854 he was admitted to the studio of a disciple of Ingres, Louis Lamothe, who initiated him into the cult of the master (shortly after, through Valpinçon, he made Ingres' acquaintance) and had him enrolled in 1855 in the Ecole des Beaux-Arts. But Degas cut short his academic training and declined to compete for the Prix de Rome; he preferred to go directly to the classical sources. Between 1854 and 1859 he made regular trips to Italy, staying at Naples with his grandfather and at Florence with his uncle Baron Bellelli, while in Rome he frequented the art circle of the Villa Medici. He also visited Assisi, Perugia, Viterbo,

and Orvieto where, in the cathedral, he copied the nudes in Signorelli's *Last Judgment*. His travel diaries, which have much to tell us of his youthful tastes and temperament, close with the following entry: "I shall go back and join in the Paris movement—who knows what will come of it? But I shall always be an *honnête homme.*"

In April 1859 he settled into a studio of his own in the Rue Madame, where he began by making portraits and history paintings. His discovery of Japanese prints, his friendship with Manet and about the same time with Edmond Duranty, novelist and art critic, a strong advocate of realism in painting, with whom he had many discussions on aesthetic problems, took effect and he now resolved to concentrate on the study and expression of contemporary life. He played an active part in the famous evening gatherings at the Café Guerbois, where Manet, surrounded by the new generation of Impressionists, was the presiding spirit. In one of Duranty's novels, purporting to be an objective description of the Paris art world in the sixties, the writer mentions Degas by name and describes him as "an artist of most unusual intelligence, greatly preoccupied with ideas—which makes him seem an oddity to many of his brother artists." His culture, his scathing retorts, his blunt sincerity and disinterestedness, the fundamental "honesty" he spoke of in his diary, soon ranked him as an outstanding, somewhat formidable personality.

In the Franco-Prussian War of 1870 he was called up and served in the artillery, where his captain proved to be his school friend Henri Rouart, of whom he had lost sight for years, a brilliant scientist and inventor and one of the first connoisseurs of the day; this was the beginning of a lifelong friendship. It was about this time that his eyesight was affected by a chill and began to give him serious cause for worry. In October 1872, desiring to escape from the depressing atmosphere of Paris after the defeat and needing a change of air, he sailed for New Orleans, where one of his uncles and his two brothers had a cotton factory, and he remained in the United States until the following spring. Back in Paris in April 1873 he set up house in the Rue Blanche, in the Montmartre district, where he was to reside for the rest of his life. He was now definitely converted to bright colors and the modern way of seeing. Though both his temperament and his views on art were far removed from those of the Impressionists, he (unlike Manet) championed their cause with generous enthusiasm and like Pissarro, whose moral rectitude he much admired, spared no pains in helping to promote and organize the successive impressionist exhibitions of the years 1874-1886. In 1877 he moved to the Rue Frochot and sometimes was to be seen at the Café de la Nouvelle Athènes, where the groups of painters and writers, who had now deserted the Guerbois, were in the habit of meeting. But, as his eyes began to fail him, Degas was more and more cut off from the outside world. He gave up oil painting and turned to pastels, with which he obtained some striking effects. He tried his hand at etching, drypoint and monotypes, took to modeling, and continually experimented with new forms and techniques in dealing with the themes in which he specialized in later life: dancers and women washing and dressing. Though it always cost him an effort to leave off work, he made a few brief journeys in Spain and Switzerland, some excursions in Burgundy and the South of France, and in 1896, with his friend, the sculptor Bartholomé, visited the Ingres Museum at Montauban. The Rouarts and the Halévys (whose weekly dinners in Paris he enlivened with his wit) were among his few intimates and he sometimes joined them on their summer holidays.

His last years were saddened by almost total blindness and the impossibility of keeping up his life's sole interest. "Everything's tiresome to a blind man who wants to believe he sees." The death of his old friend Henri Rouart in 1912 was a terrible blow to Degas, and to make things worse he was turned out of the house in the Rue Victor Massé where he had lived for twenty years, and which was now pulled down. He moved to a near-by apartment in the Boulevard de Clichy, found for him by one of his former models, Suzanne Valadon, who had now taken up painting, but he never succeeded in feeling at home in it. The outbreak of war

in 1914 depressed him still more, and he took to roaming the streets of Paris, at the constant risk of being run over, "our old blind Homer of painting," as one who knew him then described him, or a King Lear exiled from his secret kingdom. He died on September 27, 1917.

Degas's personality coupled with his undoubted genius inspired a sort of awe in all who met him. "One feels respect, an absolute respect for Degas," Odilon Redon once remarked. Though not inclined to moralizing and chary of his praises, Gauguin too spoke highly of him: "In the man himself as in his art, everything's exemplary." And finally Pissarro, a shrewd, if generous observer of his contemporaries, stated in a letter to his son Lucien (May 9, 1883) that Degas was "unquestionably the greatest artist of our time." Assuredly the most complex, both in his aims and in his achievements, so much so that definitions of his art, however just, tend to contain a touch of paradox: "a cold fever" (Huysmans), "ruthless logic" (Elie Faure), "realistic fiction" (René Huyghe), "visionary analysis" (Henri Focillon).

The formative period of his career spanned the years from 1854 to 1859. The dazzling virtuosity of a Manet did not come naturally to Degas, and, like Cézanne and subsequently Matisse, he had to "work out his own salvation" stage by arduous stage. "No art," he once confessed, "is less spontaneous than mine. Everything I do is the outcome of long reflection and my study of the great masters." His brief experience of the Ecole des Beaux-Arts convinced him that the official teachers were incapable of transmitting the true tradition; this could only be acquired by dint of personal efforts and by direct acquaintance with the masterpieces of the past. He made many copies in the Louvre and the Italian museums of works of very varied types, "trying," as he put it, "to combine the spirit and loving care of Mantegna with the verve and colors of Veronese." As for the moderns, his passion for Ingres was soon coupled with an equal admiration of Delacroix. The problem he set himself to solve was that of technically reconciling—without sacrificing any of the basic principles of art—the demands of a thoroughly classical culture with a keen sense of actuality. This is conveyed by an entry in one of the early notebooks: "Ah Giotto, let me see Paris, and you, Paris, let me see Giotto!"

He put his abilities to the test in a large group portrait, *The Bellelli Family* (Louvre), a wonderfully successful work, despite a touch of formalism, and a series of five history paintings made between 1860 and 1865: *Young Spartan Girls challenging the Boys* (National Gallery, London), *Alexander and Bucephalus* (Hänggi Collection, Basel), *Semiramis building a City* (Louvre), *Jephthah's Daughter* (Smith College Museum of Art, Northampton, Mass.), and the *Misfortunes of the Town of Orleans* (Louvre). Too stiff and incoherent to be wholly satisfactory, these works, which might be described as brilliant failures, are none the less extremely interesting. While singularly pleasing to the eye, if regarded individually, the figures (based on admirable preliminary studies in the artist's sketchbooks) fail to harmonize among themselves and, what is more, betray a concern for literal veracity out of key with the idealist conventions purporting to govern the ensemble.

In 1865 Degas realized that this anachronistic genre was a blind alley and abandoned it for good in favor of an unqualified allegiance to the contemporary scene. The years 1865-1872 witnessed the creation of his personal style and his adherence to the revolutionary movement launched by Manet and based on a methodical investigation of what Baudelaire called "modernity." At this time Manet himself followed the lead of Degas in some respects, notably as regards their common predilection for themes connected with horse racing. This was no longer, as it had been with Géricault, due solely to the beauty of the horse; Manet and Degas were equally interested in the fashionable crowds attending the races—survivals of the age of aristocracy—for which there was a great vogue under the Second Empire. Each registered and suggested in his own way effects of headlong speed and light; Manet with a spontaneous uprush of composite patches alternating in bright and dark zones, Degas by a multiplication of expressive lines and planes skillfully interwoven.

Edgar Degas (1834-1917).
The Rehearsal, 1877. (23 × 33″) The Burrell Collection, Glasgow Art Gallery and Museum.

Pictures of the races and a few beach scenes dating to 1869 were Degas's only ventures into open-air painting. Impervious alike to the picturesque life of the city streets and the natural beauties of landscape ("the air we find in the Old Masters' pictures is not the air we breathe"), he was interested primarily in human beings and aimed at rendering them more objectively, more truthfully, than any of his predecessors. Moralist and psychologist in the best French tradition, he painted some fifty portraits (none of them to order) between 1865 and 1870, showing his sitters in appropriate settings and catching them at unguarded moments. "The thing is to make portraits of people in typical, unconstrained attitudes and above all to give their faces the same range of expression as one gives their bodies." Thus his character studies are interior scenes as well, in which atmospheric ambience is enhanced by novel light effects. "I must put in lots of work on effects of lamplight, candlelight, etc. The point is, not always to show the source of light, but the effect of light. This branch of art may well develop enormously in our time—so how can one disregard it?" Among his most successful works in this field were the *Woman with Chrysanthemums* (1865, Metropolitan Museum, New York), the *Portrait of a Young Woman* (1867, Louvre) and *Madame Camus* (1870, National Gallery, Washington). Meanwhile his friend Désiré Dihau, bassoonist in the Opera orchestra, initiated him into the milieu of the ballet and theater life, and he embarked on "a series of studies of musical instruments and of musicians—their attitudes, for instance the way the violinist twists his hand, arm and neck, the way the cheeks of the bassoon and oboe players are alternately puffed out and retracted, and so on." We see all the performers in action, differentiated and convergent, in the *Orchestra at the Paris Opera* (c. 1868-1869, Louvre). Here, greatly

daring, the artist has confronted, for the first time, two totally different worlds: that of the musicians in the penumbra of the orchestra pit and that of the pink and white corps de ballet brilliantly illuminated by the footlights.

In April 1873, the year that marked a turning point in Impressionism, Degas returned from his six months' stay in New Orleans. The *Cotton Office* (Pau), with its traditional linear realism, brought to a close the first phase of his artistic evolution. He had been enraptured by the Louisiana countryside and the people he saw there. "Here everything delights me," he wrote to his friend, the painter Lorens Frölich (November 27, 1872), "everything I see holds my eye. I'm particularly delighted by the Negresses (of various shades) holding little Whites—so white!—in their arms." But there is nothing exotic about the picture; on the contrary, it is perfectly matter of fact, showing buyers and sellers fingering samples in a large airy office. "One mustn't," he explained, "practise indiscriminately the art of Paris and that of Louisiana," and it was to "the art of Paris" that he intended to devote himself, though without any pandering to the Salon and its effete academicism. On his return, his studies of dancers performing or resting, seen from various angles and in different lights, revealed a

Edgar Degas (1834-1917).
At the Races (Jockeys beside a Carriage), 1877-1880. (26 × 32¼″) Louvre, Paris.

change of manner and his conversion to the new *peinture claire*. He was too keen a draughts-man not to recognize the primordial value of line, but he ceased to regard this value as absolute, and gave more and more attention to color, light and movement.

The years 1873-1886 witnessed the full flowering of his art, in which amazing mastery was allied with a diversity of technical means. During this period he actively championed the cause of the Impressionists, though without falling in line with the movement, and he made no secret of his disapproval of the practice then coming into vogue of painting in the open air. He was equally unmoved by the revival of interest in the still life and he differed from his fellow artists as much in his choice of subjects as in the spirit of his works. For while the others were all for scenes of nature and a sensuous, frankly optimistic type of painting, he took city life and human beings as his subjects and treated them with almost brutal objectivity. He did not share Monet's and Renoir's rather sentimental interest in the streets of Paris, and the glittering façade of the great city (then undergoing a total transformation) left him indifferent. It was on the artificial life going on indoors, behind the scenes, that he fixed his keenly scrutinizing gaze, anticipating Lautrec. When Edmond de Goncourt visited Degas in February 1874, he was delighted to find him concentrating on the most characteristic types of contemporary humanity (as the Goncourts themselves and the other realistic novelists were doing in their writings), and he noted admiringly in the famous *Journal*: "I have yet to see anyone who, in reproducing modern life, better captures the *soul* of that life."

Degas's psychological acumen was no less remarkable than his searching power of visual analysis. With his zest for reality and love of movement—"If the leaves of trees never moved, how sad the trees would be, and we too!" he said one day to his friend Rouart—and gifted with the "mimetic sensibility" that Paul Valéry attributes in part to his Neapolitan blood, he investigated indefatigably all the ways and by-ways of Parisian life. There was scarcely a sphere of activity to which he did not try to give expression (often for the first time); not one significant gesture that he did not seek to render in all its immediacy. His sketchbooks contain any number of drawings of the most surprising kinds, proving how thorough was his prepara-tory work before embarking on a picture. He was particularly attracted by people having a definite "job" and engaged in it—musicians, laundresses, women ironing, milliners, singers, acrobats—whose characteristic attitudes and mannerisms he recorded with loving care.

As time went on he became more and more engrossed in the strange enchantments of the dance, with its mingling of exquisite refinement and popular appeal, of aerial lightness and rigorous precision. It provided an inexhaustible supply of graceful movements and contortions, of paradoxes and contrasts, and in this "world of exact forces and studied illu-sions" (Valéry), where miracles were born of an incessant vigilance, he found a living image of his own art, in which instinct at its most impulsive was allied with the strictest mental discipline. "One has to do the same subject a hundred times over," he wrote. "Nothing in art, not even movement, must seem accidental." Watching from above or from one side the mazy gyrations of the gaily spangled dancers weaving an endless skein of colorful arabesques in the full glare of the footlights, he was fascinated by a scene that corresponded so exactly to the controlled complexity he aimed at in his art. "A picture," he once said, "is an original combi-nation of lines and tones, each of which pulls its weight." The ballet breaks up movement into its component parts while rendering it in its entirety, and both space and the performers are subjected to systematic flexions that enhance the play of light, flooding the air with broken gleams. "After making portraits seen from above," we read in his notebooks, "I'll make them from below. Seated beside a woman and looking up at her, I shall see her face haloed by the crystals of the hanging lamp." Elsewhere he writes: "The thing is to study a figure, an object, no matter what, from all perspective viewpoints. A mirror can be used for this." The circus, theaters, cafés and concerts with their odd perspective effects and artificial lighting gave endless opportunities for experiments on these lines. Such little masterpieces in a technique

Edgar Degas (1834-1917).

Woman Ironing seen against the Light, 1882. Oils thinned with Turpentine. (31⅞ × 25½″) Private Collection, Paris.

of which Degas alone had the secret, as *Women on a Café Terrace* (1877, Louvre) and the famous *Café-Concert at "Les Ambassadeurs"* (1876-1877, Lyons), convey far better than any realistic novel the atmosphere of Paris in the 1870s with its picturesque night life, and at the same time conjure up a fantastic world.

After the re-opening in 1854 of the Japanese market, which had been closed to the outside world for centuries, the first Japanese prints had found their way to Europe in the form of wrapping paper. Like his contemporaries, Degas benefited by the study of these prints, as also by developments in the art of photography. One of his friends was the engraver Félix Bracquemond, who discovered Hokusai in 1856 and showed Degas a set of his color prints. Degas was one of the first to frequent the famous shop, "La Porte Chinoise," opened by Madame Soye in 1862 under the arcades of the Rue de Rivoli, where Japanese prints were on sale. Thanks largely to the eulogies of distinguished writers and to the success of the Oriental sections at the World's Fairs of 1867 and 1878, there developed a widespread vogue in Paris for all things Japanese. Artists decorated their studios with fans and had their models pose in kimonos. Of this rather superficial *japonaiserie*, which may be regarded as a prolongation of the romantic taste for exotic themes and styles, Whistler was the most accomplished representative. But there were other artists who looked deeper and found suggestions in Japanese art which each interpreted on his own lines. Thus Monet achieved a new limpidity and Manet exploited the tensions set up by contrasting dark and light areas, while Degas drew inspiration from the deliberate asymmetry of Japanese surface patterning, its bold foreshortenings and off-center layout, with figures cut short on the margins or thrust forward, as if about to plunge into the spectator's space. But, like all truly pregnant influences, Japanese art served less as a direct source than as a catalyser of implicit tendencies. Another influence was the camera's vision. Himself an amateur photographer, Degas learnt from it the possibilities of "close-ups," vertical bird's-eye "shots," disintegrations of space and perspective, and effects of side-lighting and back-lighting. Several of the photographs from which he got ideas for his portraits and compositions have been discovered and we know that he studied the snapshots by Major Muybridge, published in 1881, which registered the exact movements of a galloping horse. But, far from inciting him to an unelastic, mechanized vision, the camera served to fortify his style and activate his approach to visual reality, at once analytic and imaginative.

From 1880 on, he gradually gave up oil paints for pastels which, having greater flexibility and allowing subsequent retouchings, were better suited to his exacting temperament and ingrained perfectionism. By employing ingenious procedures devised by himself and a special fixative, he completely renovated pastel technique, giving it a new density and richness. He combined pastel colors with gouache, tempera, and oils thinned with turpentine and used them to touch up his famous monotypes. Sometimes, too, instead of applying them dry, in the normal way, he moistened his pastel sticks with steam—a completely new departure. "Thus," as Denis Rouart observes in his valuable study of Degas's techniques, "by soaking it with water he converted the powdery color into a semi-liquid paste which he worked over with a brush having fairly hard bristles. Elsewhere, when the coat of pastel was thin, by moistening it he obtained a wash which he spread with an ordinary painter's brush." This enabled him to vary the surface of the picture in accordance with the elements represented, for example the skin of a ballerina, her costume, the setting, and differences of lighting.

Two new themes make their appearance in this period: that of milliners, on which Degas rang the changes to such wonderful effect in the years 1882-1883, and that of women in the attitudes of their toilet, which became almost an obsession with him in his last phase. The scenes of milliners and their customers trying on hats and gazing at their reflected selves provided endless opportunities for variations of layout, color schemes, gestures and facial expressions. At the eighth and last group exhibition of the Impressionists (1886) he showed "a series of nudes of women bathing, washing, combing their hair or having it combed."

Though many disapproved of the "vulgarity" of the subject, these pictures won admiration for the amazing skill of their technique and their effects of colors seen against the light. Degas ranks beside Rodin as the true inventor of the modern nude, set free from studio conventions and mythological idealization, and depicted with unflinching objectivity and probity, without any concession to the erotic or picturesque appeal commonly associated with the theme. As he once told George Moore, the woman in question is just a human animal at her ablutions, like a cat licking herself. Hitherto the nude had always been given poses that implied a public. But Degas's women were simple, decent persons thinking of nothing except their physical occupation of the moment. Huysmans' angry denunciations of his "misogyny" seem to us singularly out of date; these masterpieces imbued with a truly classical serenity bring, rather, to our minds the words of Baudelaire (in *La Fanfarlo*): "He loved the human body for what it is: material harmony, beautiful architecture, with movement added." In the plenitude and density of their forms—despite their realistic contortions and modernity of spirit—his pictures of women at their toilet retrieve the rhythm of classical antiquity. Renoir was well aware of this. "There lingers in my mind's eye," he said, "a nude by Degas, a charcoal sketch. That was the only thing one saw in the room. It was like a fragment of the Parthenon."

Paul Cézanne (1839-1906).
Self-Portrait, about 1877. (24 × 18½″) The Phillips Collection, Washington, D.C.

Cézanne and the Position in 1884

CÉZANNE belongs to the generation of the impressionist painters, whose struggle for recognition and whose essential convictions he shared. But his work cannot be envisaged on the same plane as theirs, nor can his initial phase (which falls within the scope of this book) be fully studied without a comprehensive analysis of his evolution as a whole, which forms part of a much broader context. In fanatically carrying to its ultimate conclusion the specific intention of the painters of his time (i.e. the representation of the visible world), Cézanne in the end towered above his contemporaries and created an art of all time and no time. Nearer to Poussin or Giotto than to the Impressionists, he left behind him, in an indivisible body of work, the leavening influences that went to shape twentieth-century art, whose orientation, however, Cézanne himself would no doubt have sternly disapproved of.

He was well aware of the unfathomable mystery underlying his painting. On October 15, 1906—the very day when, having sworn to die brush in hand, he collapsed while painting in the open fields, under the downpour of a sudden storm—he wrote, in his last letter to his son, what has come down to us as his last message, impugning in effect any theoretical interpretation of his work. He was convinced of his inscrutability: "Sensations being my chief concern, I believe I'm impenetrable." By "sensations," which term designates the passive visual receptivity basic to Impressionism, Cézanne also meant the obscure forces at work in any creative personality, which he himself called "temperament." Each of his self-portraits —the one on the opposite page, dating from the period of his change of style, is not the most monumental but it is one of the most moving, in the surging fervor of the brushwork—brings us face to face with the inscrutable grandeur of a man who sought to "possess" himself by surrendering to the phenomena of the outside world.

A native of Aix-en-Provence, Paul Cézanne (1839-1906) links up in his early work with the "southern Baroque" illustrated by Daumier and Monticelli, whose Caravaggesque sources he reactivated and whose emotional violence he intensified. His inner conflicts and repressed sensuality, on which his letters to Zola throw light, found an outlet in dramatic dream-pictures, scenes of murder, lust and orgies, whose treatment and content prefigure modern expressionism. Cézanne is a striking confirmation of the dictum that true classicism is always based on romanticism overcome and mastered. For all the tumult and anguish of these early canvases, the handling of color and chiaroscuro and the organization of the picture surface exhibit already a power of invention, a breadth of conception and an authority of execution

Paul Cézanne (1839-1906).
The Railway Cutting, about 1870. (31½ × 50⅜″) Bayerische Staatsgemäldesammlungen, Munich.

characteristic of his later work. To the major influences of Delacroix and Courbet—assimilated with the immense range of effects each was master of—was added that of Manet in the course of the transition period of 1869-1871; Manet's influence is particularly noticeable in the *Portrait of Boyer* (Metropolitan Museum, New York) and *The Black Clock* (Niarchos Collection, Paris) in which the passionately romantic yearnings of his youth have subsided into a grave, majestic harmony. From the same period dates his first important landscape, *The Railway Cutting* (Munich), an astonishing masterpiece, which looks almost like an aftermath of Fauvism (it would have come as no surprise, one feels, to find Derain's signature on it). Its very baldness and rugged strength—and its exquisite refinements!—spring from a direct and forthright handling of the paints that even Courbet never approached. Its colors, still low in pitch, give off a strange sheen, a light quite different from Corot's, like the revelation of a primeval world untouched by man, though we see obvious signs of his presence. Beyond the strongly marked features of the terrain, whose rhythm is brought out with masterly simplicity, in volumetric masses sustained by horizontal planes, there looms up in the distance, swathed in a blue light tinged with pink, the majestic cone of the Montagne Sainte-Victoire, keynote of the artist's future work. All Cézanne, prior to Impressionism, is summed up here.

In the autumn of 1872 he settled at Pontoise, working side by side with the "humble and colossal Pissarro" (as he called him), whom he had known for ten years and venerated for his noble nature and artistic integrity. There took place the decisive conversion to which we have referred, from unrestrained subjectivism to the most intransigent objectivization. From now on his sole thought was to "penetrate what he saw in front of him," without any preconceived ideas or sentimental detours. But as he found nature "very complex" and was deter-

mined to sacrifice nothing of the integrity of his "sensations," his "realization," proving slow and laborious, assumed a character very different from that of the Impressionists, whose fundamental approach however he accepted. He also kept to the two essential elements of their technique, bright colors and the divided brushstroke, but applied them with an absolute coherence, built up his canvas with a serried succession of regular planes distinctly straining this way or that, which at once render mass and tone, organic structure and "light modulation," and, without breaking up or blurring its unity, impart rhythm to the two-dimensional picture surface. Illusionist values of atmosphere and perspective are reduced in the interests of an ordered monumentality and color saturation, the one indissolubly linked with the other. "When color is at its richest," he declared, "form is at its fullest." His romantic obsessions and sensual ranklings still show through in compositions painted as late as 1877, before being absorbed and sublimated in the grandiose architectonic theme of *Bathers*. But it was in the still life, to which he attached particular importance, that Cézanne began to gain control over himself and to discover his new principles of construction. If from 1880 to 1930 the still life came to play in European painting the same leading role that landscape played from 1830 to 1880, it is no doubt Cézanne who was responsible for this shift of emphasis, although he

Paul Cézanne (1839-1906).

Dish and Bowl with Fruit, 1879-1882. (16¾ × 21¼") Ny Carlsberg Glyptotek, Copenhagen.

Georges Seurat (1859-1891).

Bathing at Asnières, 1883-1884. (79⅛ × 118⅛") By Courtesy of the Trustees, National Gallery, London.

himself, in his own work, maintained a unique equilibrium between these two categories, for he united Poussin's genius for landscape with Chardin's genius for still life. His study of the twelve still lifes by Chardin in the Lacaze bequest, exhibited at the Louvre from 1870 on, aroused and intensified his interest in an art form lending itself better than any other to the concrete density and ordered stability by which he set so much store. The relations between planes, volumes, colors and space, and the interplay between surface and depth, go to create a mysterious and indefinable unity ensuring both the reality of the representation and the living autonomy of the picture. His choice of simple, primordial volumes answers to a new need for concentration. "In an orange, an apple, a ball, a head, there is a culminating point; and this point—despite the terrible effect of light and shade, color-producing sensations—is always the one closest to our eye. The edges of objects recede towards a center lying on our horizon." The same elementary and cohesive forms regulating space and light also enter into landscape, in which gay and fleeting vibrations give place to a grave and solemn silence. "The countryside is really amazing," he wrote in September 1879, while still working in the vicinity of Paris. "There seems to be a deeper silence. Here are sensations I can't express. Better only to experience them." After 1882 he lived almost entirely at Aix and there achieved a concord between his style and the landscape of his native Provence, and achieved it with a lofty grandeur that can only be called sublime and justifies Rilke's profound observation: "It was necessary for this painting to go beyond love."

In December 1883, while working at L'Estaque, near Marseilles, he received a visit from Monet and Renoir, who were traveling together in the South of France, each seeking a change

of air in an effort to end the crisis both were passing through simultaneously. "I find it harder and harder to produce work that satisfies me," wrote Monet to Durand-Ruel, and Renoir later confessed to Vollard: "About 1883 there occurred a kind of break in my work. I had carried Impressionism as far as I could, only to realize that I didn't really know how to paint or draw. In a word, I was in a fix." In the early eighties, just at the time of Manet's death, the inevitable crisis was upon them (affecting also Degas and Pissarro), involving not so much the breaking up of Impressionism as a "classical" enlargement of it; a new and disturbing realization had come over them of the astonishing powers Impressionism had released. In 1884, their work and that of many of the younger artists of the day being rejected almost en bloc by the jury of the official Salon, the momentous step was taken, under the chairmanship of Odilon Redon (1840-1916), of organizing an annual exhibition of independent artists, known as the Salon des Indépendants. Here, in 1884, Georges Seurat (1859-1891) exhibited his first large composition, *Bathing at Asnières* (1883-1884, National Gallery, London), which, though badly hung, attracted the attention of two unprejudiced critics, Roger Marx and Félix Fénéon, and aroused the enthusiasm of Paul Signac (1863-1935), who analysed the technique as follows: "This picture was painted in great flat strokes, swept in one on top of another and coming from a palette composed, like Delacroix's, of pure colors and earthy colors. By means of these ochres and browns the picture was deadened and appeared less brilliant than those painted by the Impressionists with a palette limited to prismatic colors. But the observance of the laws of contrasts, the methodical separation of elements (light, shade, local color, and the interaction of colors), and their proper balance and proportion gave this canvas its perfect harmony." This systematic application of impressionist brushwork and its "divisionist" technique offers the best modern example of a painted surface entirely homogeneous, organized like a mosaic and founded on an adjustable basic unit, which is at once an element of texture and an element of sensation. It exerted a decisive influence on the evolution of Van Gogh, Lautrec and Gauguin, and all subsequent colorists from Matisse to Delaunay passed through a pointillist phase before achieving a style of their own. Seurat kept to the open-air themes of leisure and relaxation favored by his predecessors, but with a significant emphasis on an industrial, urban environment, and raised them to a monumental scale in which we recognize today a modern transposition of Puvis de Chavannes and an underlying kinship with the frescoes of Piero della Francesca, copies of which he may have seen at the Ecole des Beaux-Arts. The illusion of perspective and atmospheric vibration is attenuated, as it is in Cézanne's work, and tends to become a kind of crystallization. Light no longer floats hazily in space but again clings to objects, to strangely stylized figures, and from an ephemeral dance is transmuted into a solemn architecture. The rapturous contemplation of reality takes on a magic and a poetry all the more pure for being geometrically concerted. Thus Cézanne and Seurat, by basing their work on direct sensations experienced to the full, by doing away with outlines (which after all were only a convention) and giving color its full force and radiance, achieved each in his own way a perfect unity of style and regained, by means diametrically opposed to his, the grandeur of the antique to which David aspired. Having in a sense come full circle, nineteenth-century painting ended on a note that marks both a fulfillment and a reversal of values. The obsessive confrontation between art and nature had resolved itself into what Cézanne called "a harmony parallel to nature." Impressionism had sown its seeds throughout the world and they were fast sprouting. Paris was no longer merely the center of French painting but the extraordinary focal point of world art.

Select Bibliography - General Index

List of Color Plates - Contents

Select Bibliography

GENERAL

E. Chesneau, *L'art et les artistes modernes en France*, Paris 1864. — C. Blanc, *Les artistes de mon temps*, Paris 1876. — P. Burty, *Maîtres et petits maîtres*, Paris 1877. — J. Gigoux, *Causeries sur les artistes de mon temps*, Paris 1886. — Thoré-Bürger, *Les Salons (1844-1868). Etudes de critique et d'esthétique*, Paris 1893. —P. Signac, *D'Eugène Delacroix au néo-impressionnisme*, Paris 1899. — R. Muther, *Ein Jahrhundert französischer Malerei*, Berlin 1901. — L. Dimier, *Histoire de la peinture au XIXᵉ siècle*, Paris 1914. — A. Fontainas and L. Vauxcelles, *Histoire générale de l'art français de la Révolution à nos jours*, Paris 1922. — J. Meier-Graefe, *Entwicklungsgeschichte der modernen Kunst*, 3 vols., 4th ed., Munich 1924. — T. Silvestre, *Les artistes français*, 2 vols., Paris 1926. — H. Focillon, *La peinture au XIXᵉ siècle. Le retour à l'Antique. Le Romantisme*, Paris 1927. — H. Focillon, *La peinture aux XIXᵉ et XXᵉ siècles. Du Réalisme à nos jours*, Paris 1928. — R. Schneider, *L'art français au XIXᵉ siècle. Du classicisme davidien au romantisme*, Paris 1929. — W. Friedländer, *Von David bis Delacroix*, Leipzig 1930; English edition, *David to Delacroix*, Cambridge, Mass., 1952. — E.P. Richardson, *The Way of Western Art 1776-1914*, Cambridge, Mass., 1939. — R. Escholier, *La peinture française, XIXᵉ siècle*, 2 vols., Paris 1941-1943. — L. Venturi, *Peintres modernes*, Paris 1941. — K. Scheffler, *Die grossen französischen Maler des 19. Jahrhunderts*, Munich 1942. — A. Hauser, *The Social History of Art*, London 1951. — P. Francastel, *Peinture et Société*, Lyons 1951. — M. Raynal, *The Nineteenth Century, From Goya to Gauguin*, Geneva 1951. — J.C. Sloane, *French Painting between the Past and the Present (1868-1870)*, Princeton 1951. — K. Berger, *Le style de Poussin et le XIXᵉ siècle*, Gazette des Beaux-Arts I, 1955. — P. Francastel, *La peinture française du Classicisme au Cubisme*, Paris 1955. — F. Fosca, *La peinture française au XIXᵉ siècle*, Paris 1956. — L. Hautecœur and P. Jamot, *La peinture au Musée du Louvre, Ecole française, XIXᵉ siècle*, 2 vols., Paris n.d. — P. Francastel, *Les grandes tendances de l'art européen au XIXᵉ siècle*, Cahiers d'Histoire mondiale, III, 4, 1957. — P.J. Jouve, *Tombeau de Baudelaire*, Paris 1958. — F. Novotny, *Painting and Sculpture in Europe, 1780-1880*, London 1960. — K. Clark, *Looking at Pictures*, London 1960. — W. Hofmann, *Das irdische Paradies, Kunst im Neunzehnten Jahrhundert*, Munich 1960; English edition, *The Earthly Paradise, Art in the Nineteenth Century*, New York 1961. — C. Sterling and H. Adhémar, *La Peinture au Musée du Louvre, Ecole française, XIXᵉ siècle*, 4 vols., Paris 1958-1961.

NEOCLASSICISM

L. Hautecœur, *Rome et la renaissance de l'Antiquité à la fin du XVIIIᵉ siècle*, Paris 1912. — E. Wind, *The Revolution of History Painting*, Journal of the Warburg and Courtauld Institutes, II, 1938-1939. — R. Zeitler, *Klassizismus und Utopia*, Stockholm 1954. — F.G. Pariset, *Le Néo-classicisme*, Bulletin d'Information d'Histoire de L'Art, Paris, March-April 1959.

ROMANTICISM

C. Baudelaire, *L'art romantique*, Paris 1868. — A. Chesneau, *Peintres et Statuaires romantiques*, Paris 1879. — L. Rosenthal, *La peinture romantique*, Paris 1901. — L. Hautecœur, M. Aubert etc., *Le Romantisme et l'art*, Paris 1928. — L. Rosenthal, *L'art et les artistes romantiques*, Paris 1928. — P. Colin, *Le romantisme*, Paris-Brussels 1935. — F. Antal, *Reflections on Classicism and Romanticism*, Burlington Magazine, 1935, 1936, 1940, 1941. — M.P. Boyé, *La mêlée romantique*, Paris 1946. — E.H. Gombrich, *Imagery and Art in the Romantic Period*, Burlington Magazine XCI, 1949. — L. Réau, *L'ère romantique. Les arts plastiques*, Paris 1949. — M. Brion, *Romantic Art*, London 1960. — P. Courthion, *Romanticism*, Geneva 1961.

ORIENTALISM

R. Escholier, *L'Orientalisme de Chassériau*, Gazette des Beaux-Arts, 1921. — J. Alazard, *L'Orient et la Peinture française au XIXᵉ siècle*, Paris 1930. — J. Alazard, *L'Exotisme dans la peinture française au XIXᵉ siècle*, Gazette des Beaux-Arts II, 1931.

LANDSCAPE

J.W. Mollet, *The Painters of Barbizon*, London 1890. — G. Lanoë and T. Brice, *Histoire de l'école*

française du paysage depuis Poussin jusqu'à Millet, Paris 1901. — P. DORBEC, L'art du Paysage en France, Essai sur son évolution de la fin du XVIIIe siècle à la fin du Second Empire, Paris 1925. — C. ROGER-MARX, Le paysage français de Corot à nos jours, Paris 1952. — K. CLARK, Landscape into Art, London 1949.

REALISM

C. PERRIER, Du réalisme, L'Artiste, Paris, October 1855. — M. BUCHON, Recueil de dissertations sur le réalisme, Neuchâtel 1856. — CHAMPFLEURY, Le réalisme, Paris 1857. — E. BOUVIER, La Bataille réaliste, Paris n.d. — L. ROSENTHAL, Du romantisme au réalisme, Paris 1914.

IMPRESSIONISM

E. DURANTY, La nouvelle peinture, Paris 1876, reprinted 1946. — G. RIVIÈRE, L'impressionniste, Journal d'art, Paris 1877. — T. DURET, Les peintres impressionnistes, Paris 1878. — G. GEFFROY, Histoire de l'Impressionnisme, Paris 1894. — J. LAFORGUE, Mélanges posthumes, Paris 1903. — J. MEIER-GRAEFE, Impressionisten, Munich 1907. — R. HAMANN, Der Impressionismus in Leben und Kunst, Marburg 1908. — W. WEISBACH, Impressionismus, 2 vols., Berlin 1910-1911. — P. FRANCASTEL, L'Impressionnisme, Paris 1937. — W. UHDE, Les impressionnistes, Paris 1937. — L. VENTURI, Les archives de l'Impressionnisme, 2 vols.,

Paris-New York 1939. — R. HUYGHE, L'impressionnisme et la pensée de son temps, Prométhée, February 1939. — B. DORIVAL, Les étapes de la peinture française contemporaine, Vol. I, Paris 1943. — E. SCHEYER, Far Eastern Art and French Impressionists, The Art Quarterly, Spring 1943. — J. REWALD, The History of Impressionism, New York 1946. — G. BAZIN, L'époque impressionniste, Paris 1947. — C.L. RAGGHIANTI, Impressionismo, Turin 1947. — G. BAZIN, L'époque impressionniste, Paris 1947. — J.L. VAUDOYER, Les Impressionnistes, de Manet à Cézanne, Paris 1948. — M. RAYNAL and J. LEYMARIE, History of Modern Painting, From Baudelaire to Bonnard, Geneva 1949. — R. COGNIAT, Au temps des impressionnistes, Paris 1950. — F. NOVOTNY, Die grossen französischen Impressionisten. Ihre Vorläufer und ihre Nachfolger, Vienna 1952. — O. REUTERSWALD, Impressionisterna inför Publik och Kritik, Stockholm 1952. — L. VENTURI, De Manet à Lautrec, Paris 1953. — F. NOVOTNY, Die grossen französischen Impressionisten, Vienna 1953. — J. LEYMARIE, Impressionism, 2 vols., Geneva 1955. — R.T. STOLL, Die französischen Impressionisten, Zurich 1957; French edition, Lausanne 1957. — W. BALZER, Der französische Impressionismus, Die Hauptmeister in der Malerei, Dresden 1958. — G. BAZIN, Trésors de l'impressionnisme au Louvre, Paris 1958. — M. SERULLAZ, Les peintres impressionnistes, Paris 1959. — F. MATHEY, Les impressionnistes et leur temps, Paris 1959. — R. COGNIAT, Le siècle des impressionnistes, Paris 1959.

MONOGRAPHS

Auguste: C. SAUNIER, Gazette des Beaux-Arts, Sept. 1910.

Barye: C. SAUNIER, Barye, Paris 1925. — C. O. ZIESENISS, Les aquarelles de Barye, Paris 1954.

Bazille: G. POULAIN, Bazille et ses amis, Paris 1932. — F. DAULTE, Frédéric Bazille et son temps, Geneva 1952.

Boilly: P. MARMOTTAN, Le peintre Louis Boilly (1761-1845), Paris 1913.

Boudin: G. CAHEN, Eugène Boudin, sa vie et son œuvre, Paris 1900.

Cézanne: R. FRY, Cézanne. A Study of his Development, London 1927. — G. MACK, Paul Cézanne, New York 1935. — J. REWALD, Cézanne et Zola, Paris 1936. — L. VENTURI, Cézanne, son art, son œuvre, 2 vols., Paris 1936. — J. REWALD, Cézanne, Correspondance, Paris 1937. — F. NOVOTNY, Cézanne und das Ende der wissenschaftlichen Perspektive, Vienna 1938. — R. HUYGHE, Paris 1936. — R. M. RILKE, Lettres sur Cézanne, Paris 1944. — L. GUERRY, Cézanne et l'expression de l'espace, Paris 1950. — M. SCHAPIRO, Paul Cézanne, New York 1952. — B. DORIVAL, Cézanne, Paris 1952. — G. SCHMIDT, Aquarelles de Paul Cézanne, Basel 1952. — K. BADT, Die Kunst Cézannes, Munich 1956.

Charlet: A. DAYOT, Charlet et son œuvre, Paris 1893.

Chassériau: H. MARCEL and J. LARAN, Théodore Chassériau, Paris 1911. — L. BENEDITE, Théodore Chassériau, sa vie et son œuvre, 2 vols., Paris 1931. — P. JAMOT, Théodore Chassériau, Paris 1933.

Corot: A. ROBAUT and E. MOREAU-NÉLATON, L'œuvre de Corot. Catalogue raisonné et illustré, précédé de l'histoire de Corot et de son œuvre, 4 vols., Paris 1904-1906. — J. MEIER-GRAEFE, Corot, Berlin 1930. — A. SCHOELLER and J. DIETERLE, Corot. Supplément au catalogue de l'œuvre par Moreau-Nélaton, Paris 1948. — G. BAZIN, Corot, Paris 1951.

Courbet: H. D'IDEVILLE, Gustave Courbet, Paris 1878. — E. GROS-KOST, Courbet, Souvenirs intimes, Paris 1880. — J. A. CASTAGNARY, Fragments d'un livre sur Courbet, Paris, Gazette des Beaux-Arts I, 1911, and II, 1912. — G. RIAT, Gustave Courbet, Paris 1906. — A. FONTAINAS, Courbet, Paris 1921. — J. MEIER-GRAEFE, Courbet, Munich 1921. — G. DE CHIRICO, Courbet, Rome 1925. — C. LÉGER, Courbet, Paris 1929. — P. COURTHION, Courbet, Paris 1931. — G. BOAS, Courbet and the Naturalistic Movement, Baltimore 1938. — M. SCHAPIRO, Courbet and Popular Imagery. An Essay on Realism and Naïveté, Journal of the Warburg and Courtauld Institutes, IV (1940-1941). — K. BERGER, Courbet in his Century, Gazette des Beaux-Arts II, 1943. — R. HUYGHE, G. BAZIN and H. ADHÉMAR, Courbet, l'Atelier du peintre, allégorie réelle, 1855, Paris 1944. — H. NAEF, Courbet, Bern 1947. — P. COURTHION, Courbet raconté par lui-même et par ses amis, 2 vols., Geneva 1948-1950. — G. MACK, Gustave Courbet, London 1951. — P. MacORLAN, Courbet, Paris 1951. — L. ARAGON, L'exemple de Courbet, Paris 1952. — M. ZAHAR, Gustave Courbet, Geneva, 1952.

Couture: T. COUTURE, Méthodes et entretiens d'atelier, Paris 1868. — J. J. SEZNEC, The "Romans of the Decadence" and their Historical Significance, Gazette des Beaux-Arts II, 1943.

Daubigny: L. BOURGES, Daubigny: Souvenirs et croquis, Paris 1900. — E. MOREAU-NÉLATON, Daubigny raconté par lui-même, Paris 1925.

Daumier: A. ALEXANDRE, Honoré Daumier, l'homme et l'œuvre, Paris 1888. — E. KLOSSOWSKI, Honoré Daumier, 2nd ed., Munich 1923. — A. RUMANN, Honoré Daumier, Berlin 1926. — R. ESCHOLIER, Honoré Daumier, 2nd ed., Paris 1923. — E. FUCHS, Der Maler Daumier, 2nd ed., Munich 1930. — E. BOUVY, Daumier: L'œuvre gravé du

maître, 2 vols., Paris 1933. — J. LASSAIGNE, *Daumier*, Paris 1938. — C. SCHWEICHER, *Daumier*, London 1954. — J. ADHÉMAR, *Honoré Daumier*, Paris 1954. — K. E. MAISON, *Daumier Studies*, Burlington Magazine 1954 and 1956. — N. KALITINA, *Honoré Daumier*, Moscow 1955. — G. ZILLER, *Honoré Daumier*, Dresden 1957. — J. CHERPIN, *Daumier et le théâtre*, Paris 1958.

David: R. CANTINELLI, *Jacques-Louis David, 1748-1825*, Paris 1930. — A. HUMBERT, *Louis David peintre et conventionnel*, Paris 1937, 2nd ed. 1947. — K. BERGER, *David and the Development of Géricault's Art (The Beginnings of Modern Art)*, Gazette des Beaux-Arts II, 1946. — A. MAUROIS, *J.-L. David*, Paris 1948. — D. L. DOWD, *Pageant Master of the Republic: Jacques-Louis David and the French Revolution*, Lincoln, Nebraska 1948. — J. ADHÉMAR and J. CASSOU, *Jacques David, naissance du génie d'un peintre*, Paris 1953. — L. HAUTECŒUR, *Louis David*, Paris 1954. — W. PACH, *The Heritage of J. L. David*, Gazette des Beaux-Arts I, 1955.

Decamps: A. MOREAU, *Decamps et son œuvre*, Paris 1869. — C. CLÉMENT, *Decamps*, Paris, n.d.

Degas: P. A. LEMOISNE, *Degas*, Paris 1912. — P. LAFOND, *Degas*, Paris 1918-1919. — J. MEIER-GRAEFE, *Degas*, Munich 1920. — M. GUÉRIN, *Lettres de Degas*, Paris 1931. — P. VALÉRY, *Degas, danse, dessin*, Paris 1938, New York 1948. — P. JAMOT, *Degas*, Paris 1924. — G. JEANNIOT, *Souvenirs sur Degas*, La Revue Universelle, 1933. — D. ROUART, *Degas à la recherche de sa technique*, Paris 1945. — P. A. LEMOISNE, *Degas et son œuvre*, 4 vols., Paris 1946-1949. — L. BROWSE, *Degas Dancers*, London 1949. — D. C. RICH, *Edgar-Hilaire-Germain Degas*, New York 1951. — D. COOPER, *Degas. Pastels*, Basel 1952. — F. FOSCA, *Degas*, Geneva 1954. — P. CABANNE, *Edgar Degas*, Paris 1957.

Delacroix: A. ROBAUT, *L'œuvre complet d'Eugène Delacroix* (avec commentaire de E. Chesneau), Paris 1885. — J. GUIFFREY, *Le voyage d'Eugène Delacroix au Maroc*, Paris 1909. — J. MEIER-GRAEFE, *Eugène Delacroix: Beiträge zu einer Analyse*, Munich 1913. — E. MOREAU-NÉLATON, *Delacroix raconté par lui-même*, Paris 1916. — E. DELACROIX, *Œuvres littéraires. I, Etudes esthétiques; II, Essais sur les artistes célèbres*, Paris 1923. — R. ESCHOLIER, *Delacroix: Peintre, graveur, écrivain*, La vie et l'art romantiques, 3 vols., Paris 1926-1929. — F. GYSIN, *Eugène Delacroix, Studien zu seiner künstlerischen Entwicklung*, Strasbourg 1929. — L. HOURTICQ, *Delacroix*, Paris 1930. — R. PIOT, *Les palettes de Delacroix*, Paris 1931. — R. RÉGAMEY, *Eugène Delacroix*, Paris 1931. — V. CHRISTOFFEL, *Eugène Delacroix*, Munich 1931. — L. RUDRAUF, *Eugène Delacroix et le problème du romantisme artistique*, Paris 1942. — E. DELACROIX, *Journal*, 3 vols., edited by A. Joubin, Paris 1932; new edition, Paris 1959. — A. JOUBIN, *Correspondance générale d'Eugène Delacroix*, 5 vols., Paris 1935-1938. — K. BADT, *Eugène Delacroix: Drawings*, Oxford 1946. — J. CASSOU, *Delacroix*, Paris 1947. — R. JULLIAN, *Delacroix et Baudelaire*, Gazette des Beaux-Arts II, 1953. — U. APOLLONIO, *Delacroix*, Milan 1956.

Fantin-Latour: L. BENEDITE, *Fantin-Latour*, Paris 1903. — V. FANTIN-LATOUR, *Catalogue de l'œuvre complet (1849-1904) de Fantin-Latour*, Paris 1911.

Fromentin: L. GONSE, *Eugène Fromentin, peintre et écrivain*, Paris 1881.

Gérard: H. GÉRARD, *Œuvre du Baron F. Gérard*, 2nd ed., Paris 1852-1857.

Girodet-Trioson: J. ADHÉMAR, *L'Enseignement académique en 1820: Girodet et son atelier*, Bulletin de la Société de l'Histoire de l'Art français, Paris 1933. — G. LÉVITINE, *Girodet-Trioson, An Iconographical Study*, Harvard University Press 1952. — G. LÉVITINE, *L'Ossian de Girodet et l'actualité politique sous le consulat*, Gazette des Beaux-Arts II, 1956.

Géricault: C. CLÉMENT, *Géricault: Etude biographique et critique avec le catalogue raisonné de l'œuvre du maître*, Paris 1867. — L. ROSENTHAL, *Géricault*, Paris 1905. — R. RÉGAMEY, *Géricault*, Paris 1926. — M. MILLER, *Géricault's Paintings of the Insane*, Journal of the Warburg and Courtauld Institutes, IV, 1940-1941. — K. BERGER, *Géricault: Drawings and Watercolours*, New York 1946. — K. BERGER, *David et le développement de l'art de Géricault*, Gazette des Beaux-Arts, II, 1946. — P. COURTHION, *Géricault raconté par lui-même et ses amis*, Geneva 1947. — K. BERGER, *Géricault und sein Werk*, Vienna 1952; French edition 1952. — D. AIMÉ-AZAM, *Géricault et son temps*, Paris 1956. — L. EITNER, *The Sale of Géricault's Studio in 1824*, Gazette des Beaux-Arts, February 1959. — R. LEBEL, *Géricault*, n.d. (1962).

Gros: J. B. DELESTRE, *Gros et ses ouvrages*, Paris 1845; new edition 1867. — E. DELACROIX, *Gros*, Revue des Deux-Mondes, Paris, September 1, 1848. — P. LELIÈVRE, *Gros, peintre d'histoire*, Gazette des Beaux-Arts, II, 1936.

Ingres: AMAURY-DUVAL, *L'atelier d'Ingres*, Paris 1878. — H. LAPAUZE, *Ingres, sa vie et son œuvre*, Paris 1911. — L. FRÖHLICH-BUM, *Ingres, sein Leben und sein Stil*, Vienna 1924. — L. HOURTICQ, *Ingres*, Paris 1929. — R. LONGA, *Ingres inconnu*, Paris 1942. — ALAIN, *Ingres*, Paris 1949. — G. WILDENSTEIN, *Ingres*, London 1954.

Jongkind: P. SIGNAC, *Jongkind*, Paris, n.d.

Lami: P.-A. LEMOISNE, *Eugène Lami 1800-1890*, Paris 1912.

Manet: A. PROUST, *Edouard Manet, Souvenirs*, Paris 1913. — P. JAMOT, G. WILDENSTEIN and M. L. BATAILLE, *Manet*, 2 vols., Paris 1932. — J. REWALD, *Edouard Manet, Pastels*, Oxford 1947. — A. TABARANT, *Manet et ses œuvres*, 3rd ed., Paris 1947. — D. COOPER, *Manet*, London 1949. — G. H. HAMILTON, *Manet and his Critics*, New Haven 1954. — J. L. VAUDOYER, *Manet*, Paris 1955. — G. BATAILLE, *Manet*, Geneva 1955. — K. MARTIN, *E. Manet*, Basel 1958. — J. RICHARDSON, *E. Manet*, London 1958.

Méryon: P. BURTY, *Charles Meryon: A Memoir and Complete Catalogue of his Works*, London 1879.

Michel: A. SENSIER, *Etude sur Georges Michel*, Paris 1873.

Millet: A. SENSIER, *Millet*, Paris 1881. — W. GENSEL, *Millet und Rousseau*, Bielefeld-Leipzig 1902. — A. THOMSON, *Millet and the Barbizon School*, London 1903. — E. MOREAU-NÉLATON, *Millet raconté par lui-même*, 3 vols., Paris 1921. — P. GSELL, *Millet*, Paris 1928. — R. L. HERBERT, *Millet revisited*, Burlington Magazine, July and September 1962.

Monet: G. GEFFROY, *Claude Monet: Sa vie, son temps, son œuvre*, Paris 1922. — G. CLEMENCEAU, *Claude Monet*, Paris 1928. — K. H. USENER, *Claude Monets Seerosen-Wandbilder in der Orangerie*, Wallraf-Richartz-Jahrbuch, XIV, 1952. — D. ROUART, *Claude Monet*, Geneva 1958. — W. C. SEITZ, *Claude Monet*, New York 1960.

Pissarro: A. TABARANT, *Pissarro*, Paris 1924. — L. R. PISSARRO and L. VENTURI, *Camille Pissarro, son art, son œuvre*, Paris 1939. — C. PISSARRO, *Lettres à son fils Lucien*, Paris 1950.

Prud'hon: C. CLÉMENT, *Prud'hon*, Paris 1872. — E. DE GONCOURT, *Catalogue raisonné de l'œuvre peint, dessiné et gravé de P. P. Prud'hon*, Paris 1876. — A. FOREST, *Pierre-Paul Prud'hon: Peintre français*, Paris 1913. — J. GUIFFREY, *L'œuvre de P. P. Prud'hon*, Collection de la Société de l'Histoire de l'art français, Paris 1924. — R. RÉGAMEY, *Prud'hon*, Paris 1928. — G. GRAPPE, *Prud'hon*, Paris 1958.

Puvis de Chavannes: R. JULLIAN, *L'œuvre de jeunesse de Puvis de Chavannes*, Gazette des Beaux-Arts, II, 1938.

Renoir: G. RIVIÈRE, *Renoir et ses amis*, Paris 1921. — J. MEIER-GRAEFE, *Renoir*, Leipzig 1929. — J. REWALD, *Renoir Drawings*, New York 1946. — M. DRUCKER, *Renoir*, Paris 1944. — D. ROUART, *Renoir*, Geneva 1954. — W. PACH, *Renoir*, New York, Paris 1958.

Rousseau: A. SENSIER, *Souvenirs sur T. Rousseau*, Paris 1872.

Sisley: G. GEFFROY, *Sisley*, Paris 1927. — F. DAULTE, *A. Sisley*. Catalogue raisonné de l'œuvre peint, Paris 1959.

Valenciennes: L. VENTURI, *P. H. de Valenciennes*, The Art Quarterly, IV/2, 1941. — G. BAZIN, Gazette des Beaux-Arts, 1962.

General Index

Where no museum is specified, works listed in the index are to be found in the principal public collection of the city indicated, as follows: Aix-en-Provence, Musée Granet; Baltimore, Walters Art Gallery; Boston, Museum of Fine Arts; Cambridge (Mass.), Fogg Art Museum; Chantilly, Musée Condé; Chicago, Art Institute; Cleveland, Museum of Art; Copenhagen, Ny Carlsberg Glyptotek; Detroit, Institute of Arts; Glasgow, Art Gallery and Museum; Hartford (Conn.), Wadsworth Atheneum; Minneapolis, Institute of Arts; Montpellier, Musée Fabre; Munich, Staatsgemäldesammlungen; New York, Metropolitan Museum of Art; Philadelphia, Museum of Art; Stockholm, Nationalmuseum; Toledo (Ohio), Museum of Art.

List of Color Plates

Contents

THIS VOLUME OF THE COLLECTION "PAINTING ○ COLOR ○ HISTORY" WAS PRO-
DUCED BY THE TECHNICAL STAFF OF EDITIONS D'ART ALBERT SKIRA. FINISHED
THE THIRTY-FIRST DAY OF OCTOBER NINETEEN HUNDRED AND SIXTY-TWO.

TEXT AND ILLUSTRATIONS PRINTED BY

COLOR STUDIOS
IMPRIMERIES RÉUNIES S.A., LAUSANNE.

PLATES ENGRAVED BY GUEZELLE ET RENOUARD, PARIS.

PHOTOGRAPHS BY

L. Adrion, Paris (page 91), Maurice Babey, Basel (pages 10, 12, 14, 15, 16, 17, 19, 23, 24, 26-27,
28, 30, 34, 36, 39, 41, 42, 43, 44, 48, 50, 53, 54, 55, 56, 59, 60, 62, 66, 70, 71, 72-73, 77, 84, 86, 87,
93, 104, 106, 107, 115, 116, 118, 119, 121, 126, 129, 130, 134, 135, 136, 138-139, 141, 145, 146, 154,
156, 177, 183, 185, 187), Henry B. Beville, Washington (pages 61, 79, 94, 109, 111, 149, 150, 158,
163, 186, 188, 206), Joachim Blauel, Munich (page 208), Werner Bruggmann, Winterthur (pages 33,
98, 181), Henry Ely, Aix-en-Provence (pages 37, 38, 105), A. Frequin, The Hague (page 173),
Louis Laniepce, Paris (pages 75, 160, 162, 182, 194, 195, 201, 203, 210), Louis Loose, Brussels
(pages 20, 64, 81), Rainbow, Paris (page 124), Walter Steinkopf, Berlin (page 169), Zoltán Wegner,
London (pages 69, 117, 151, 166-167, 172, 179, 190, 200), and by courtesy of the magazine "Du",
Zurich (page 176), Editions du Cercle d'Art, Paris (page 178), the Ny Carlsberg Glyptotek, Copenhagen
(page 209) and the Toledo Museum of Art (page 143).

Jean-Dominique Ingres (1780-1867). Antiochus and Stratonice (detail), 1840. Musée Condé, Chantilly.

The Classical Nostalgia

and Flemish traditions and the fascinations of the East, painters turned to color in their search for new means of expression, and this in spite of Ingres' persistent championship of line. Created in England with Constable and in Spain with Goya, modern painting, with its new vision of the outer world and its new awareness of man's inner life, was developed and matured in France by artists who based their work on direct visual experience and uncompromising sincerity of pictorial statement. As compared with Constable and Goya, his contemporaries, David may seem almost a reactionary, but we today can better gauge the greatness of his work and its necessary place in the internal evolution of French painting. Delacroix, who recognized the part played by David as being one "of immense consequence within the general renewal of ideas and politics," described him as "a singular compound of realism and idealism." Here we have the main line of cleavage which runs through the century and from which all its contradictions spring, though these were triumphantly resolved by Courbet in The Painter's Studio, *the central painting of the nineteenth century, which he himself boldly called a "real allegory" and intended as a glorification of creative activity.*

We have followed here the traditional division into movements, Neoclassicism, Romanticism, Realism, and Impressionism. We have attempted throughout, however, to interrelate them and to keep the reader aware of their continuous interaction, while at the same time making it clear that these are not hard-and-fast divisions, but merely a framework, a convenient means of ordering and grouping the works of a century particularly rich in great artists, every one of whom transcends the historical, theoretical and technical limitations which go to define their achievements. Personalities such as Géricault, Corot or Daumier do not lend themselves to classification. Of the four movements which followed each other, the first three sprang from common sources; the fourth alone, whose scope and significance—originally at least—were exclusively pictorial, involved a new way of seeing which marked a radical break with the vision of the past. We felt it necessary to devote a special chapter to landscape painting, which has always been one of the purest reflections of the French genius, and which now came into its own and for several decades overshadowed all other branches of painting. The key to its rise and unprecedented development (and to the lucid and searching exploration of the inner man that ran parallel with it) lies in the cult of nature, which also explains the specific character and optic magic of painting in this period. In the cult of nature we have the unifying principle behind all the apparent contradictions of nineteenth-century painting, for even the boldest flights of the imagination and the highest exigencies of idealism were linked with that cult.

Introduction

*F*rench painting of the nineteenth century, whose cardinal importance is universally recognized, requires a volume to itself. But if it is true that in art history the centuries overlap and do not necessarily coincide with their chronological limits, any other division may well be equally arbitrary. The two key dates chosen as the limits of this study span a period of exactly one hundred years which, however, for all its variety and richness, seems indeed to form a unified whole. These dates correspond to the two key pictures that open and close the sequence of illustrations. In 1784 David executed the last official commission of the old régime, The Oath of the Horatii, a resounding manifesto of the new age ahead, which all at once made Paris—as Goethe observed—the center of gravity of modern art. In 1884, a year after Manet's death, the younger, independent artists banded together in Paris to found the Salon des Indépendants, which for the first time enabled painters freely to exhibit their work to the public. And there, at the opening exhibition of 1884, Seurat showed his first large-scale composition, Bathing at Asnières, which had been rejected by the jury of the official Salon, and which at once summed up and superseded Impressionism. Seurat's work, together with that of Cézanne, marks a decisive turning point in the orientation of modern art and inaugurates the twentieth century. Though France maintained its leadership, painting from now on became definitely international, with Paris as its center of focus.

The French Revolution destroyed not only the economic and social structure of the old régime, but also the transcendental ideology that had made for the unity of Baroque culture. By giving free rein to democratic aspirations, it also released the pent-up energies and conflicting forces of individualism. The whole trend of history in the nineteenth century, as events seemed to follow each other with gathering speed, went to emphasize the relativity of values and their dialectical sequence; it heightened the tension between the urgency of the present and the nostalgic sense of the past, creating an acute awareness of that peculiar quality which was henceforth to be inseparable from contemporary art and which Baudelaire called "modernity." Standing more and more apart from the plastic arts, which were now entering on a decline, and quickened by the inspiring example of the Old Masters to be seen in the museums, painting asserted its pre-eminence and autonomy. Along with poetry and music, with which it came to vie in suggestive power, painting developed into a mirror and touchstone of modern life, of the modern sensibility. Responsive as never before to the lessons of the Venetian

INTRODUCTION

★

THE CLASSICAL NOSTALGIA

DAVID AND HIS FOLLOWERS
CHARM OF PRUD'HON
INGRES AND STYLIZATION

★

ROMANTIC EXALTATION

GROS AND THE NAPOLEONIC SAGA
BRILLIANCE OF GÉRICAULT
DELACROIX AND THE POETRY OF COLOR
ORIENTALISM AND DECORATION

★

THE RISE OF LANDSCAPE PAINTING

FROM NEOCLASSICISM TO COROT
FROM ROMANTICISM TO THE BARBIZON GROUP

★

THE BATTLE OF REALISM

MILLET AND THE SOIL
COURBET AND THE MAJESTY OF LIFE
HUMANITY OF DAUMIER
MONTICELLI AND PROVINCIAL PAINTING
FANTIN-LATOUR

★

THE IMPRESSIONIST REVOLUTION

MANET AND THE MODERN WAY OF SEEING
MONET AND LIGHT
PARADISE OF RENOIR
COMPLEXITY OF DEGAS
CÉZANNE AND THE POSITION IN 1884

Translated from the French by James Emmons

★

Distributed in the United States by
THE WORLD PUBLISHING COMPANY
2231 West 110th Street, Cleveland 2, Ohio

★

PRINTED IN SWITZERLAND

FRENCH PAINTING

The Nineteenth Century

BY JEAN LEYMARIE

SKIRA

PAINTING ○ COLOR ○ HISTORY

COLLECTION PLANNED AND DIRECTED BY
ALBERT SKIRA